从西天到中土 ⊙ 印度当代新思潮读本
West Heavens: Readers of Current Indian Thought

从西天到中土 ⊙ 印度当代新思潮读本

West Heavens: Readers of Current Indian Thought

丛书主编 ⊙ 张颂仁 陈光兴 高士明

Series initiated by: Chang Tsong-Zung, Kuan-Hsing Chen, Gao Shiming

WEST HEAVENS

Tejaswini Niranjana

Nationalism Refigured

[印] 特贾斯维莉·尼南贾纳 著

重塑民族主义

特贾斯维莉·尼南贾纳读本

上海社会科学院出版社

SHANGHAI ACADEMY OF SOCIAL SCIENCES PRESS

缘起

"从西天到中土"是一个综合的文化交流方案,由中国美术学院展示文化研究中心和汉雅轩发起,梦周文教基金会资助研究,从学术思想和当代艺术两个角度去亲近印度,进行视觉文化和亚洲现代性的文化比较。读本中的学者于2010年秋的上海双年展期间陆续来华演讲;为了让听众进一步了解他们的思想,每位学者为我们精挑了这个选集,以中英双语出版。

当今的印度离我们既近且远,除了被西方传媒渲染的新兴经济的龙象之争和模糊偏见之外,印度不在一般国人的视野之内。印度咸称古国,但作为当代文明,一个甚至在现代西方思潮中举足轻重的印度学界,并不在普遍意识之中。作为人口的大国和现代国家,印度的经济、文化、科技皆有不可估量的前景;作为中国近邻与久远的故交,印度早就应该被中国关注。但与印度交流的当务之急不在此;中国须要深切思考印度、亲近印度是为了自明。

中国走上现代化的道路已逾一世纪,从革命到冷战到自由资本全球化，我们的道路一直摆脱不了欧美的世界想象，话语也固定在"东西"和"中西"之说法。无怪中国百年来的各种自强运动的结果，都脱不了西方制度的模式。作为典范的欧美，中国钦羡为"先进文化"——于今天的国情已不适宜无条件借鉴。但面对中国的历史资源时，我们又往往囿于欧美范式而无法善用。如何在冷战的两种西方历史计划以外找到中国的位置，如何发掘被欧美视野冷落的历史资源，就必须放眼其他的发展经验。如果要寻找在亚洲现代化道路上与中国采取截然另途，但依我们的"富强"尺度又是成就可观的例案，我们则无法不审视印度。

中国引以自豪的现代之路是民族革命，彻底推翻过去，重新再造大一统，但结果我们离自己的历史文化越来越远。印度的道路则是摆脱殖民帝国，但在民族独立后依然承继了殖民时代机制。然而，当中国的"后革命"经验与印度的"后殖民"相遇时，我们又不能不讶于左翼革命在印度至今不衰的事实。目前各种倾向的共产党在印度尚有四十多个组织，革命经验不可谓不丰富；可是印度又是世上最大的民主国家。这让我们无法不想：中国的革命是否也与印度的殖民经验相通？而印度的"后殖民"是否为革命的另一种方式？印度现代化的历程之多样与丰富，中国无法相比；同时，在日常生活的层面，新旧文化传统并行不悖。雅利安文明的婆罗门学者和各式传统修行人似乎与工业文明不相涉地穿插在都市节奏之中。现代中国与印度相遇，感观上最受刺激的疑惑是：现代与历史（而且是多层面的历史）到底如何并存？

印度与中国的现代都因承欧美的帝国主义和资本逻辑而致，所以中印的相遇是设在欧美的大平台上，绕开欧美无法谈亚洲的现代，也无法深切交流双方的经验。但要脱略于欧美的历史经验来重新自明，不能够自闭地缅怀过去；要打开未来，我们更必须把中国经验提升为足以让欧美也能借鉴的新知识。这可能是印度当代学术最值得国人参考的一面。这系列读本的作者大多为西方学界熟悉，而且，印度学者擅长的"后殖民"理论和城市研究至今尚是西方新思潮的显学；比方在当代艺术的领域，就直接影响了近二十年的国际趋向。

"从西天到中土"的计划源于展示文化研究中心历年的一系列工作计划。2003年许江院长倡议以"亚洲"作为中国美术学院建校七十五周年纪念的议题，嘱高士明、吴美纯两位教授主持，邀我并预其事。"亚洲的双重时间"从亚洲各国的民间历与耶稣历的并行现象着墨，作为"地之缘：亚洲当代艺术的迁徙与地缘政治"越域考察和展览的基础。2008年广州三年展由高士明、萨拉·马哈拉吉和我策划的"与后殖民说再见"再次启动了对"东西"二元框架的反思。"从西天到中土"企图推进前此的探索，在亚洲内部作近距离和实质的交往。陈光兴教授在这领域已投入多年的气力，承不弃，介入高士明和我的行列，策动了他在学术圈的老关系，论坛才得以顺利成事。此中的心意非言谢可以相报，亦惟有以谢忱言表。

2010年，为了配合论坛的开幕，我们适时推出了这一系列读本的第一版，这是其中多位作者的作品首度形诸中文。

为了使这些优秀的思想文本以最佳质量留存于中文世界，我们随后又对它们进行了再度校对、修订和少量的篇目的调整，其中六本在2012年—2013年期间由世纪文景再版；2017年另外两本则在上海社会科学院出版社副总编唐云松先生的支持下，由该社再版，并邀请两位作者——印度重要的艺术史家和批评家吉塔·卡普尔女士和印度女性主义学者特贾斯维莉·尼南贾纳为新版撰写的序言，并调整了部分内容。梁捷先生应邀对这两本书做了细致的校订。

印度和中国在现代境遇中相遇，不独是现代西化大潮的因缘。远在西风东渐之前，中土惟一的一次文化大变革来自汉唐的佛教东渡。佛学来华虽然远远未有近百年源自西洋的现代革命的残酷惨烈，但其影响之深远，也要历数百年的反刍，直到宋代才被彻底消化，被纳入中华文化的主体。在百年西化的意识形态革命之后，再访天竺可以提醒中国自我改造的历史记忆，并提醒我们在想象世界版图的"西方"时，尚有一个离感官更远而脚程更近的"西天"。

张颂仁记于二〇一二年秋
修订于二〇一七年夏

序：作为方法的印度

或许是因为过去十二年主编《亚际文化研究》(*Inter-Asia Cultural Studies: Movements*)国际学刊，与亚洲各地（特别是印度）的批判知识圈产生了工作关系，所以张颂仁与高士明两位先生会找我一起组织在2010年10月至12月于上海举办的"从西天到中土：印中社会思想对话"的系列活动，由于理念相通，当然就义不容辞地参与了规划工作。他们分派给我的任务之一是替来访的印度学者的读本写序，给了我这个机会说清楚投入这次印中对话的思想背景。

十几年前推动建立《亚际文化研究》学刊的动力，是在有限能力的范围内去改变既有的知识状况，在学术生产的层面上推动亚洲各地的互动与整合。那个时候我们来自亚洲各地十几个地区二十余位的编辑委员，对客观情势进行分析所产生的共识是：总的来说，在整个20世纪的历史进程中，亚洲各地的知识圈都是把眼睛往欧美看，一个世纪下来，所有事物的基本参照体系都是以欧美经验为主。百年之中，这个逐步建立起来、极其稳固的知识结构，造成了学术思想上巨大的问题，不仅是分析视野的窄化，把欧美之外该参照的多元历史经验割除，更糟糕的是欧美的知识方式几乎变成了惟一的典范。但是，历史已经证明这套知识根本无法有效地理解、把握与解释我们自身的生存环境。如何透过亚洲不同次区域之间知识圈的互动，能够彼此看到，进而能使得各地的历史经验成为彼此的参照点，多元转化既有的参照坐标，才有可能创造出新的、更具解释力的知识方式。就是凭借着这个认识论的共识，我们一起走了十二年。

回头来看，这条路没有白走。虽然基本格局没有太大的变化，但是上述的知识结构正处在被快速地松动当中。过去十二年世界情势的变化，正在确立世界是在走向多元并存的时代：拉美地区政权左转、东盟加三的形成、中国与印度的崛起、非洲经济持续成长、奥巴马取代布什政权、欧盟成员的继续增加，等等。相较于1980年代末期，东欧、苏联社会主义阵营的解体，美国强权一枝独秀主宰世界的"全球化"感觉结构，过去十二年走向多元政治经济区域的变化，仿佛意味着一元世界的结束。在思想上，原来已经确定、凝固的知识体系，及其所深信不疑的价值观，正在快速地崩解当中，以欧美历史经验为基地形成信心十足的解释框架都面临着前所未有的挑战。处于变动的时代，放慢脚步、重新找回世界各地根植于现代历史经验的思想资源,于是成为开创新的知识状况难以跳过的路径。十二年很短,《亚际文化研究》还没做出值得彰显的知识方式,但是至少我们已经上路了,尝试着走"亚洲作为方法"的知识路线。

在亚洲,乃至于其他的第三世界地区,既有主流的知识结构之所以会长期以"欧美作为方法",还是得归咎于世界史的走向,在以欧美为中心向外旋转的力道下,中国也好,印度也罢,都是以"超/赶"(超英赶美)的基本姿势,学习欧美的事物(当然包括了它的价值观),学术思想、知识生产于是被定位成国家民族现代化工程中的主要环节。姑且不要追究"超/赶"的知识方式中暗藏的陷阱,它是否混淆了规范性的目的与客观的历史解释力,至少可以开始问的问题是,一个多世纪下来,现代化的工程到底把原有的这些所谓后发国家变成了什么长相?民主也好,科学也罢,在学习后的搅拌中,实践出了什么新的模样?换句话说,是不是该停下脚步互相交换一些"超/赶"的经验,在欧美之外的地区之间,互相照照镜子,发现自己从过去变到现在的长相的路径?看清楚了,解释到位了,才能继续走下去,甚至进而发现"超/赶"的知识路线已经走到尽头,该是调整方向的时候了。

如果说知识的目的不是挑空了、为了知识而知识(首先预设了大写真理超越于历史的存在,用来笼罩整个世界),而是为了在世界史的范围内,从多元历史经验的视角,解释各地面对的不同的问题与处境,在相互参照、比较之中,慢慢提炼出具有世界史意义的知识命题，那么，可以说当前所有声称具有普遍主义的理论命题，都不成熟，以欧美经验为参照体系的理论，能够充分解释欧美自身历史就不错了，哪里能够解释其他地区的历史状况？反过来说，对于欧美以外地区的解释必须奠基在其自身历史发展的经验、轨迹当中，不能够简化地、错误地以欧美经验来丈量、解释自身。我想这正是应邀来访的著名的庶民研究（Subaltern Studies）历史学家迪佩什·查卡拉巴提（Dipesh Chakrabarty）称之为"将欧洲地方化"（provincializing Europe）的思想方案，或是2010年7月刚刚过世的沟口雄三教授之所以提出"以中国为方法，以世界为目的"的思想精神之所在。

如果说欧美的历史经验只是一种参照的可能性，特别是它的发展经验与后发地区差距更大，那么在知识转化过程中需要被重新调整的，来访的印度女性主义理论家特贾斯维莉·尼南贾纳（Tejaswini Niranjana）提出的策略，就是必须在欧美之外的地区开展出"替代性的参照框架"（alternative frame of reference），也就是把原来以欧美为参照，多元展开，以亚洲内部、第三世界之间的相互参照，经由参照点的移转，从差异中发展出对于自身历史环境更为贴近的解释。这里思想方案的前提是：关起门来，以本土主义的自闭方式所产生的国粹主义，无法看清楚已经卷入现代的自我，只能沉溺在光辉的过去让自己继续感觉良好而已；打开门来，只以欧美为超赶的参照方式，已然失效，必须在民族国家内部的本土主义（nativism）与欧美中心的世界主义（cosmopolitanism），此两者之外，寻求新的参照体系。

我认为在上述开启新的知识方式的问题意识下，"作为方法的印度"将会对中国学术思想界产生积极的作用，但是中印之间能够产生对话的前提在于抛弃过去"超/赶"的认识论与知识方式，不能再是以落后/进步、现代化与经济发展的速度等，这些表象来进行比较。用我自己的话来说，就是得先摆脱、搁置规范性的比较，从分析上入手，看清差异，再开始提出内在于历史的解释。

印、中都是世界级的大国，农民占了人口最大的比例，资料显示印度目前是仅次于中国的第二人口大国，将在2026年达到15亿，超过中国的13.5亿成为最大人口国；2015年印度经济的扩展速度将超过中国。换句话说，抛开其他历史、文化的异同，在社会科学的意义上来说，在世界上所有国家中，对中国最具可比性的就是印度，很难找到其他的地方。

但是，这两个国家也有庞大的差异，印度是多语言、多文化的国家，至今没有统一的语言，国会开会是要经过翻译的，所以很多印度的重要知识分子，如来访的阿希斯·南迪（Ashis Nandy），从来就不认为印度是欧洲意义下的民族国家，而是一个文明体。1947年从殖民地的身份独立，在被大英帝国征服以前，印度地区没有统合的政体，所以独立以后也很难编织出数千年统一的民族历史，必须更为多元复杂地理解它的过去。因为多民族的过去，其中在部分的人口中留下了所谓的种姓制度（caste system），到今天这个社会组织的原则还在运作，政治体制必须要去处理，无法简单地消灭，而是创造机制让底层的人口参与在政治过程当中。由于多语言的社会生存，文化差异与政治运作交叉重叠，不仅形成许多所谓区域性政党，连一些地方性政治人物（如省长），都是以特定语言产生的电影工业中制造出来的明星，以区域性的高知名度，经过普选选出。在此意义上，印度是世界上最大的民主国家，民主运作根植于地方，全国性的政党都必须想办法跟区域性政治力量结合，才能进行有效的统治。

对我个人而言，过去十几年进出印度，每次交流都有问不完的问题，因为南亚经验与东亚实在不同，摆在一起后者的情况变得相对单纯，各个国家地区语言统一，民族国家面貌表面清晰，又不是多元政党，等等。这些有趣的差异，原来该是可以好好研究的，但是我大部分的中国朋友，大陆、香港、台湾都一样，把这些差异在已经习惯使用的"超/赶"的思路逻辑下，作了球赛式的比较：印度太长时间是殖民地，所以中国比较好；印度政治制度是殖民体制的遗留，所以中国比较好，是经过孙中山、毛泽东革命建立起来的（反映的是再次贬低殖民地经验，把战后第三世界主义的世界观丢了）；印度有种姓制度，所以中国比较好，封建制度已经消除（但是并不去追问印度过去的因子是如何与当代社会接轨，反过头来看看自己的社会中是如何与过去衔接，这个社会真是不再封建了吗？）；印度是多党的问题谈得比较少，台湾地区的人会暂时忘掉欧洲的多党制，把美国两党制搬出来，说只有两党才进步（但是没法儿去问历史问题，印度的多党，乃至于区域政党是为何形成）；还有些人说，印度今天牛还在大城市马路上跑来跑去，哪有中国来得进步，不可以以印度为参照的。总之，如果还是要用简单的"超/赶"逻辑，以欧美树立起来的简单的现代化指标来评比，那就只有等到印度经济超过中国，国力强大的时候，才会进入中国人的视野，现在就继续向天上看吧！

其实，交流必然是双向的，其中会有许多难以避免的错位与误解，举例来说，印度的知识界许多朋友对中国感兴趣，并不是由于它的经济崛起，而是中国二战后的社会主义阶段与今天经济发展的关系，长远形成的农民文化与政治的关系（这是以帕沙·查特吉［Partha Chatterjee］为代表的庶民研究关切的核心议题），社会主义体制与女性解放的问题至今产生了哪些变化，中国如何看待经济发展与资本主义体系之间的关系，中国广大的知识界对于世界的未来有什么不同于欧美的看法，知识界如何在自身的历史实践中提炼出对世界史的解释，等等。总之，以印度为代表的第三世界知识分子，对于中国有基本的尊重，对中国知识界有一定的期待，都与中国社会主义的政治传统有着密切的关系，而与中国是否现代或是进步没有关联，但是，上述这些问题似乎并不是中国知识界感兴趣，或是准备好可以充分对话的。（更让人难过的是，当第三世界地区期待与中国对话时，常常发现中国许多的知识分子对他/她们根本不感兴趣，眼里只有欧美跟自己，还有人跟你说，别搞政治正确了，亚洲根本不存在，第三世界有什么值得对话的。）

我希望已经说清楚了"作为方法的印度"的前提，认识印度是为了去重新认识中国自身与世界,但是也知道当前的知识状况还是处于难以撼动的"超/赶"方式当中,欧美的价值观深入学术思想界,就连是社会主义国度的大陆知识界都很快在赶过港台地区战后"脱亚入欧/美"的知识状况,拥抱欧美知识体系的速度之快,远远超过经济发展,令人惊吓,所以对于这次试图开启的印中对话,我并不抱持很大的希望。

这次活动邀请到的学者,除了杜赞奇(Prasenjit Duara)因为是研究中国历史的专家,很多著作都已经译成中文外,其他几位,无论是否生活在印度,他们的知识构成都根植于印度社会与历史,在国际学术界都是非常有分量的学者,年龄上也横跨了三代,从1937年出生、1980年代就早已在国际上赫赫有名的老将阿希斯·南迪,到在印度与国际思想界备受尊重、刚刚退休的帕沙·查特吉,以及1990年代初以后结构主义翻译理论成名的、壮年一代的文化理论家特贾斯维莉·尼南贾纳。读本的翻译工程不小,为的是让中文世界的读者在与他们会面之前或是之后,能够对他们身后的印度社会、历史与文化有更进一步的认识的机会。根据我的理解,这几位重要的思想者大都不是第一次来到中国大陆,对中国有一定程度的认识与想法,我们期待他们的来访,可以让中国的知识界能开始对印度也有相对应的深度认识,成为我们自我转化的契机。

最后,得感谢受邀来访的几位我个人长期的印度友人:女性主义理论家特贾斯维莉·尼南贾纳、社会思想家阿希斯·南迪、底层研究的政治理论家帕沙·查特吉、底层研究的历史学家迪佩什·查卡拉巴提，与在中国已经很有名气的历史学家杜赞奇；以及还没缘分会面的著名的艺术理论家萨拉·马哈拉吉（Sarat Maharaj）和在台湾地区见过一次闻名全球的后殖民理论家霍米·巴巴（Homi Bhabha）教授，感谢他们在百忙中来访，并授予他们著作的翻译出版权。

同时，得特别感谢好友王晓明与王安忆的拔刀相助，以及许江院长与陆兴华两位先生的大力支持，承担起各场与印度学者对话的任务。也谢谢来自香港特区、台湾地区及大陆应邀参与不同场次，担任特约讨论人的朋友们。

第一次有机会跟原来素昧平生的张颂仁与高士明两位先生一起工作，感觉很好，有点像是老友重逢一样，我个人很珍惜，他们的心胸、气度与智慧，让我重新发现很多事情只要有心人凑在一起，分工合作，截长补短，都还是有希望的，感谢二位的信任！

陈光兴记于二〇一〇年八月二十日于新竹交大
二〇一二年七月修订

特贾斯维莉·尼南贾纳

特贾斯维莉·尼南贾纳 (Tejaswini Niranjana) 目前担任香港岭南大学文化研究系教授和系主任，她也是印度艾哈迈达巴德大学艺术与科学学院的访问学者。她是印度班加罗尔文化与社会研究中心的联合创办人，该中心在 2000—2012 年期间开设了创新性的跨学科博士项目。2012—2016 年期间，她是孟买塔塔社会科学院印度高等教育语言中心的主任，也是维基百科的印度语言顾问。她的著作包括《为翻译定位：历史，后结构主义和殖民语境》(伯克利，1992)、《调动印度：在印度与特立尼达之间的女性，音乐与移民》(杜伦，2006 年)，以及即将出版的关于孟买音乐热的专著。她最近同王晓明共同编辑出版《现在的谱系：定位亚际文化研究》(德里，2015)。

第二版前言

2016年初，印度首都新德里，有所一流大学意外地卷入了一场政治纠纷中。当年2月9日，学生们在贾瓦拉哈尔·尼赫鲁大学（简称JNU）组织集会，抗议政府对两名克什米尔人的首领判处死刑。这二人都被印度政府视为分裂分子。就在集会即将开始前，JNU的行政官员撤销了此次活动的许可。即便如此，学生们依旧按原计划行事，而且，据信有几个戴面具的人——事后确认他们是校外人员——喊出了反印度口号。当时，有两家在集会现场拍摄的电视台遭到了右翼印度教民族主义学生组织（Akhila Bharatiya Vidyarthi Parishad，简称ABVP）领导人的警告。这段录像据称被"动了手脚"，导致一家主流媒体播出了"假新闻"，暗示JNU的学生是恐怖分子和反民族者。不同学生组织之间也发生了冲突。四日之后，JNU的学生会主席、博士生坎亥亚·库马尔（Kanhaiya Kumar）被捕，罪名是煽动叛乱和刑事阴谋。指控他所依据的是1870年殖民统治时制订的印度刑法第124条。JNU的管理层还禁止库马尔和其他几个学生上课或在学校宿舍留宿。此外，校方又对这些学生处以了不同程度的罚款。

由于全国性的抗议、国际社会对印度政府镇压异见的批评，还有学生们的绝食抗议，德里最高法院终于中止了学校的禁令。但是库马尔等了近一个月才得到保释。保释后，他做的第一件事就是向聚集在 JNU 的大批人群发表演说，呼吁"azaadi"，即**印度之内的**自由（freedom *within* India）——包括免于种姓不平等限制的自由、免于宗教不宽容的自由，还有免于贫困的自由。库马尔和他的同事谢赫拉·拉希德（Shehla Rashid）等左派领袖非常注意把他们自己和克什米尔分裂分子区分开来。他们宣称，自己不是"反民族者"，但他们同时确信自己拥有提出异议的权利，并且在面对限制言论自由的社会政治措施时，他们支持批判的声音，认为这很有必要。所以当他们高呼"azaadi"或自由的时候，他们并不是像克什米尔分裂分子那样呼吁**不受制于印度的**自由（freedom *from* India），他们呼吁的是**印度之内的**自由。[1]

JNU 的学生和他们遍布全国的支持者都在强调自由的问题，这一现象悄然同自由概念在印度的形成联系在了一起。150 年的历史中，被殖民的人们和独立后没有实质性地获得自由的人们，都将自由视作某种强烈的愿望。值得注意的是，这种自由的观念和民族的观念在概念上紧密地结合在一起，人们希望借此保证该自由可以获得实现。

---

[1] http://www.hindustantimes.com/india/is-this-anti-india-read-full-text-of-jnu-leader-kanhaiya-s-speech/story-rlhVQ9XVALS3Oc5h1UCOmK.html. ——此为原注，全书同。

本书中的论文来自我过去20年的写作，讨论了翻译、流行电影、女权主义语言的转变等问题。准备这篇前言时，我重读了它们，这让我很惊讶地发现民族的观念一直贯穿于印度思想界的辩论中，也让我好奇这是否需要向非印度的读者们作一些说明。

这本论文集首次出版后的7年里，我自己对这本书所切入的智识、政治和社会背景有了更多的了解。西天中土项目曾在2010年把我带到上海，后来一直在继续它卓越的工作，为印度和中国的画家、学者甚至音乐家们策划了一系列不同的对话。而亚际文化研究项目，不仅把西天中土介绍给我，更持续通过各种活动和出版物传播思想，对区域内的学者和实践者们有着变革性的影响。我提到西天中土和亚际文化研究这两个项目，是为了点明亚洲思想圈环境的改变，并且想说，我这本书现在重新进入的空间和2010年的那个空间已然不同。我不清楚，当我把论文的关怀改得更好读，这会不会让文章更容易被接受，因为有些联系在几年前可能还很新，但现在看来会更明显。

2010年在上海和其他地方巡回讲座的时候，我曾觉得有些挫败。很常见的一点是沟通交流的无力感。这不仅仅是因为不同的语言，而是由于很难找到共同的参照点。印度的很多学术著作都带着后殖民的设定，这很明显和中国的语境大不相同。请让我指出一些可能很难介绍给中国的方面——其中之一就是民族这个在印度知识界辩论中不断涉及的理念。

虽然在印度，不论在独立前后，我们的民族主义思想家都有着悠久的传统，但是当代印度的批判学术研究涉及了对民族和民族主义的批判，我把这种质问称为"民族—现代（national-modern）的政治与文化逻辑"。简单说来，印度精英们领导了这么一个项目，在女性、达利特（贱民）、农民、部落和工人等各个人群的斗争之前，就已经对民族的构建达成了共识。1947年从英国独立看上去好像加强了这种共识，但是政治和社会权力依然留在精英们手中，他们最终对物质或无形资源的重新分配并没有多少兴趣。

对中国读者发言的时候，我总得提醒自己要强调，印度没有像中国一样经历过大革命。发生在印度现代时期的，更准确地说是一个改革的过程。在改革过程中，很多改变确实发生，但是社会却没有根本地或者剧烈地转变。于是，社会和政治结构很大程度上都原样地保留了下来，导致了不满和持续的斗争，要求为许多被剥夺了权利的群体去争取权利和承认。所以独立后大约70年，坎亥亚·库马尔关于自由的言论，依然能够在1947年以后出生的人群中获得巨大的反响。

坎亥亚所要求的也是对民族的新想象，它不依靠单一的印度概念，不会简单地认为印度属于占大多数人口的印度教徒，而是需要利用语言、地域、宗教实际的多样性。他还要求我们重新关注种姓和性别的不平等，这两点都是当今右翼民族主义——以2017年当权的政府为代表——所努力淡化的问题。关于"文化"的争论标志着民族概念的诞生与扩张，这可以帮助我们理解这场21世纪发生在社会领域的骚动。

就在JNU事件发生的前几周，2016年1月17日，在南印度的海德拉巴大学，一位达利特博士学生罗希特·维穆拉（Rohith Vemula）自杀了。在这起事件后，紧接着发生了学生在校园里的抗议，还有一部分师生被捕。维穆拉的同学们普遍认为他的自杀是在抗议学校冷漠而残酷的行政部门，也是在抗议这个系统——它不能为来自底层社会的学生提供新颖的机会。国家未能兑现承诺，未能履行它自己的宪法所规定的义务，这是那些致力于社会变革的人们长期关注的一项议题。20世纪五六十年代，包括印度在内的许多民族国家都曾尝试进行法律领域的干预，然而海德拉巴学生的自杀又一次表明,.这种干预不足以影响文化的转型。自杀案变成了催化剂，刺激了全国包括JNU学生在内的许多年轻人，认为有需要与那些也在各自尝试批判国家的社会边缘人士结为同盟。有评论员将政府在JNU事件中对学生的惩罚，视为对形成更大规模批判同盟之可能性的直接回应。

在我写下这些的时候，执政党的学生分支，就是那个在JNU学生遭到煽动叛乱的起诉中扮演了核心角色的ABVP，于2017年2月21日攻击并殴打了在德里拉姆加斯学院（Ramjas College）和平抗议的师生。这所学院是德里大学的一部分，它组织了一场名为"抗议的文化"的研讨会，邀请的嘉宾中包括一位JNU的学生乌马尔·卡里德（Umar Khalid），他在上一年曾因为煽动叛乱的指控被捕。因为预料到了可能会发生的问题，组织者事前已请求卡里德不要参会。尽管如此，在德里警方的支持下，ABVP仍旧打断了研讨会。而且当师生们进行示威游行时，他们遭到了ABVP的袭击,一部分人受伤严重,被迫住院治疗。ABVP成员宣称,他们在拉姆加斯学院听到了支持克什米尔"azaadi"或独立的口号。一位在场的教师澄清说,那些口号所呼吁的是表达"azaadi",即言论自由。再一次地,关于民族不同概念之间的竞争被摆上了前台——有些人争论道,一个民族的成员必须一直保持相同的信仰、相同的行为;另一些人争论道,一个民族包含了不同的言论、不同的可能性,包括了批判主流观点的可能性。从这些关于"印度文化"之定义的争论中,我们也能看到更广泛的对立势力,比如本集中收录的论文《文化为什么重要》(*Why Culture Matters*)里就讨论了粉红内裤运动(Pink Chaddi Campaign)所反映的论争。

为了讨论民族和文化的问题而构建一套公共语汇,这并不容易。这是因为在印度,自然科学占有学科统治地位,而且指望所有"聪明的学生"都热心向往以科学为事业,把在学校表现不那么好的学生留给其他学科。即便是那些从事社会科学的人,说话最有底气的还是经济学家。印度占统治地位的社会科学一直都是经济学,不管是马克思主义的变种还是新古典主义及其发展的派别。独立后70年以来,国家对科研的投入严重地集中到了主要聘请经济学家的机构那里,而且在他们当中很少能发现历史学家、社会学家或者文化理论学者。

不过,那些对批判地思考文化问题和民族再现问题作出了重要贡献的学者,他们的著作也有了一定的发行量。这里我只提几个名字。他们当中有一些包含在西天中土的系列丛书里，比如政治思想家阿希斯·南迪或帕沙·查特吉，以及其他如文化理论学者苏茜·塔鲁（Susie Tharu），历史学者罗米拉·塔帕尔（Romila Thapar）和塔尼卡·萨尔卡尔（Tanika Sarkar）。我认为我自己的论点是在与这些学者的著作的对话过程中浮现的，即便我转向了他们中有些人没有涉足的领域，例如翻译理论、南印度流行电影，或加勒比音乐和文化。我认为，我自己的工作，从不同的方向和上面提到的那些学者一起尝试了批判民族——现代的常识——认为有某种继承而来的"印度的"文明精髓。我从我的书《为翻译定位》(*Siting Translation*)中摘录了部分，在那里我表明，这种批判在殖民时期需要建立在作为实践和哲学的翻译之上。该批判还有一种方式，即另行建立参考框架，不把"西方"当作唯一的比较点，我在以印度学者的身份研究加勒比的论文里探讨了这个理念。在另一篇论文里，我讨论了1990年代早期全球化时期印度流行电影对女性主人公的再现，展示了民族在当代是如何被重新塑造的，以及女性是以何种方式被呈现为这个重塑过程的核心的——虽然经常是通过很有疑问的方式。

民族的空间及其在20世纪学术著作中的核心地位是个意义重大的现象，常常被理所当然地视为合适的研究框架。我想说，不仅对于南亚和东南亚这样的后殖民社会，而且对于战后的冷战区域，以及像中国这样有着后内战与后革命设定的国家，都是如此。这个世界见证了前所未有的人民运动，这些运动既有被迫的也有自发的，它们不仅揭示了关于排斥的新语言已经出现，也让民族的理念在当下重新获得了大众的适切性。

从 20 世纪进入 21 世纪，中国令世人震惊的转变把我们许多同在亚洲的人们钉在了期待的观众席上，几乎像是在大银幕上观看电影。由于中国对世界开放了，不仅创造了新的市场，而且，通过探索智识世界、视觉艺术和表演艺术领域里的联系，中国人保持开放地思考其他历史、其他空间，并对差异的意义保持警觉，这是非常重要的。所以，中国不只是需要理解和衔接"西方"，更需要重新塑造新的模式来联系"其他"，或者用帕沙·查特吉的话说，是"绝大多数的世界"。朝着这个方向的第一步也许可以是观察民族和文化的理念在亚洲有怎样的意义，并且去理解对这些概念的批判开辟了哪些可能性。

特贾斯维莉·尼南贾纳

2017 年 3 月

（翻译：周展）

目 录

1 / 替代性框架？为第三世界的比较研究提问 / 王立秋 译 陈恒 校

29 / 语言，斗争之所 / 袁伟 译 许宝强 黄德兴 校

87 / 为什么文化重要：重新思考女性主义政治的语言 / 王立秋 译

105 / 重新塑造民族主义：当代南印度电影和女性主义主体 / 周展 译

替代性框架？
为第三世界的比较研究提问

爱德华·格里桑*对我说："我从未在巴巴多斯见过你，你从未在马提尼克岛见过我。为什么？"我回答说："因为那些旅行不在我们的议程上。"——乔治·拉明**：《对话录》

这篇论文旨在论述，为第三世界不同地点的知识分子之间持续进行的对话，创造一个批判空间的可能性。部分地出自我自己赴西印度群岛的旅行，这些反思将聚焦于我们当代历史—政治语境中对此类对话的需要。在此语境中，旧的边界正被抹除与重划，而穿越地理距离的移动正变得某种程度

---

* 爱德华·格里桑（Edouard Glissant, 1928— ），当代加勒比作家兼理论家。——此为译注，全书同。
** 乔治·拉明（George Lamming, 1927— ），诗人和小说家，生于巴巴多斯。

上既更困难又更容易——这取决于你要去的是哪里。

我的一些朋友和我在20世纪80年代晚期着手进行的计划，在《亚际文化研究》(Inter-Asia Cultural Studies, IACS) 领域中迅速激起反响。当我第一次与陈光兴和IACS期刊组的其他成员会面的时候，我意识到，他们的问题尽管为不同的脉络所塑造，在其概念和政治内涵上，却与我和我朋友们的问题吊诡地相似。因此，尽管这篇文章原本不是为这个期刊的潜在读者群而写的，但看起来，把这个关于那些为我的问题提供触发原因的"旅行"故事放到这里，某种程度上来说也是合适的。此外，IACS期刊组选择在"主题化"时所进一步"问题化"的对象是"亚洲"这个概念，而我自己早期的研究，以相当类似的方式，探讨的则是"第二世界"的问题。[1]

尽管如此，我对今天使用"第三世界"这个术语可能遭遇的许多困难并不是毫无意识的——现在，这个术语已经不再负载，以我们共同的殖民主义经验、以我们为自决和主权而共同进行的斗争为基础，来锻造团结的积极任务。显然，在我们后冷战的当下，形态结构与20世纪五六十年代——去殖民化与不结盟运动的年代——已截然不同；那时，"第三世界"还有可能作为一个积极的政治范畴而发挥作用，即便这个术语本身是在"二战"后的殖民母国（metropolis）中发明的——为的是认可那些将旧帝国主义取而代之的援助和发展

---

[1] IACS期刊的编者寄语试图在这两个术语的相互联结中对二者进行探究。不过，这并非本文关注的焦点。

计划（Singham and Hune，1986年）。今天若再将第三世界这个词汇当作毫无疑义的反帝国主义概念加以提出，很可能把人放到他自己民族国家内部的统治精英的一方，这个精英群体寻求为从西方跨国公司——这些公司日益渗入先前"封闭"的各个经济体系——那里收回（自己的）市场—空间，而早已试图与非殖民母国的精英建立联系。

我提议的用法，正如我希望展示的那样，意在向知识分子和其他在他们自己的社会中投身于对支配统治进行批判的人，建议不同种类的团结和交流（而不只是那些在统治群体之间发生的团结和交流）的可能性。出于我的目的，我将使用"第三世界"[1]这个术语来指涉那个由"万隆计划"（不结盟运动）所塑造的地域及其后此地域的分解。此外，该术语还将描绘一种后殖民政治的主体——一种由马克思主义和形形色色的民族主义所塑造的主体——近年来，这个主体已不得不自问在去殖民化辩论中不曾居于（确实也不可能）核心地位的种姓、种族、共同体和性别的问题，而这些问题在今天严重地影响了精英民族主义的种种计划。

只要快速地勾勒当代的"国族"批判——以印度为例——直接的历史—政治语境，人们就可能会想起，对于20世纪七八十年代的激进政治（特别是那些由马克思列宁主义

---

[1] "第三"也是因为不是第一，甚至也不是第二。此外，在历史（战后）意义上的"第三"，指的（尽管是在一种有限的意义上，请记住像中国和古巴那样的例外）是带有某种"混合制"经济，不那么社会主义，也不那么资本主义的"不结盟"的国家。

群体和女性运动所发起的政治）来说，民族国家是重要的批判对象。尽管民族批判是激进政治的核心，这种批判，在许多方面，却仍是民族现代性（the national-modern）的政治和文化逻辑的一部分。正如我们现在能够看到的那样，政治的世俗主义和现代性依赖于对种姓、宗教认同、族群、区域和语言差异的拒斥。确实，似乎正是这些拒斥使得女性主义或马克思列宁主义运动的能量及其触及的范围成为可能。然而，在20世纪90年代，像"反曼达尔鼓动"（anti-Mandal agitation）*、印度人民党（Bharatiya Janata Party）的兴起、成功的区域政党的形成等等这样的政治事件，与私有化、自由化印度经济的驱力结合在一起，已经扰乱了民族—现代性的叙事——今天，我们许多人的作品，正处于这种扰乱之中。对于像我这样，在社会中对支配性的语言进行批判的人来说，重新改造和使用"第三世界"这个概念可以为普世现代性（the universal-modern）这个问题引入另一个切入点。

因此，我要为第三世界的"重新世界化"（reworlding）**而辩；为更新严肃探讨我们社会（在文化、政治和经济上）的依附地位和"低度发展"状态的企图而辩。既然民族／国家对我们许多人来说仍然是切实可行的单位，也考虑到过去统治精英对"第三世界"这个术语的使用——以此来寻求对受害者地位的承认并要求"援助"——我建议，我们应该重

---

* 1978年，曼达尔委员会提出一种方案，建议在招生、招工方面为低种姓族群提供额外的保留名额。

** 原文reworlding，系仿照rewording而生造的单词。——校注

新思虑这种批判—政治的用法：将"第三世界"这个术语放置在每个民族—国家之内。通过坚持提出成为"第三世界"实际上意味着什么这个问题，以及受此情势影响最巨大的是社会的哪个部分（比如说，对谁而言"低度发展"是一个问题？）这个问题，我们可以迫使我们的统治群体澄清他们的反帝修辞，并迫使他们进入那些更可被问责的、更具代表性的政治选择。在国际论坛上乞灵于"第三世界"的行为赖以为根基的假设——即在统治者与被统治者之间存在一种共性（commonality）——是需要被问责的，而统治者亦必须被要求接受这一假设的题中之义。对平等和公正的多样化的诉求，可以通过来自同样地变成"第三世界"（third-worlded）地区的成功案例的存在来加以强化。我们可能意欲要求的，是透过"第三世界"这个术语的部署来扩展帕沙·查特吉所谓的"民主"（在他的术语里民主属于政治社会 [political society]，在这个领域中，今日种种的政治要求由许多不同的 [庶民群体] 所表达），这个宣称也可以被看作"现代性"（现代性这个词指的是第三世界中的公民社会：一个专为那些少数有资格成为"公民"的人而保留的领域）的对立物（Chatterjee，1996 年）。

对"民主"[1]的重新关注也理应导致我们工作中的学科复兴及民主化。我自己的学科，英语研究，至今也有一段时间经历了各种方面的政治质问了。回顾今日已被称

---

1 现在，查特吉对这个术语的使用应该是明白无误的了，我在这里沿用了这种用法，它与新世界秩序的执法者所意味的那种用法大不相同。

作"印度英语研究批判"的那一切，人们会看到某些我们不得不承认的僵局，在相关性的问题（the question of relevance）上尤其如此。独立后的一代英语教师——如帕坦卡（R.B.Patankar）、潘尼迦（Ayyappa Panikkar）和阿兰瑟莫西（U.R.Ananthamurthy），这里我只点出一些在20世纪70年代活动的人物的名字——他们透过这样的方式来解决该学科专业的相关性问题：在教室里进行如同以往的教学工作，但活跃地以马拉地语（Marathi）或马拉雅拉姆语（Malayalam）或卡纳达语（Kannada）等地方语言为主，介入他们所属的智识生活。然而，在20世纪80年代，一些教师——比如说，在海得拉巴、德里和加尔各答——开始在英语教室里提出不同的问题，这很大程度上与他们对女性主义的参与有关。在20世纪90年代，在民族/国家问题、共同体问题和种姓以及性别问题上的冲突尖锐化，看起来更直接地把老师和学生的不满和不安带进了教室，导致人们对在学校接受的课程训练、教学方法的实践以及研究强调的重点产生了持续的质疑。纲举目张地来看，我们可以说，在英语系里，两类工作开始受到持续上升的关注：（a）力图检视印度语言、文学和文化实践，考查不同种类的写作（比如说女性写作或贱民写作），或通过研究到目前为止被认为无甚价值的文化形式（比如说大众电影或儿童文学）来扩大学科领域的研究；以及（b）对"前大英殖民地"（commomwealth）甚至是第三世界的文化和文学进行研究。尽管第一类的研究议程看起来确实需要方法论和政治方面重大的重新定向，但说到底，印度的学生/老师，在研究中对什么在某种意义上是"他们的"并不是特别地无知。（考虑到印度独立后社会科学所负载的民族主义包袱——这在他们的总课程计划中是清晰可见的——以及，考虑到这一包袱在转移到英语研究时必然会有些延迟，当我说我教授加勒比和非洲文本时可能会得到的最可预见的回应是："可是为什么不是印度的文本？"对此问题有多种可能的答案，但出于篇幅的考虑，在这里我就不再继续这个话题。）第二部分，教授"第三世界"文学的议程，一开始就先天不良。稀缺的制度资源几乎不能提供这个学科所要求的常规材料，更不用说转向对那些来自非都会区域的不太为人所知的文本的购买了。与研究者对一手和二手材料的接触受到极大限制的处境相比，教师遭遇到的困难则更为艰巨。尽管存在这些问题，在这些领域，教学与研究两者皆一直在持续，因此，我在这里想为我们在印度用来展开对其他第三世界语境的教学和研究的那些隐含前提重新进行检视和辩解，并提出这样的建议，即当下的时代要求我们对新研究议程进行批判性的塑型，这些议程将会在强调比较研究的重要性时，更新对比较研究所采纳的种种假设进行再思考。

印度人，无处不在的印度人

我们时代的标志之一，就是"印度"令人叹为观止的国际可见度（不仅有选美皇后，还有技术专家、科学家、艺术家、经济学家、历史学家甚至文学理论家！）由于某种压倒性的自我庆祝的文化民族主义，我们绝少停下来思考这个"印度人"和他/她由全球资本主义经济的政治经济学来完成的部署。这种我们不需要强调的经济,也是一种学术界和知识生产的经济。在20世纪中期,在尼赫鲁式的社会主义以及不结盟运动的年代,印度宣告与其他前殖民地人民的团结,并对比他们处境更为不妙的国家给予了各种各样的支持。然而,在这个千禧年的末尾,印度人却不仅仅是另一个后殖民地的人民,相反它是一个号称自己已获得某种例外性(exceptionality)或特殊地位的人——这是一项日益将其同其他后殖民地国家的居民区分开来的成就。在中产阶级印度人——甚至就在她自己大声强调自身的文化差异的时候——成为跨国资本循环的中继点的时候,先前的认同轴心已经得到转化,旧有的团结也遭到了背弃。尽管新近许多学术批判把注意力集中在印度公民主体的形成上——把承担这个阶级出现的种种(比如种姓、社群和性别上的)排除作为主题来进行分析,发生在跨国空间的"印度人"之构造中的那些微妙的变化,至今仍然没有得到认真的研究。

我提到这个,是因为从我几次加勒比之行中,产生的一个顾虑。在加勒比,我在牙买加和特立尼达遭遇了许多对"印度人"的看法,这些看法和认识常常特别是被新印度移民群体,像全球印度教组织(Vishwa Hindu Parishad)——它是涵盖印度人民党的同盟"家族"(Sangh Parivar)的一部分——那样的国际组织,甚至是印度的民族国家通过其高级专员公署(英联邦成员国大多数元首为英女王,所以相互之间派驻的最高使节为高级专员)来积极促成的。身处印度大学的人，能够轻而易举地把西印度的文本读作是"新英语"写作的连续统一体中的其他文学创作中的一种；但在加勒比或非洲工作的印度研究者，可能也得厘清他或她与在那些地域生活的印度裔人士的关系，并对他或她从事比较研究的动机作出解释。这个要求可能与"文化"这一个观念——由来自印度的印度人，以及西印度群岛生活的印度裔——的运用有关，他们征引遥远的过去和荣耀的文明作为自己种族优越性的证据。正如一位圭亚那朋友说的那样，"印度人永远说文化是他们有而黑人没有的东西"。[1] 我在其他地方已经讨论过，加勒比地区对印度特质的征引，存在一种复杂的政治，其细节常常为到当地访问的印度研究者所忽视，这部分地是因为他/她自己未经检视的关于"印度文化"意味什么的观念（Niranjana，1995年）。

在加勒比的教学

我在加勒比地区感受到的另一种深刻的方向错失感（disorientation）是置身于一种非西方的西方的迷误。早期在印度外的出访总是去往第一世界，无论去的地方有多大的差异，对我来说，这些地方都不是印度，都不是第三世界。我与加勒比的遭遇迫使我开始在习以为常的那些问题——比如就印度与西方的关系问题——之外提出另一些关于同一和差

---

[1] 当我们有来自印度的印度人进行"东印度群岛的西印度人"的研究时，遇到的情况要复杂得多。这些离散共同体的文化形式经常被印度人想象为片段的、欠缺的或衍生的。

异的问题——无论是在政治领域（关于民族/国家和区域的观念），经济领域（"依赖"和"发展"的问题）还是文化领域（与传统对现代性的争论）。不仅如此，那些遭遇还对我在课堂里提出的问题、我采纳的教学策略以及我讲授的文本产生了决定性的影响。[1]

几年前，我写过一篇论文——基于我1989年讲授的有关非洲和加勒比的一门课程——在这篇论文中，我试图探索在印度的英语系讲授非西方文学文本意味着什么。[2] 对我来说，对我的学生来说，接触这些文本、语境和历史都还是第一次。考虑到大多奉行欧洲中心主义的图书馆中材料稀缺，讲授这门课程是十分艰难的，而与这些文本的接触，每一步都不得不进行认真仔细的反复商讨。

显然我们的关注点不只在于"内容"，即仅仅用那些新的文本来取代旧有的文本。我在那篇论文中提出，这种简单的替换并没有对一个由伟大文本组成的"正典"（canon）的需求提出质疑，这种需求带着以特定的方式来讲授这个正典的命令。我的观点是，进入（被包含和被容纳）现存范式的要求并没有对范式本身构成威胁，"因为它从不质疑那个一开始就决定了要排除什么的标准"（Niranjana，1995年：249页）。

---

[1] 我把对这些改变的细节性探讨推迟到以后再进行，这里我只示范性地指出，我不得不寻求向学生介绍——至少是听起来是这样——西印度大众文化的方式，同时试图在加勒比发起关于语言政治的讨论。

[2] 这篇论文，题目是《历史，真正地开始：后殖民教学的动力》(History, really beginning: compulsions of postcolonial pedagogy)，稍后刊载于 Rajan（1992年）。

相反，我提议，我们必须审视我们**如何**教学/阅读，检视我们带给非洲和加勒比文本之阅读的期待。我强调了教授非殖民母国文本的重要性，这样的教学必须同时通过不使用"惯常的阅读方式"来抵抗"被正典吸纳"的问题。（Niranjana，1995年：249页）

因此，我的主张是，非殖民母国文本对学科和常规的文学批评方法提出了根本的挑战，这不是因为这些文本所具有的内在品质，而是因为——从一些方面来看，它们内嵌于其中的历史某些方面与印度相似——我们的问题和兴趣与这些加勒比和非洲的作品相契，或者说，相耦合。当然，也有这样的风险，在强调相似性的时候，我们可能会忽略特定的第三世界社会之间的真实差异。尽管如此，我们与这些文本的接触，"迫使我们把注意力从美学转向政治的维度"，"让我们不在诗学的形式中，而是在文化、政治和历史的领域中寻找一致和不一致"（Niranjana，1995年：250页）。在某种程度上说，我们能够实现的是"把文本更加稳固地置入物质与社会实践，而非纯文学的传统之中"。（Niranjana，1995年：250页）。

回顾这些关注，在我看来，重点还是落在了文学文本上，对于文学文本得以在其中形成的话语网络，以及其他类型的文化创造，人们的关注还是不够。也许这仅仅是一个信息不充分的问题。也许成为障碍的还有问题的形构本身——问题被形构成一个文本及其语境的问题——的表述问题，因为这种形构使得文本最终可以脱离其语境，而语境则被想象为仅仅是环绕文本的那种东西。如何界定一个文本边际的分野（或者说，首先是什么构成了一个"文本"），这个问题并没有得到处理，除了被一笔带过的情况，结果是在课堂上展示的那些文本恰好就是那些英语研究这一学科很容易接受的作品（沃尔科特［Derek Walcott］的戏剧、布拉斯维特［Kamau Brathwaite］的早期诗歌、拉明［George Lamming］的小说），同时又完全地忽视，例如对一切研究西印度群岛文化政治的努力来说，都极为重要的加勒比流行音乐。[1]

现在，在我看来，问题与我们第三世界主义（third-worldist）力图发现"我们自己"的文化创造的努力有关，这些文化的创造，用夸美·安东尼·阿皮亚（Kwame Anthony Appiah）的话来说，是值得受到尊敬的。此外，像"政治"和"美学"这样的概念在事后之明看来，对它们的征引就好像它们的意义是"给定的"一般，而人们又往往太早地确立它们之间的区别，尽管同时这些术语也有可能对整个的方法论的探讨起到了速记（shorthand）的作用。1990年，学科转型的需要确定无疑地在不同的区域得到了表达，但对我来说，至少，对于这种学科转型所涵盖的更重要的意义，到现在为止仍没有得到充分的思考。只有在1990年代后期戏剧性的民族事件之后（我这里指的特别是高种姓青年拒绝接受政府为低种姓反歧视所采行的平权政策［affirmative action］而

---

[1] 沃尔科特，布拉奇维特和拉明的文本常常以这样的方式为文学课程所吸收，在这种同化方式中它们与大众文化的关联——这既是形式上的又是主题上的——受到了掩盖，而这又导致它们像其他一切现代主义文本一样被阅读。

进行的反曼德尔鼓动），在印度挑战"英语"意味着什么这个问题，才能够以别样的形式出现，而人们也才能够从不同的批判视角，来探究使主导性的"美学"得以建构的整个地基。作为一个事件，"曼德尔"，把许多中产阶级的、左倾的世俗印度人的注意力吸引到公民—主体的构成中种姓的"藏匿"（invisibilizing）上。在为一种在许多方面与后独立时期的世俗主义一致的现代主义支配下的文学研究中，直接面对——有时是通过对早期的贱民和女性主义的动议的整合——那些帮助形成美学领域的被排除之事物，成为可能。探究美学领域的历史形成，在我看来，对第三世界文化的比较研究来说，就我们着手比较的是什么，以及我们如何开展我们的工作而言，可能具有重大的意义。

民族志的问题

第三世界比较研究者的任务之一，在于将那些不属于研究者自己的第三世界空间重新概念化。这项任务可能涉及反对这些空间约定俗成的殖民母国式的描述，而这种描述必然预设了特定的民族志视角，特定的人类学态度。

尽管文学/文化的比较研究者常常不具备人类学方面的正规训练，人类学的论述模式和思维习惯却注定要影响一切像比较研究那样的事业。比较研究，把对文化构成的研究看作是区别于为研究者所寓居其中的那种文化构成的研究。可以预见，在印度的学生，比如在研究英美文学时，人类学的问题永远都不会出现。支持"现代"知识生产的框架和定位确保了这个问题仅用于非西方——或者也许我们应该说"南方"——文化的研究。[1]然而，在去殖民化之后的几年间，人类学一直受到了来自不同源头的对其原动力和进程的持续探问，其中值得注意的——就我们的目的来说——是由后殖民主体变成的人类学家（the postcolonial-turned-anthropologist）（Asad，1973年；Scott，1989年）。由于经典人类学的计划是通过对"他者"文化的研究来生产某种西方的自我理解，人类学研究者也就倾向于预设了西方文明的中心地位。考虑到这个学科为研究者提供的这种定位，第三世界的"人类学家"怎能开始质疑这个中心地位呢？

当这样的人类学家（显然我是在用这个描述命名一整套的主体—位置，无论这位研究者所受的是何种学科训练）冒险步入另一个第三世界空间的时候，她/他的定位——因此也是主体—位置——的规范化/正常化也就向这样的质问开放，而批判支配性知识型（episteme）的可能性，我要说，也就会开始出现。这种批判，必然在对他或她的特权（区别于在"民族/国家"语境中发生的那种忘却）抛弃（unlearning）和对他或她与殖民母国知识生产的体制和学科框架的合谋的承认中，涉及第三世界的知识分子——特别是通常本身就是

---

[1] 有趣的是，不仅是对南方文化创造物的阅读被看作人类学的活动。民族志的问题也紧紧粘住创作的生产。比如说，对钦努阿·阿契贝那样的非洲作家的标准的文学批判上的否定，是（因为）它们"太过于人类学"。有时，同样的问题也附着在第一世界的少数民族文学（我最先想到的是非裔美国人的写作）或印度的贱民写作或妇女写作上。

上层阶级和高种姓的印度知识分子。

到目前为止，这点已经十分明确：包括人类学在内的现代学院学科，与欧洲扩张的新阶段是同时产生的，它们既支持（underwrite）着殖民治理计划，又被殖民治理的计划所担保（underwritten）(Said，1978年；Asad，1973年)。无论学者在殖民时期是帮助生产关于被殖民者的刻板印象，还是提供习俗和实践方面的细节性的信息，在这两种情况下他们都在建构一个在各方面都被描述为非现代的、传统的或原始的世界，因此也是一个顺从于"更高级的"文明统治的世界。正是由殖民母国学院体制所认可的学者所宣称的专业知识或技能（即詹姆斯·克利福德［James Clifford，1983年］如此恰当地称之为"民族志的权威"），持续地在为这种知识的"真理性"和事实性背书。

民族志学者履行着如**翻译者**一般的功能——确实，人类学的计划就像是把一种文化翻译为对另一种文化来说可理解的语汇的计划（Asad，1986年，Niranjana，1992年）。直到最近，这个学科内才应对了这个问题：像那些在殖民或新殖民统治下的权力关系如何决定翻译的方向与性质——正如塔拉尔·阿萨德（Talal Asad）指出的那样，常有投向更强势的那种语言/文化而简单化的趋势（Asad，1986年；Fabian，1986年）——的问题。这也再一次提出了受众问题和民族志学者的主体—位置的问题：谁写作？为谁写作？殖民母国与第三世界语境的再现、与第三世界对该语境的再现，这两者之间可能会存在什么样的差异？

比较研究的基础

到现在为止，常常秘而不宣的比较研究的基础，一直是某种人文主义和普世主义，预设了某种共通的人性：尽管它们表面上有所差异，世界上的人民在根本上，被认为是一样的，或者，处于趋于互相相似的进程当中。然而，这在某种程度上，可以说是一种居高而下的论断。比如说，"自由主义的"西方民族志学者能够声称研究客体和研究者的共通的人性，即便在"客体"那边，他们的人性有待通过民族志学者把他们的言语和行为翻译成他/她欧洲—美国的语言来被发现。那么，能够被拿来相比较的，就是非西方的语境与人类学家自己的西方语境。这种比较中隐含的——尽管有着人类共通性的声明——是阿奇尔·姆邦伯（Achille Mbembe）在谈到非洲语境的时候，所称的"失败了的普世性的视角"：

> 比较计划的共通的单位、根本的基础，**甚至是比较计划的内在的决定性都是西方的现代性**，无论这种现代性被理解为被用来衡量其他社会的标准，还是被理解为其他社会前进的最终目的地。每一次"非洲"被引入这种操作，这种比较的活动就被简化为"优等"与"劣等"之间的运算关系。高低等级的区别偷偷地滑入以类似、形似、相似的三个虚妄的幻象之间，确立了以一种任意的方式定义的价值次序，而后者正起到了使歧视与（太

过于经常的）暴力合法化的作用。

——Mbembe 1992 年：142—143 页

正如我在关于翻译之政治的著作中论述的那样，一种普世的历史的前提——在比较研究中，人类意识的统一乃是基于这个前提——允许——就像在黑格尔式的世界历史模式中那样——把第三世界文化放到欧洲—美国文化之下的一种内在的等级秩序而出现（Niranjana，1992 年：69—70 页）。

结果，甚至当第三世界知识分子自己在从事比较工作的时候，他们也成为将**他们自己的**文化产物拿来与殖民母国文化产物相比较的这种工作的一部分——迦梨陀娑成了印度的莎士比亚，图图奥拉（Amos Tutuola）成了非洲的菲尔丁。这是在我们被殖民的文化中找到某种，就像夸美·安东尼·阿皮亚写到的那样，"达到［某种标签的］高标"（无论是哲学的还是文学的标签）的东西，找到某种我们"**值得**受尊敬"的东西的渴求的一部分（Appiah，1992 年：148 页，强调部分来自原文）。事实是，阿皮亚说，以非洲为例，"在西方的阴影中受教育的知识分子"注定"要采纳一种本质上的比较视野"（Appiah，1992 年：151 页）。为这些术语框定的比较计划所固有的不对称，在两个不同的第三世界语境被主体—位置和定位处于第三世界的人比较或放到一起研究的时候，至少被移走了（由于它不可能仅仅因此而消失）。

19

在殖民母国的回圈之外？

因此，这就是一种与视角之构造有关，与个人的所在地如何有助于批判个人与知识和表征的殖民母国体系之合谋有关的论述。尽管人们从中说话的空间，其历史、其问题，都决定性地设定了研究者的视角，这点现在已经得到了广泛的承认，但是，这样一种视角结构在第三世界的比较研究上的意义，尚未得到详尽的讨论。如果民族志研究工作——按定义这种研究永远是比较的——至今已经不但在字面意义上而且在象征意义上都内嵌于统治结构的话，那么我们也可以推测，当这奠基的动力（founding impulse）不再是更大的和具备更有效的控制力的时候会发生什么。如果人们不再为了治理或管理而再现或生产知识的话，替代性的动力可能是什么？

如果那些动力中的某一种，是拆解欧洲中心主义的政治计划的有意识的表述的话，那么，除却其他的第三世界空间，人们还要到哪里（在他们自己本土的语境之外，本土的语境出于种种原因可能是不充分的）去寻找资源呢？这项计划不可能是一项孤立的、仅位于单个后殖民地（postcolony）的计划。尽管我当然不会否定在许多地区殖民与后殖民的轨迹彼此互有差异，当代语境中支持例外论的论述只会削弱人们迫切需要的新的团结出现的可能。[1] 关于我们共同历史的沉默，

---

[1] 比如说，举两个例子，印度人和巴西人，常常主张在不同语境中的例外。这种生成只能是普世范畴生产中的合谋。

反映了某种为我们所共享的未来之可能的沉默。因此，也许某种程度地把共享的历史呈现出来可以是有益的，因为作为这些历史之产地和留存地的殖民地和学科网络一直以来都是殖民主义/新殖民主义全球事业的一部分。至于可能"得到"的是什么，只有比较计划的结果才能给出建议。只有通过担起提出问题——其中不止一个国家有类似的利害关系——的风险，我们才能争取对我们的研究范式进行重新配置的机会。

就像有关印度文化的研究需要把东方主义的再现结构纳入考虑范围之内那样（Niranjana，1993年；Niranjana，1992b），我们也得为我们正在尝试介入的第三世界语境进行类似的整地工作。正如我在西印度群岛旅居期间发现的那样，我对"印度"，比如说在殖民话语中被生产的方式的觉知，并没有为我提供感觉到与加勒比相关的类似——如果尚有所差异的话——的再现结构的保证。开始在自己所在的空间之外思考第三世界空间的第三世界知识分子，需要提出这些不同的区域如何被话语建构为知识的客体的问题，需要进一步地检视使这些知识的客体得以出现的技术与理论，理解在哪种程度上我们当下对彼此的阅读受到了那些论述框架的框定。[1]

---

[1] 通过书写非洲语境并使用V.Y.穆丁比创造的"殖民图书馆"术语，阿奇尔·姆邦伯（Achille Mbembe 1992年：141页）声称，先于一切关于非洲的当代话语，存在一个"图书馆"，一种落成的偏见，后者摧毁了一切有效比较的根基。

替代性的框架

如果迄今为止这些学科一直受这些支配的范式所限定，那么，在这些议程被扰乱的时候，可能被生产出来的是何种第三世界的再现呢？我们可以问，当一个西印度人阅读尼日利亚人钦努阿·阿契贝（Chinua Achebe）的时候，会发生什么？当一个南亚人阅读西印度人卡姆·布拉斯维特的作品时又会发生什么？在南非的杜比（Lucky Dube）吟唱牙买加风格雷鬼乐（reggae）的时候又会发生什么？这些新的再现的意义是什么？它们发出何种文化转变的信号？它们的功能与第三世界环路中传播的殖民母国文化产品的功能有何不同？它们可能在它们开始传播的新场所中协助开启什么批判的空间？

还能提出更多的问题：为什么我们南方各国确实应该彼此交谈？为什么我们必须介入跨越第三世界地点的比较研究？也许新的比较工作的"目的"是间接的。也许这种工作可以做到的，是对参考坐标的替代性框架的发展作出贡献，这样，西方现代性就不再被视为合法化或比较的唯一立足点。让我对此作出强调，我不想提出，我们能够消除第一世界的知识结构或直接生产完全不以"西方"为中介的主体性。我的论点只是，需要对比较之轴的规范化进行质疑。在我们许多批判性的工作中，在我们的大众文化概念中，这个轴线上对立的两极自我展示为"印度"和"西方"。承认在我们的日常生活层面之外，存在有别于西方的地理和政治空间，存在总是与我们的文化交叉——但通过殖民主义的逻辑这些空间与我们的过去的相互叠盖却不可能得到承认——的空间,实现这种承认是重写我们的历史,以及预想并扩充我们的未来——一起构筑的、更新的未来——的第一步。[1]

对其他第三世界空间的批判性的介入可能有助于在南方开创一种新的国际主义,(在其动机、欲望及其想象的未来上)区别于为第一世界所驱动的侵略性的全球化国际主义。植入本文的论点是关于视角和智识/政治的定位。**位于**第三世界,我们该如何互相**阅读**以确保我们不仅仅表现为西方历史的脚注(Mukherjee,1995年)?我们该如何学会质疑那种关于第三世界人民的知识藉以生产的认识论结构?这里我要引用圭亚那学者、活动家沃尔特·娄德尼(Walter Rodney)的话:

> 当一个非洲人辱骂一个印度人的时候,他重复的是所有那些白种人对印度契约"苦力"说过的话;反过来,印度人也从白人那里借用了"懒惰的黑鬼"的陈词滥调,把它用到他身旁的非洲人身上。就像除了通过一个白种人的眼光,没有一个黑人会看到另一个黑人。是开始通

---

[1] 正如大卫·斯科特评论的那样,"当然,问题不在于好像要恢复某个古老的前殖民统一体而抹除西方,好像,西方是真的可抹除的样子。相反,问题……在于建立一种反思性标记的对话交流之实践,这种实践能够使后殖民知识分子与别处的后殖民者相沟通……透过的是共享但有差异的历史和这些共享但有差异的认同"(Scott,1989年:83—84页)。

过我们自己的眼睛来观看的时候了。(Rodney，1969年：33—34页)

我们应该把何种批判意识带入我们的教学和写作，以避免生产穆丁比(V. Y. Mudimbe)所谓的"殖民图书馆"中存在的关于黑/棕/黄种人的刻板印象(Mbembe，1992年：142页)？我们怎样才能学会提出哪些与其他第三世界空间中的人民的实际关注相符的问题？我们需要建构什么样的图书馆或档案馆？我们需要获取的新的读写能力(literacy)又是什么？我们怎样才能学会克服我们那些多重的遗忘症？

这篇论文表达了一些与新的世界主义印度人的出现有关的焦虑，他们可能积极地寻求与第一世界而不是第三世界的认同。此外，我也通过聚焦于第三世界比较研究者所面临的**共同**问题，来探讨为什么这种认同是成问题的，我也间接地指出印度研究者把那些否定自己的空间并使其"去历史化"的熟练操作和再现模式，复制到他们与其他第三世界语境的关系中的危险。在这样做的时候，我并不是意图为向我们尼赫鲁时代的国际政治的简单回归而辩；相反，我要求的，是通过指出为全球化的经济增长所掩盖的团结之形式，对当下的可能性进行重新的思考。

随着新的全球化，通往第一世界的种种路径将会得到前所未有的清晰界定，同时也会变得更加易于穿越。地图上的其他场所会变得前所未有的模糊，前所未有的更难以企及。今日，我们当代政治—文化认同的批判视角，比过往更加地要求我们把其他旅途纳入我们的议程之中。

致　谢

这篇文章起源于笔者在不同场所与大卫·斯科特（David Scott），玛丽·约翰（Mary John），纳迪·爱德华兹（Nadi Edwards），萨迪斯·德什潘德（Satish Deshpande），苏西·塔鲁和韦维克·达勒什瓦（Vivek Dhareshwar）等人的持续对话。我还要感谢乌玛·马赫什瓦利（Uma Maheshwari），阿妮塔·切利安（Anita Cherian），帕普（Rekha Pappu）和斯里拉塔（K. Srilata）对这篇论文文稿的评论。我还要对一些朋友的批评表示感谢，正是他们批判性的介入，使我进一步重塑我的一些论述，他们是：克雷格·卡隆（Craig Calhoun），恩内斯托·拉克劳（Ernesto Laclau），查特尔·墨菲（Chantal Mouffe），库米·纳多（Kumi Naidoo），路易·索亚雷斯（Luiz Soares）和伟力合（Otavio Velho）。

（翻译：王立秋　校订：陈恒）

参考书目

Appiah, Kwame Anthony (1992) "Ethnophilosophy and its critics", in *In My Father's House: Africa in the Philosophy of Culture*, Methuen.

Asad, Talal (ed.) (1973) Anthropology and the Colonial Encounter, Humanities Press.

Asad, Talal (1986) "The concept of cultural translation in British social anthropology", in J. Clifford and G. Marcus (eds.), *Writing Culture: The Poetics and Politics of Ethnography*, University of California Press.

Chatterjee, Partha (1996) "Two poets and death: on civil and political society in the non-Christian world", unpublished paper.

Clifford, James (1983) "On ethnographic authority", *Representations* 1, 118—146.

Fabian, Johannes (1986) *Language and Colonial Power: The Appropriation of Swahili in the Former Belgian Congo, 1880–1938*, Cambridge University Press.

Mbembe, Achille (1992) "Prosaics of servitude and authoritarian civilities", *Public Culture* 5 (10): 123—145.

Mukherjee, Meenakshi (1995) A phrasein a talk on"The Caribbean and Us", IACLALS Annual Conference, Mysore: January.

Niranjana, Tejaswini (1992a) *Siting Translation: History, Post-structuralism and the Colonial Context*, University of California Press.

Niranjana, Tejaswini (1992b) "History, really beginning: compulsions of postcolonial pedagogy" in Rajeswari, S. R. (ed.) *The Lie of the Land: English Literary Studies in India*, Oxford University Press.

Niranjana, Tejaswini (ed.) (1993) *Interrogating Modernity*, with P. Sudhir and V. Dhareshwar, Seagull Books.

Niranjana, Tejaswini (1995) "The Indian in me: gender, identity and cultural politics in Trinidad". Paper presented at the International Conference on the Indian Diaspora, Trinidad: University of the West Indies, St. Augustine.

Rajan, Rajeswari Sunder (ed.) (1992) *The Lie of the Land: English Literary Studies in India*, Oxford University Press.

Rodney, Walter (1969) *The Groundings with my Brothers*, Bogle-l'Ouverture.

Said, Edward (1978) *Orientalism*, Vintage.

Scott, David (1989) "Locating the anthropological subject: postcolonial anthropologists in other places". In J. Clifford and V. Dhareshwar (eds.) *Traveling Theories, Traveling Theorists.* Special Issue of *Inscriptions* (No.5).

Singham, A. W. and Hune, Shirley (1986) *Non-Alignment in an Age of Alignments*, Zed Books.

语言，斗争之所

本文译自《为翻译定位：历史，后结构主义与殖民语境》（Siting Translation: History, Post-Structuralism and the Colonial Context），特贾斯维莉·尼南贾纳著，加州大学出版社（University of California Press），1992年，1—86页。本中译版最先发表于《语言与翻译的政治》，许宝强、袁伟选编，中央编译出版社，2001年，第4章。

对英语知识的热情已经渗透并扩散到了印度最蒙昧、最偏远的地方。一些土著孩子在往返于恒河中的汽艇上乞讨着，他们要的不是钱，而是书本……有一帮男孩从一个叫考麦科里（Comercolly）的偏僻地方上了船，缠住了几位要来加尔各答的先生。孩子们要起书来的那份热切劲让他们大感惊讶。一本柏拉图就放在桌子上，而其中一位先生随便问一个男孩，给他这本行不行。"行啊!"那孩子叫道,"随便什么书都行,我就是要一本书。"这位先生情急之下终于想到了一个办法:他拆开一本过期的《评论季刊》,然后把里头的文章分给了他们。

——查尔斯·特里维廉(Charles Trevelyan),
《论印度人民的教育》

定位翻译

在后殖民的脉络下,**翻译**的问题意识(the problematic of *translation*)成了引发有关再现、权力以及历史性等诸多问题的一个十分重要的场所。所谓的后殖民脉络,指的是百家辩驳争鸣,竞相试图去解释或重新描述存在于不同的人民、种族和不同语言之间的不对称和不平等关系。由于殖民事业里所蕴含的驯服/主体化(subjection/subjectification)的实践,并非仅仅是通过帝国的强制机器得以实施,它们同时也借由哲学、历史、人类学、语文学、语言学以及文学阐释等种种话语而得以推行,因此,殖民"主体/臣民"(the colonial "subject")——由权力/知识的技术或实践[1]所建构——便是在多重论述与多个场所之上所产生出来的。翻译就是这样一个场所。作为一种实践,翻译型塑了并具体化了殖民状态下不对等的权力关系。在此利害攸关的是被殖民者的再现——他们必须以一种特殊样貌给生产出来,以至于能够正当化殖

---

[1] 福柯说,"(权力)产生知识……(它们)互相直接地蕴含着彼此"(Foucault, 1979年: 27页)。他进一步指出,"个人"或主体是由权力技术或主体化的实践所"制造"出来的。

民统治,并且会自己主动地去乞求英文书籍。在这样的殖民脉络下,构成翻译问题意识的一系列相关问题便导致了某种概念经济的产生。依照惯例,翻译依赖于西方哲学有关真实、再现以及知识等的主张。真实被视为是毫无疑问、"就在那里"的东西;知识涉及对于这种真实的再现;而再现提供了直接、无中介地去接近透明真实的通道。然而,经典哲学的论述并不是简单地先生产出一种翻译实践,然后这种翻译实践再为殖民统治所用;我认为,在殖民脉络下的翻译生产并支撑了一个概念经济,而这种概念经济又同时渗入到西方哲学的论述里,成了一个哲学素(philosopheme)(哲学概念性的基本单位)。如雅克·德里达(Jacques Derrida)所论,形而上学的概念并不仅限于或单单产生在哲学的"场域"之中;相反,它们是在多种语体,从各式各样的论述中产出并流通其间,提供了一个"概念网络,哲学**本身**即是在此概念网络中构成"。[1] 在型塑某种主体的过程中,在对被殖民者以特定样貌的呈现中,翻译创造出了关于真实和再现的包罗万象的概念。这些概念、以及我们由此而能够产生的思维推断,就把伴随殖民主体建构过程中的暴力完全给遮蔽了。

因此,翻译所生产的是种种遏制的战略。通过运用再现他者的某些模式——他者也因此而得以产生——翻译强化了对被殖民者所作的霸权性(hegemonic)描述,并成为爱德华·萨义德(Edward Said)所称为的再现,或无历史之对

---

[1] 德里达,《白色神话:哲学文本中的暗喻》,收入《哲学的边缘》,阿兰·巴斯(Alan Bass)译,芝加哥:芝加哥大学出版社,1982,第230页。

象。[1]这些描述成为**事实**，进而对殖民地的事态产生影响：且看托马斯·巴宾顿·麦考莱（Thomas Babington Macaulay）[*]在1835年把印度的传统教育当作过时且不相干的东西加以排斥，此举即为英语教育的引入铺平了道路。

在制造连贯又明晰的文本和主体的过程中，翻译——跨越了不同知识幅度的论述——参与了被殖民者文化的定型过程，使其似乎是静止不变的东西，而非历史的产物。翻译的功能似乎是明晰地呈现一个原本已存在的东西，只不过这个"原本"实际上却是由翻译而生产出来的。吊诡的是，翻译也为被殖民者在"历史"里提供了一席之地。得翻译之助而出头的黑格尔历史观，鼓吹一种目的论的、等级化的文明模式，依据的便是"精神"之"觉悟"(the "coming to consciousness" of "Spirit")，而对于这种发展，非西方文化据称并不适宜或者尚未做好准备。翻译就是这样为了不同的论述——哲学、历史编纂学、教育、传教士的著述、游记等——所部署，以为更新和维系殖民统治之用。

我在此所关注的是通过对一组相关文本的解读，探讨翻译在当代欧美文学理论（在广义上使用这个"学科"之名）中所处的位置。我认为，在殖民和后殖民的脉络下，"翻译"的部署向我们展示了对后结构主义的一些理论要素的一种质疑之道。

---

1 萨义德，与尤吉尼奥·多纳托（Eugenio Donato）等人的讨论（Said, 1979年：65—74页）。

[*] 麦考莱，英国辉格党议员，著名历史学家，著有《英国史》。

第一章概述翻译的问题意识及其相关的后殖民情境。通过解读不同种类殖民译者的文本，我要表明它们是如何把对非西方他者的霸权性描述制造出来的。由于有了强有力的翻译形而上学作为根基，这些描述即便在后殖民的脉络下，也仍然被视为是对"我们土著"衰败或堕落的真实写照。在前殖民地国家，统治阶级的权力依然透过英语教育而被正当化，也正是通过英语教育，经由翻译而传布开来的占主导地位的再现，也逐渐被视作是"自然"且"真实"的东西。要能够质疑这些再现，也必须对支撑它们的历史主义信念作一番检讨。因此，我将就对历史决定论的批判与正在经历去殖民化的世界之间的相关性展开讨论。黑格尔式的对非西方的表述固然影响深远，背后还有目的论的历史发展模式的认可，但对这种模式的质疑或仍可倡导出一种新型的翻译实践来。

在第二章里，我将检讨"翻译"在传统翻译研究的论述和民族志写作里的状态。对这两方面的讨论在文学理论上或许处于边缘的地位，但对其研讨一番或许仍可帮助我们提高对翻译批判的认识。翻译研究里常用忠实和背叛一语，假定一个毋庸置疑的再现观，翻译研究困陷于此种惯用语中，不能自拔，便未能去质问翻译的历史性问题；而在另一方面，民族志最近已经开始对再现的纯真无辜、以及长期存在于翻译中的不对等关系这两个方面都展开了质疑。

在第三、第四和第五章里，我的论述将主要围绕保罗·德曼（Paul de Man）、雅克·德里达（Jacques Derrida）以及瓦尔特·本雅明（Walter Benjamin）的著作而展开（本

35

雅明乃一较早的批评家，如今对后结构主义的思想家们正变得日益重要起来）。我的分析表明翻译是如何在这三位思想家那里起着一个"哲学形象"（figure）的作用，与每个人的主要关怀同义或者相关：在德曼是寓言（allegory）或文学；在德里达是再现和意向性的问题意识；在本雅明是唯物主义的历史编纂问题。我一方面指出本雅明著作里翻译与历史之间的布置关系，一方面描述德曼与德里达对其《翻译者的任务》这篇重要论文所作的解读。我的论点是，瓦尔特·本雅明早期就翻译所作的论述都意味深长地化为一种喻说，并转入了其后期有关历史写作的文章里，而德曼和德里达都没有认识到这层转喻。[我用"喻说"（trope）一词来表示一种包含了重喻（re-figuring）和置换（displacement）的隐喻过程。]两位解构的主要倡导者拒不理会本雅明文中的历史问题，这便让人想到了他们理论中的一个重大缺陷，也许还表明了何以解构从未处理过殖民主义的问题。

在最后一章，借助从印度南部的卡纳达语译成英语的一段文字，我将讨论在后殖民空间里后结构主义的"使用"。通观全书，我的论述遍及了殖民统治下翻译"发挥作用"的所有语域：哲学的、语言学的和政治的。假使在哪里我似乎仅仅专论其一，那完全是出于一种策略性的考虑。

在一个迅速去殖民化的世界里，结构主义和后结构主义对文学研究的影响导致"英语"出现了"危机"，本书便是处在此种更为广泛的脉络之下。自由主义人文主义的意识形态鼓吹殖民主义的教化使命，其自身也因此而得以延续；此种意识形态在遵循阿诺德（Arnold）、利维斯（Leavis）和艾略特（Eliot）传统的"文学"和"批评"的话语里，也还依然被继续宣扬着。这些学科压制了自身得以合法建立的基础，此基础即德里达借海德格尔之言，称之为逻各斯中心主义的或本体神学的形而上学，而所有关于再现、翻译、真实、整体和知识的概念都包含在其间。[1]

对"英语"或文学或批评，很少有从后殖民视角给予系统性的质疑者，更不用说还吸收了当代理论洞见的后殖民视角。[2]为了能有助于对这些论述与殖民和新殖民统治之间的共谋性展开质疑，我打算以检讨翻译之"使用"作为一个适度的开场。自欧洲启蒙运动时起，翻译就一直被用来支撑种种主体化的实践，对被殖民的民族来说，尤其如此；在这样一个情境下，对翻译进行反思便成了一项重大的课题。对于试图要理解那些早已活在"翻译里"、由殖民视角想象与再想象的"主体/臣民"的后殖民理论，这项反思则具有极大的迫切性。这样一种反思，试图通过解构翻译并重新书写翻译作

---

[1] 比如，后浪漫主义文学批评所依据的文本概念是把文本看成是一个统一、连贯的象征性整体，而可以被批评家"再"现或诠释。德里达会说文本"总是已经"带上了再现的标记的，它并非是经由其"作者"的"原创性"突然就产生出来的。

[2] 但请参见高里·维斯瓦纳坦（Viswanathan, 1987年）。维斯瓦纳坦在其《征服的面具》(Masks of Conquest，哥伦比亚大学出版社，1989年)一书里，对殖民印度时期英国文学的意识形态作用做了精确细致的讨论。在此我还应该提到恩古吉·瓦·蒂翁哥（Ngũgĩ, et al., 1972年）对英语文学所提出的著名质疑。其他可参考的著作包括Achebe，1975年和Chinweizu & Madubuike, 1980年（1983年）。

为抗争策略的潜能,来重塑我们对翻译的认识。

鉴于"后殖民"是以分散形态存在的,我们将必须通过各种不同的节点去理解它:即现在与压迫历史的交汇点;[1]殖民"主体"的形成;市民社会里霸权(hegemony)的运作,[2]以及已经开始了的建设性的解构工作(affirmative deconstruction)[3]。

在着手描述后殖民的时候,我们或许可以重述一下殖民主义的一些残酷事实。自17世纪末年左右一直到"二战"以后,全世界几乎都被英国和法国,还有次一等的西班牙、葡萄牙、德国、俄国、意大利以及荷兰所控制——统治、占领和剥削。到了1918年,欧洲列强已把地球上85%的地方都变成了其殖民地。[4]一直到第一次世界大战以后(有些非西方的史学家称其为欧洲内战),非殖民化的进程才露出端倪。当然,我们在此不能说从殖民到后殖民社会存在着一个迅速或完整的过渡期,因为那样便会把殖民历史断裂的复杂性降低到了无足轻重的地步。**去殖民化**一词只能是粗略地指称那在民族解放斗争的语言里被称为"权力移交"的东西,通常是从统治的殖民政权转移到本土的精英阶层手里。

---

1 **历史**同**翻译**一样,是在本书里一直受到质问的一个词。
2 **霸权**(hegemony)和**市民社会**(civil society)是安东尼奥·葛兰西用的两个词。其定义将在后面的讨论里给出。葛兰西的名著是收在 Quaderni del carcere 里的一系列片言断语,英译文叫《狱中札记》(Gramsci, 1971年)。我所给出的关于"主体化实践"的例证,主要根据自传性的著作,其中大多是来自殖民和后殖民的印度。
3 关于翻译作为建设性解构的例子,见 Niranjana, 1992年:ch.6章。
4 关于帝国强权野心的生动描述,见爱德华·萨义德的经典名著《东方学》(Orientalism, Said, 1978年)。

政权之移交固然有其不可忽视的重要意义，但假如据此便把它看成是殖民统治"结束"的标志，则未免太天真了一些，因为殖民论述的力量正在于它所具有的巨大伸缩性。我所谓的**殖民论述**，指的是用于建构并支配"殖民主体/臣民"的那套知识体系、再现模式、权力策略，以及法律、规训等等。这里**论述**的用法，在意义上与米歇尔·福柯（Michael Foucault）的概念并无多大的不同，但是，我对这一术语的运用又不完全是建立在福柯体系之上的，这一点在本章的余下部分将会得到明示。殖民的权力关系常常就在那只能称之为新殖民的状态下又再被生产了出来，且有些时候，前殖民地的人民对"英文书籍"的渴望一如其祖先一样的强烈。[1]

因此，所谓后殖民者（主体、国家、语境），依然还深深地带着一个不在场的殖民主义（absentee colonialism）的烙印。在经济和政治上，前殖民地仍要继续依赖从前的统治者或称"西方"；在文化领域（**文化**在此不仅指文学和艺术，而且还包括种种的主体化实践），尽管民族主义的修辞广为人用，但去殖民化的成效却是极其缓慢的。我认为，通过考察翻译，我们或许能对殖民话语的持续力量理解得更加深刻一些，并进而学会颠覆之。

---

[1] 虽然许多帝国主义批评家把当代第三世界的社会描绘成"新殖民主义的"，但我将使用**后殖民**一词，以免低估了活跃于这些社会里的反抗殖民和新殖民的压迫力量。在这里我特别指的是印度这个情境，所举大部分例子也都来自那里。再者，经济学家要比文化理论家更有可能会用**新殖民主义**一词。这样说并不是要假设两个独立不同的分析领域，而仅仅是想表明在一个角度层面上适用的词在另一个之上也许就不那么准确了。

至此应该清楚明白的是，**翻译**一词在我这里并非仅指一种跨语际的过程，而是对一整个完整问题意识的指称。它是一组问题，也许是一个"场"，充斥着所有被挪用的词汇所产生的力量，甚至也包括了传统翻译论述的用语在内，以用来指名那些问题，用来**翻译**。拉丁文里 translatio 和希腊文里的 metapherein，立即使人联想到运动、扰乱和置换。德文里的 Übersetzung 也一样，法文里的 traducteur 处在 interprète（诠释者）与 truchement（代言人，媒介）之间，表明了我们或许可以合诠释与阅读之力造就一种翻译实践，而其所具有的扰乱力量要比其他两项行为大出许多。置换的要义在其他一些拉丁文词语如 transponere, transferre, reddere, vertere 里也可见到。在我的笔下，翻译指的是：（一）与某些古典的关于再现和真实的观点相互支撑的翻译问题意识；（二）由后结构主义对前一问题意识的批判所开启的问题意识，这便使得翻译总是成为一种"增益"（more），或德里达所谓的添补（supplement）。[1] 添补有两重含义，既指补缺，也指"额外"添加。德里达是这样解释的："能指的过剩（overabundance），其添补性（supplementary character），乃是一个有限性（finitude）的产物，也就是说，是一个必须得到添补的缺漏的

---

[1] 在《立场》一书里，德里达（Derrida, 1981 年）把添补界定为一种"不可确定"之物，无法再"被包含在哲学的（二元）对立之中"，但它又是在"从不建立第三项的情况下"，抵制并瓦解着哲学的二元树立。"……添补既不是加，也不是减，既不是外在的，也不是内在的补充；既不是偶然的，也不是本质之所在。"

结果。"(Derrida，1978年)不过，在有需要的时候，我会点明翻译一词的较为狭义的用法。

我对翻译的研究，完全不是要去解决什么译者的困境，不是要在理论上再给翻译另立一说，以便难够找到一个"缩小"不同文化间之"隔阂"的更加保险可靠的"办法"。相反，它是要对这道隔阂、这种差异作彻底的思索，要探讨如何把对翻译的执迷（obsession）和欲望加以定位，以此来描述翻译符号流通其间的经济学。关于翻译的论述是多种多样的，但它们却都没有，或缺乏，或压制了对历史性和不对称的意识，而就这一状况进行考察，便是我的关注所在。虽然欧美文学上的现代派如埃兹拉·庞德（Ezra Pound）、格特鲁德·斯泰因（Gertrude Stein）、萨缪尔·贝克特（Samuel Beckett）都坚持不懈地凸显了翻译问题，但由于他们的著述至少已被主流的文学批评家们广泛地讨论过，又因为我的质问核心不是诗学，而是当今被称为"理论"的诸种论述，所以我对他们的著作未有论及。

后殖民对自由人文主义关于进步的修辞和对普世性宏大叙述所持的怀疑态度，与后结构主义有着明显而密切的关联。[1]比如德里达对再现所作的批判，使我们能够对"再现"（re-presentation）这个概念进行质疑，进而对那需要得到"再现"的本源或对"本源"这一概念本身展开质疑。德里达认

---

[1] 事实上，即便是对于**后殖民**和**第三世界**这两个词汇，我用起来也不无犹豫，因为它们也可被一个无视多样性的整体化叙述所用。

为"本源"本身就是分散的,其"同一性"无法确定,因而一个再现不是"再现"一个"本源",相反,它所"再现"的总是那种已经被再现的东西。这一观点可以被用来推翻那些关于"印度人"的霸权性"再现",比如说,由 G.W.F. 黑格尔和詹姆斯·穆勒(James Mill)所提供的那些说法。[1]

后结构主义对反思翻译意义重大的另一面,在于其对历史主义的批判:这种批判揭示了传统历史编纂学所具有的发生学(追溯本源)与目的论(设定某种目的)的特征。我已经指出过,所谓"历史主义",其实是将**历史的**东西(因而既非不可避免也非不可改变)表现为**自然的**东西,这一点与我对殖民主义主体化实践的关注有着直接的关联。对历史主义的批判或许可以给我们展示一条把穆勒和黑格尔笔下那"怯懦"又"狡诈"的印度人加以解构的方法。当然,我在此关注的不是所谓对"印度人"的错误再现。确切地说,我是要对掩盖相互关联性且把"差异"本质化的态度(即约翰尼斯·费边[Johannes Fabian]称为的否认同时共代性[denial of coevaelness])进而导致对他者的刻板印象建构的做法展开质疑。如霍米·巴巴(Homi Bhabha)所说的:"刻板印象并不是因为它对某个特定的真实作了虚假的再现因而是一种简化。它之所以是简化,乃是因为它是一种固定不变的再现形式;这种再现否认差异的活动变化(经由他者而行的否定使

---

[1] 黑格尔,《历史哲学》(1837),西贝利(J. Sibree)译,纽约:科利尔出版社,第203—235页,以下称《历史哲学》;穆勒,《英属印度史》(1817;新德里:联合出版社,1972),以下称《英属印度史》。

之成为可能），对于主体如何在精神和社会关系之意义中的**再现**构成了一个问题。"（Bhabha，1983年：27页）

查尔斯·特里维廉本就是积极支持对印度人实施英语教育的，他在1838年描述的那些"土著男孩"，被殖民主义论述"召唤"（interpellated）或塑造成为了主体。特里维廉骄傲地展示了，印度的少年是如何在没有任何外力的强迫下，主动地乞求"英语"。[1]

关于对被殖民者的文明教化，黑格尔式的哲学家、穆勒式的史学家、威廉·琼斯爵士（Sir William Jones）[*]式的东方学家都制造出了霸权性的文本，部分地保证了主体对于屈从状态的"自由接受"（free acceptance）。[2] 这些"学者"（scholarly）的论述（文学翻译是其概念性的标志）帮助维系着殖民统治的压迫，而殖民统治又通过对其"主体/臣民"的召唤来支撑这些论述。殖民主体的建构要经历一个"他者

---

[1] 在殖民统治下，"个人作为一个（自由的）主体被召唤，以便能够自愿地屈从于主体的命令，也就是，（自由地）接受他的屈从状态，即他将'完全由他自己'来作出屈从的姿态和行为。"（Althusser，1971年：182页，着重号为原文所加）**召唤**是阿尔都塞用来描述意识形态用语言来"建构"主体的一个词。

[*] 威廉·琼斯，英国人，东方学家，创建了亚洲协会，提出了著名的印欧语假说，揭示了梵语与欧洲语言之间的同族关系。

[2] 我并不是要把黑格尔的唯心主义、穆勒的功利主义和琼斯的人道浪漫主义混为一谈。但是他们的文本却都建立在异常相像的关于印度和印度人的预设之上。有关这些预设是如何最终导致了英语教育引进印度的讨论，请参阅拙文《翻译、殖民主义及英语的兴盛》（Niranjana，1990年）。拉杰斯瓦里·松德·拉坚（Rajeswari Sunder Rajan）对我要把翻译同"英语"在印度的开端联系起来的尝试，提出了富有见地的批评，在此谨表谢意。

化"的过程,这涉及了一种目的论的历史观,即把殖民地的知识和生活方式看作是在"正常的"或西方社会里所有之物的扭曲或不成熟的版本。[1]因此,西方的东方学家的知识挪用了"再现东方之权力,不仅向欧美人,而且也给东方人本身去翻译并解释他(和她)自己的思想和行为。"(同上:408页)

作为召唤的翻译

18世纪末,英国想方设法地要了解东印度公司商人底下属民的情况,翻译在此即明显构成了东方主义殖民话语的一部分。爱丁堡大学一位名叫 A. 马克诺奇(A.Maconochie)的学者,在1783年和1788年两次敦促英国君主采取"或许是必要的措施来发掘、搜集并翻译所有现存的印度人的古籍"。[2]虽然马克诺奇希望透过这些翻译,欧洲的天文学、"古器物学"以及其他科学能够获得进展,然而,是要到了威廉·琼斯(他于1783年抵达印度,出任位于加尔各答的最高法院的法官)的手中,翻译才明显地服务于"驯化东方并将其转化成一个欧洲学问的国度"。[3]

作为翻译家和学者,琼斯一手把一个文本化了的印度介绍到欧洲,且影响最大。他到达印度不出三月,亚洲学会

---

[1] 罗纳德·英登,《印度的东方主义建构》,《当代亚洲研究》,20,第3号(1986),第401—446页。

[2] 引自达兰帕(Dharampal),《美丽的树:18世纪印度原住民的教育》(新德里:白布利亚出版社,1983),第9页。

[3] 萨义德,《东方主义》,第78页。

（Asiatic Society）即召开了第一次会议，琼斯任会长，而总督沃伦·黑斯廷斯（Warren Hastings）则为赞助人。亚洲学会成员本都是东印度公司组建的印度政府里的行政官员，也主要是通过这些人的努力，翻译将助上一臂之力，把东方"收拢"（gather in）并"圈围"（rope off）起来。（同上）

琼斯精通波斯语文法，做过翻译，在来印度之前，已经是享有盛誉的东方学家。他在一封信里坦陈雄心抱负，立志"要了解印度，要博大精深胜于古往今来的任何其他欧洲人"。[1] 据说，18世纪西方的文人几乎都读过琼斯的译作（Arberry，1960年：82页）。同代的作家，尤其是德国作家，如歌德（Goethe）、赫尔德（Herder）等人都仔细研读过他的作品。当琼斯有新作抵达欧洲时，各类期刊都热切地摘选一些短小的篇章，立即予以刊登。他翻译的迦梨陀娑的《沙恭达罗》（Sākuntala）一版再版；乔治·福斯特（George Forster）据此译本在1791年出了他那著名的德文翻译，其后，该剧更被翻译成其他几种欧洲语言。正如20世纪一位学者所说："说他改变了我们（即欧洲人）对东方世界的整个概念也并不夸张。如果要写一篇有关琼斯影响的论文，我们则可以自吉本（Gibbon）到丁尼生（Tennyson）的注脚里搜集到大部分的材料。"[2] 琼斯对研究印度的数代学人的持久影响，甚至在1984年印度出版的琼斯演讲和论文集里都可见

---

1 《致阿尔索坡二世斯宾塞伯爵的信》（1787年8月17日）收于（Jones，1970年：2：751页）；着重号为原文所加。
2 R.M. 荷威特（R.M. Hewitt），引自 Arberry（1960年：76页）。

到。在文集的前言，编辑莫尼·巴格齐（Moni Bagchee）指出，印度人应该"沿着威廉·琼斯爵士所规划的道路，去努力准确地保存并阐释其民族的遗产"。[1]

我研究琼斯的文本，主旨并非是要拿琼斯的《沙恭达罗》或《摩奴法典》的译本去与所谓的原著作一番比较。确切地说，我要做的是研究琼斯译作的"外围文字"——如前言、他每年向亚洲学会所作的演讲、他给加尔各答大陪审团的指示、他的信件，以及他写下的"东方"诗词——以便展示他是如何参与建构一个历史主义式的、目的论的文明发展模式；这种模式与以透明再现为先决条件的翻译观融会合一，协助建立起了关于"印度人"的强大叙事版本，使得后代的论者，纵使其哲学和政治流派各有不同，但却都把这种描述几乎是浑然一体地纳入到了他们各自的文本之中。

琼斯著作里最富意味之处包括：（1）由于土著对其自身的法律和文化的诠释不足为信，所以必须由欧洲人来作翻译；（2）成为一个立法者的欲望，给印度人制定他们"自己的"法律；以及（3）对于印度文化进行"净化"并为其代言的欲望。这些执迷与欲望之间的内在关联极其复杂，但它们都可被视为是注入于一个更广泛的关于改善和教育的论述之中，用以召唤殖民主体。

琼斯构建出来的"印度人"是一副懒懒散散、逆来顺受的样子，整个民族无法品味自由的果实，却祈盼被专制权力

---

[1] 巴格齐（Bagchee）为琼斯的《演讲及文章》（Jones，1984：xvi 页）所写的前言。

所统治,且深深地沉溺在古老宗教的神话里。他在一封信里指出,印度人"无法享有公民自由,"因为"他们当中极少有人有此概念,而知道的人也并不想要自由"。[1] 琼斯本乃 18 世纪一正直的自由派人士,反对"邪恶",但却承认印度人有"接受专制权力统治的必要性"。看到土著在英国统治下比在他们从前的统治者手下要"快乐"得多,他的"悲伤"得到了"极大的抚慰"。在另一封信里,琼斯告诫为他所羡慕的美国人,别"像我身边这些上当受骗、迷迷糊糊的印度人那样,你若把自由给了他们,他们非但不以为福,反以为祸;他们会把它当作一瓶毒药那样甩掉,而如果他们能够品尝一下,再消化掉,其实是会成为生命之源的。"[2]

英国的统治是必要的;自由是"不可能"交给印度人的,琼斯有此信念,那厌恶之情便不断得到了缓解。他反复提出了"东方人"习惯于暴虐统治的观点。在对亚洲学会发表的第十年度演讲中,他说,一个"历史"的阅读者"必然会注意到,由于长期暴政统治的作用,人们之所以异于食草牲畜的那些官能都已麻木退化了。这位读者必然会把古往今来大多数亚细亚民族那明确无疑的劣根性都归因于此"。[3] 印度人是"顺从的"、他们没有自由的能力,以及土著的法律不容提出关于自由的问题等等——这些想法就这样被集合在了亚洲专制主义的概念之下。这样的专制统治,再由英国人接

---

[1] 琼斯,《威廉·琼斯爵士书信集》(1970),第 712 页。
[2] 《威廉·琼斯爵士书信集》(1970),第 847 页。
[3] 琼斯,《演讲及文章》(1984),第 99 页。

掌下来，只能用以填满东印度公司的金库："印度人的这些领土，上苍将其投入英国人的怀抱以给予保护和福祉，其土著的宗教、风俗和法律将政治自由的想法全都给杜绝掉了。不过……从这个温顺民族的勤勉之中，吾国所获甚丰甚巨。"[1]

依照琼斯的说法，印度辉煌灿烂的过去是包裹在迷信之中的，"被神话和隐喻的奇形怪状的长袍标识妆点着"（Jones，1984年：100页），但如今这些"退化"且"堕落的"印度人也确曾经"以知识渊博著称于世"承认印度曾有黄金时代，[2] 这种看法似乎与琼斯所坚称的印度社会的不变性相互矛盾："我所谓的印度，指的是印度人的原始宗教和语言在今天依然多少带着其远古纯洁遗风所盛行的整个国土。"[3] 然而，他似乎想要以下面的方式来避开这种矛盾，即通过把未经改变的"宗教和语言"同衰败了的"艺术""政府"和"知识"（同上，7—8页）区分开来，虽然此二者之间的界限极为含糊暧昧。琼斯的区分似乎维持了殖民话语的那种自相矛盾的做法，即一边把土著的没落"自然化"（事情一直未变），一边又将其"历史化"（事情**变得**糟糕了）。我们在史学家詹姆斯·穆勒那里也会看到同样的手法，不过他没有接受琼斯关于印度早先存在一个黄金时代的观点，而是设想了某种一成不变的野蛮状态。

印度人不仅狡诈，而且"天生地"女人气——这样的表

---

[1] 琼斯，《演讲及文章》（1984），第99—100页。

[2] 琼斯，《演讲及文章》（1984），第7—8页。

[3] 琼斯，《演讲及文章》（1984），第6页。

述在琼斯的著述里时常是一并出现的。在一篇论述东方诗歌的文章里,他描绘波斯人的特性是"**柔弱、追欢逐乐、好逸恶劳,还女人气十足**,这些特征使得他们轻易就成了所有西方和北方民族蜂拥侵袭的猎物。"[1] 照琼斯的说法,波斯诗歌对"柔弱、纵欲,但却狡猾又虚伪的"印度人影响甚大。[2] 土著的虚伪和不可靠令琼斯念念不忘,萦绕于心,成了他著作里通常与翻译相关的一个喻说(trope),最早出现在其1777年的《波斯语文法》一书中;塞缪尔·约翰逊(Samuel Johnson)还给沃伦·黑斯廷斯送了一册去。在这本语法书的前言里,琼斯强调了东印度公司官员学习亚洲语言的必要性。在论及对波斯语日益增长的兴趣时(波斯语在印度是法庭用语),他把这归因于英国官员在收到他们看不懂的信件时所产生的挫折感。琼斯道:"现已发现,土著们的精确忠实不足以采信,雇用他们做翻译是件极其危险的事。"[3]

身为印度最高法院的法官,琼斯担当起了翻译印度法的古老文本——《摩奴法典》的任务,这也成了他最为重要的工作之一。事实上,他开始学习梵文,主要就是为了能够核对协助他工作的印度婆罗门学者对印度法所作的解释。他在一封信里写道,很难对好几部法典的土著译员进行核查和控

---

[1] 琼斯著:《东方语言译文集》(Jones, n.d: 348页)以下简称《译文集》。"土著"的女性化在殖民话语是个极有趣的喻说,不过在此将不作展开讨论。
[2] 《译文集》第2卷第358页。
[3] 琼斯著:《波斯语文法·前言》(Jones,1771年[1823年]:vii页)。对"不忠"的反复强调间接表明,在被殖民者这一存在着一个虽被压制但是历史悠久的抵抗传统。我希望在别处探讨这个问题。

制，他说，"在婆罗门学者（精通梵文与印度教的法律、哲学和宗教）和大毛拉（印度伊斯兰教的法律专家）里，几乎难寻诚实正直之士，没有谁给出的意见里不带有该当责备的偏见"。[1] 在开始学习梵文之前，琼斯给已经把《摩奴法典》译出三分之一的查尔斯·威尔金斯（Charles Wilkins）去信说，"印度法的源流要纯净，这一点至关重要，因为我们对梵文一窍不通，全凭土著律师的衷心尽责"（同上，666页）。有趣的是，这位著名东方学家要揭示印度昔日伟大辉煌的企图，常常表现为英国人或欧洲人负有把没落了土著民的文本翻译过来并进而使之净化的职责。这种浪漫的东方学家的宏图大业，几乎是毫不为人所察觉地就滑入了以英语教育来"改进"土著的维多利亚时代功利主义的事业里。[2]

甚至在到印度之前，琼斯就已经制定出了一个解决印度法翻译难题的方案。在1788年写给康沃利斯勋爵（Lord Cornwallis）的信函里，他再次提到了土著律师的狡诈和他们的意见不足为信。"离开英国之前，"他写道，"我就已经想到

---

1 琼斯，《威廉·琼斯爵士书信集》(1970)，第720页。
2 "东方学家"和"英国语言文学专家"对于殉夫自焚（Sati）的习俗有一些共同的假设。有关这一方面的讨论，请参阅Mani（1987年）。维斯瓦纳坦在《英国文学研究之开端》(Viswanathan，1987年）一文中提出，把对印度人的教育英国化的措施实际是利用了东方学的种种"发现"。有关詹姆斯·穆勒与托马斯·麦考莱两个态度之精细区分比较，这可参阅Stokes（1989年[1959年]）。斯托克斯认为穆勒根本就不是个英国语言文学专家，因为他并不认为英语教育符合"功利"的标准。他也绝对不相信正规教育的效用。但是，我在此所关注的是一种较为宽广的功利主义关于教育的话语，这种话语贯穿于英国在印度教育方针的变革之中。

了革除这一恶习的明显的一招"（Jones，1970年：795页）。当然，这明显的一招就是用英国人自己的翻译来代替印度人。与他的赞助人沃伦·黑斯廷斯一样，琼斯坚决赞成以印度人自己的法律来治理印度人。然而，由于这些"上当受骗"又"迷迷糊糊"的印度人不以自由为福反以为祸，由于他们肯定不能管理自己或行使好自己的法律，所以得首先把这些法律从他们手里拿走，经"翻译"之后，才能使他们受益。土著不诚实的另一个表现是琼斯所说的"伪证频仍"（Jones，1999年［1979年］：vol.7）。"一个低贱的土著所发之誓"，几乎没有任何效力，因为作起伪证来，人人都"全无一丝内疚之意，仿佛能作伪证便是机灵智慧的证明，甚或还是一种美德"（同上，7章：280页）。琼斯希望通过再借翻译之力，一劳永逸地解决从印度人那里取"证"的办法（同上，682页），使得这种伪证行为会受到自家（经过翻译的）法律的制裁。

琼斯把编纂和翻译《摩奴法典》看作是"（他的）印度研究的成果"，这一点是明白无疑的，因为他希望，对于生活在这个国度的"八百万纯朴有用之人来说，它能够成为正义的标准，"而这个国度乃是英国于睡梦中、由命运女神抛掷进英国的管辖之下的（Jones，1970年：813页）。法律的论述在此的作用是把殖民冲突的广泛暴力掩盖起来。经过翻译的法律将会规训并调教"数百万印度臣民"的生活，"其勤劳勉力经妥善引导将会大大增加英国的财富"（同上，927页）。因为，按照这位翻译家的说法，"那些法律实际是被对欧洲政治和商业利益极为重要的一些国家当作上帝（the Most High）之言加以敬奉的。"[1] 琼斯的翻译出过四版，重印了数次，最后一次于1880年在马德拉斯面世。虽然在东印度公司治下的后期岁月里，以及在不列颠王国政府的直接管辖下，印度法表面上是依据西方模式来制定的，但时至今日还存在着的因应不同宗教而制定的不同民法规则却表明，这些法律实际是从东方学家对"印度教徒"和"穆斯林"之经文的释义建构和翻译中所得出的。

按照琼斯的逻辑，给印度人以他们自家的法律会带来更高的效率，因而也会给英国带来更大的利益；除此而外，使用印度法或许还有另一层原因。在其第十周年的演讲里，琼斯指出："土著的法律将政治自由的想法全都给杜绝掉了。"（Jones，1984年：100页）这种观点被认作是对"原"文本的一个可靠的（因为是西方的）解释，经由一个与"透明"再现论相互支撑的翻译观的启动之后，便开始在各式各样的论述里流传开来。我认为，翻译的如此部署，是配合了一个目的论的等级文化模式的建立，或为之创造了条件；这种模式把欧洲置于文明的顶端，如此也为被殖民者提供了一个位置。

威廉·琼斯想要净化印度的法律、艺术和哲学的欲望，乃是英国人的进步论述的翻版，这一点我先前已有提及。一心想为"印度人恢复其自家文明之辉煌"的琼斯，在《太阳颂》（1786年）里描述了他的使命。《太阳颂》是琼斯一系列"印度"颂歌里的一首，在欧洲广为流传，由逝去了的黄金时代里

---

[1] 琼斯：《印度法典·前言》，载于Jones（1999年［1799年］vol.7: 89页）。

的人物、衰败且无知的现在和来自远邦的翻译者组建成章:

> 要是他们（神祇）问:"声声慢慢是何人?"
> ……
> 你就说:银色的鸟上天颜温柔更开怀,他从那遥远的地方来。
> 不吐梵天语,
> 自是潺潺圣堂曲;
> 路过了亘古之偏道僻径,穿越过久远之堵塞洞穴。
> 深潭清泉里把东方知识来汲取。[1]

在有些诗如《恒河颂》(1785—1786)里,琼斯改变了用第一人称代词称谓自己的做法,转而给被殖民者开出了一个主语的位置,让"印度人"夸英国人,说他们"保存了**咱们**的法律,又终止了**咱们**的恐惧"(Jones,n.d.:第 2 章:333 页,着重号为笔者所加)。这里,法律的论述似乎凸显了暴力,但结果却是把这暴力放在了殖民**以前**的年代里;或者,换一种说法,是为了表明英国人的到来导致了印度人自家法律的**正确**贯彻和实施,结束了"专制的"暴力和"恐惧"。

在 18 世纪末和 19 世纪初,印度文献的译者分为两大类,一类像是威廉·琼斯这样的行政官员,另一类是像威廉·凯里(William Carey)和威廉·沃德(William Ward)这样属瑟

---

[1]《译文集》第 2 卷第 286 页;原文标点法。

兰波浸信会会教派（Serampore Baptist）的基督教传教士。这后一类属于最早把印度教著作译成欧洲语言的人之列。那些个文本常常是被他们通过编订"标准本"而亲自校勘过了的，其基本准则便是西方关于统一性和连贯性的经典概念。依据这些权威的译本，传教士们斥责印度教徒没有虔诚地实践印度教。[1] 传教士们会接着声称，他们惟一得救的希望就是**改宗皈依**到西方更加高级、发达的宗教。传教士的神学乃是源于一种在传统与现代、落后与发达之间建立一系列对立的历史主义模式。这种把线性的历史叙述强加于不同文明的做法，明显是把殖民压迫合法化并推展了开来。

威廉·沃德在其三卷本的《印度人的历史、文学及神话综述》（Ward，1822年）的前言里，恶毒地攻击土著的堕落和不道德，读来很能说明问题。在沃德的笔下，土著的宗教、生活方式、风俗习惯和制度，一如其他异教徒的一样，都带有"淫秽"和"残忍"的特征，这一点在"印度人"的身上表现得最为"令人恶心"和"骇人"（Ward，1822年：xxxvii页）。作者对"土著"的性活动念念不忘，声称曾亲眼目睹过无数个"淫秽"场景，因为印度的习俗制度就是"淫秽之温床"，且庙堂里的礼拜仪式都呈现出"淫秽的诱惑"（xxxvi—vi页）。然而，与威廉·琼斯所不同的是，沃德并不把印度人的现状看作是背弃了从前那个黄金时代的堕落。相反，同

---

[1] 有关以殉夫自焚为背景而对印度宗教文本化的讨论，请看 Mani（1985年，1：107—127页）。

詹姆·穆勒一样（穆勒经常赞同地引用沃德的话），沃德眼中的印度人天生腐败，缺乏教育和改进的办法。他提出印度人的"精神和道德之改进"乃是不列颠民族的"崇高使命"。一旦印度"文明开化"起来，哪怕是独立了，她也会"大量地消费英国的产品"，从而"更好地促进英国的大繁荣"。沃德论及一件"非常奇怪之事"，即印度每年从英国购买的产品，"连从我们港口里开出的一艘货船都填装不满"：

> 但是，且让印度得到她所需要的那更加高等的文明吧，她是可以开化的；且让欧洲的文学注入到她所有的语言里去吧；然后，你再看，从英伦各港口到印度之间的海面上，将会布满我们的商船。精神教化和科学将会从印度的中心向亚洲各地延伸扩展开，一直到缅甸王国和暹罗，到百千万民众的中国，到波斯，甚至远及阿拉伯半岛去。
>
> （Ward，1822年：liii页）

然后，整个"东半球"都会信仰基督教。在资本主义扩张的时代里，口译和文本翻译协助着为欧洲的商品开拓市场。传教士的文本有助于我们明白的是，翻译自出现伊始，便为宗教、种族、性及经济等论述所多重决定（overdetermined）了。这是一种多重决定，不仅仅是因为多重的力量作用于它，而且还是因为它也带来了多种多样的实践。由翻译所肇始的种种遏制之策因而为一系列的论述所部署，因而我们可以把翻译称为殖民压迫的一项重要技术手段。

沃德著作里所流露出来的那种自以为是的厌恶之情，在詹姆斯·穆勒的"世俗"历史编纂学里得到了非同寻常的回应。穆勒从沃德、琼斯、查尔斯·威尔金斯、纳撒尼尔·哈尔海德（Nathaniel Halhed）、亨利·科尔布鲁克（Henry Colebrooke）以及其他人翻译的文字里构建出了关于"印度人天性"的一种说法。其所著《英属印度史》于1817年以三卷本的形式面世，直到最近一直被当作印度历史的一个范本。[1] 在穆勒看来，印度人，不论印度教徒还是穆斯林，都有着不诚实、撒谎、背信弃义和唯利是图的品行。他说，"印度教徒就像太监一样"，"具有做奴隶的非凡品质。"他们同中国人一样，"言行虚伪、奸诈无信、好撒谎，其品行之卑劣甚至超出了野蛮社会的通常标准"。他们还很怯懦，冷酷无情，自以为是，且身体不干不净（Mill，1817年：486页）。[2] 在界定印度人的过程中，穆勒企图在对比之下，画出一幅"高等"欧洲文明的高尚风貌。如萨义德所指出的，"东方作为可资对照的形象、观念、人格和经验，帮助了对欧洲（或西方）自身的界定"（Said，1978年：1—2页）。

穆勒声称，"弄清印度人在文明等级上的确切状态"对英国人来说具有极大的现实意义。要先弄懂他们，然后才能恰

---

[1] 穆勒的著作今天仍被用在印度历史的课堂上。人们多半甚少提及他的种族主义立场，而对其在描述印度人性格上所表现出来的智慧倒是每每可悲地表示了赞赏之意。

[2] 德国印度学家麦克思·穆勒（Max Müller）宣称，詹姆斯·穆勒的《历史》"要对在印度发生的一些最大的不幸负责"，见古哈（J.P. Guha）为《英属印度史》1972年重印版所作的卷首语，第xii页。

当地治理他们；若是以为他们已经高度文明开化了，那将是一个十分严重的错误（Mill，1817年：456页）。为了证明自己的观点，穆勒常常巧妙地引用持有黄金时代论的东方学家们自己的著述，来把他们置于可疑之地。他的策略是，首先要推翻印度曾有历史的说法，然后提出，印度人的状态堪与证明人类处于其孩提时代的原始社会相比（包括英国自身的过去）。这成熟——幼稚、成年——童年的对立正好增强了殖民脉络维系下的改进和教育论述的生命力。

穆勒有言曰："原始的民族爱称自己拥有一个遥远的古代，似乎从中得到一种特别的满足。东方民族特好浮夸虚荣，爱自吹自擂，所以，它们在大多数情况下都把自己的历史追古溯源得离谱之极"（Mill，1817年：24页）。穆勒的《英属印度史》就是建立在此种言论的框架之上的。书中从头至尾，一而再，再而三地用**原始**、**野蛮**、**凶残**和**粗野**这些字眼来形容"印度人"，就这么全凭重复之力，形成了与东方学家的古老文明假说相对抗的一种论述。

穆勒声称，东方学家们提供的证明印度人有过高度文明的那些描述，都是"虚妄的证据"。比如，印度人所具有的"女性的柔弱"与温和，过去被看作是一个文明社会的标志。然而，在穆勒这里，他却提出文明的**开端**既与举止的"温文尔雅"相符，也不排斥行为的"粗暴有力"。如同北美的"野蛮人"和南海的岛民们所表现的那样，温和常常是与"人类生活最原始野蛮的状态"联系在一起的（Mill，1817年：287—288页）。至于印度教所规定的那些禁欲苦行，则往往是与一个原始民族的宗教里对"最为松弛的道德观"的鼓励并生共存的（同上，205页）。对于印度人使用的工具虽然粗糙但活却做得熟练又利索，一个东方学家或许会知道几句；但穆勒对此的评论则是，"能够熟练地使用自己那些并非完善的工具，乃是原始社会的一个普遍特征"（同上，335页）。要是有谁提出印度人有优美的诗歌，穆勒则回答道，诗歌表明的是人类文学的初始阶段，印度人的文学似乎还依然停留在那里（同上，365页）。

人性之外表虽然多种多样，但在不同的社会阶段却呈现出一种"惊人的一致性"（Mill，1817年：107页），穆勒就是利用他所谓的自己对人性的这种了解，来进一步地巩固他的世界历史的目的论发展模式。比如，印度法所规定的酷刑审判，就常见于"我们野蛮祖先的习俗制度里"（同上，108页）。穆勒似乎是捡起了，比如说，威廉·琼斯关于欧洲文明的印度—雅利安人的起源理论，且如此运用起来，实际是给我们道明了这些理论的意识形态基础。东方学家和功利主义者的话语，最终产生的都是同样的历史主义模式，且是以一种非常相似的方法来把殖民主体加以构建的。穆勒说摩奴那里的创世记述乃是"一片模糊晦暗、语无伦次、前后矛盾又混乱不堪"（同上，163页），且印度人的宗教思想也是"含混、模糊、摇摆不定、隐晦不明又前后不一的"；说这番话时，他实际上是直接援引了琼斯对印度法的看法。"无边的神话"和"那标志着无知之人宗教的一连串无谓的颂扬"（同上，182页），乃是原始的头脑喜好制造离谱、"荒诞又愚蠢"

之物的典型特征（同上，163页）。且把这些观点同琼斯在其《摩奴法典》译本前言里对由"描述和祭司权术"所创造之体系的描写比较一下吧——"它充满了玄学和自然哲学的奇思怪想，充满了无聊的迷信……到处都是微不足道又幼稚的繁文缛节，充满了通常是荒诞且常常可笑的仪规虚礼"（同上，88页）。

穆勒所著《英属印度史》的第一章有28个脚注，其中近一半提到了威廉·琼斯；第二章的脚注主要为哈尔海德翻译的《原住民法典》（Halhed，1777年）和琼斯翻译的《摩奴法典》所占。穆勒从这两个文本里（还有科尔布鲁克的《印度合同与继承法汇编》）（Colebrooke & Tarakapanchanana，1864年）慎征妙引，论证了印度法律的荒诞不经又不公正。他引用哈尔海德在《原住民法典》译者前言里的话，说印度人的道德同印度人的法律一样粗鄙无文，因为后者之劣乃前者之果（Mill，1817年：125页注90）。从查尔斯·威尔金斯翻译的《五卷书》（一本寓言选集）里，[1] 穆勒获得了一幅"卑贱可鄙""卑躬屈膝"的印度人的画像，其自惭形秽之状向他证明了印度的暴虐状况；此外，从威廉·沃德那里，穆勒当然获得了"大量有关印度宗教伤风败俗"以及由此而产生的"深重堕落"的证据。

穆勒对铭文碑颂之翻译的运用是有选择性的（Mill，1817年：496页，504页注30）。溯古或称贵之词立即被当作胡编

---

[1] 见亨利·科尔布鲁克的《五卷书》校勘本，Colebrooke（1804）。

乱造打发掉，而任何显示了印度人堕落的东西，都被视作是正当合理的证据。穆勒把《往世书》（神话传说）贬为一钱不值的伪历史，但却愿意从《沙恭达罗》这出戏里接受有关那个时代的政治协议和法律的证据（同上，133页，473页）。历史被斥为虚构而见弃；但虚构——经过翻译的——却被当作历史来接受。穆勒在文中从威尔福德上尉（Captain Wilford）（威氏也是一位研究黑格尔的权威）刊登在《亚细亚研究》上的文章里摘引出几句，写道："印度的地理学、编年史以及历史学体系都是同样可怕而又荒谬绝伦的东西"（同上，40页）。因此，有关印度人的历史知识全部加起来也超不出几张四开印刷纸的篇幅（同上，423页）。其言辞同不到十年后的麦考莱谴责印度教育所用之语极其相像。正如史学家拉纳吉特·古哈（Ranajit Guha）所指出的那样，穆勒于其《历史》的开篇一章说的是印度人的古老历史，然后便中断行文，接着用了近500页（或九章）的篇幅来谈论印度人的"天性"（也就是说，他们的宗教、习俗、生活方式等）。[1] 这九章里普遍用的是现在式时态，其作用是把印度人的处境去历史化，从而既为他们在文明的等级上确立了一个位置，也固定了他们永恒不变的本质。

不仅世俗的历史编纂学和历史哲学参与到了殖民论述里，西方的形而上学本身（"历史主义"正是其象征标志），似乎也在某个年代从殖民翻译里浮现出来。比如，黑格尔的世界

---

[1] 拉纳吉特·古哈，《评殖民印度下的权力和文化》（手稿）第59页。

历史理论，就是建立在 18 和 19 世纪移译非西方文本的翻译家所传播开来的再现观之上的。

保罗·德曼说，不管我们承认与否，不管我们知不知道，我们都是"正统的黑格尔派"。[1] 德曼所关心的是对传统的历史主义展开批判，这种历史主义是由黑格尔关于精神之觉悟的目的论体系所提出来的。黑格尔说，在印度，"绝对的存在表现得……像是在一种梦境的痴迷状态下"，且由于"印度人天性的一般要素"就是这种"精神处于梦寐状态的特征"，所以印度人还没有获得"自我"或"意识"（Hegel，1837 年：204—225 页）。由于在黑格尔看来，"历史"指的是"精神的发展"，又由于印度人不是能够产生行动的"个体"，所以"印度文化的传播"是在"史前"，是"一种哑然无声、没有行动的扩张"（Hegel，1837 年：206 页）；所以"亚细亚帝国屈从于欧洲人便是其必然的命运"。（同上，207 页）

黑格尔一方面愿意承认印度文学把其人民描写得性情温和、纤弱且多愁善感，另一方面却又强调说这些特征常常是和绝对地欠缺"灵魂的自由"以及"个体的权利意识"联系在一起的（Hegel，1837 年：225 页）。所谓印度人"胆小怯懦"，"女人气"，受着亚洲暴虐统治者的压迫，最终将不可避免地为西方所征服——这种看法乃是黑格尔式历史哲学的组成部分，这种历史哲学不仅召唤殖民主体，而且也为殖民翻

---

[1] De Man（1982）。桑吉·柏什卡尔（Sanjay Patshikar）就这一问题以及第一章中的其他相关点同我作过讨论，在此谨表谢意。

译所支撑认可（authorized）。黑格尔谴责印度人狡猾奸诈、惯于"欺骗、偷窃、抢劫、谋杀"，这与詹姆斯·穆勒的著述，以及科尔布鲁克、威尔金斯和其他东方学家们的翻译是同声一气的。

我已经指出过，穆勒的历史模式参与到了英国人的改进论述（discourse of improvement）里，而这种论述为麦考莱和特里维廉热情地支持着。"功利"和"效用"的意识形态的鼓吹者们，利用了部分是由东方学家的翻译事业所造就的传统与现代之间的对立，来达到取消本土教育和引入西方教育的目的。

詹姆斯·穆勒自1830年起担任东印度公司在伦敦的检察官或首席行政长官，对公司一系列方针的修订发挥了影响。其子 J.S. 穆勒在《自传》里写道，其父发往印度的信函，"继其所著之《历史》之后，对促进印度之改进，教导印度官员弄清其职责，可谓贡献良多，前人所为无出其右。"[1] 当威廉·本汀克（William Bentinck）在1828年就任总督之时，他承认自己是詹姆斯·穆勒的门徒，深受其影响。穆勒对正规教育的效用虽然表示怀疑（Stokes，1959年［1989年］：57页），但对"有用的知识"，却很是热衷，因而对本汀克引领的教育改革的努力，还是给予了支持。在本汀克看来，"英国的语言"是"通往一切改进的钥匙"，且"普通教育"的实施将会促成"印度的再生"。[2]

---

[1] J.S. 穆勒《自传》，引自斯托克斯著《英国功利主义者与印度》（Stokes，1959年［1989年］）。

[2] 本汀克（Bentinck），引自 Spear（1970年，2: 126页）。

福音会教徒出于对雅各宾派无神论的恐惧，在迅速巩固的大英帝国的版图内，四处推广传教活动，激进的或功利主义的论述因此而得到了增强。像威廉·威尔伯福斯（William Wilberforce）和查尔斯·格兰特（Charles Grant，克拉彭派［the Clapham Sect］的成员）这样的福音会教徒及其支持者们，不仅在东印度公司，而且也在政府里占据着要津。然而，由于英国人害怕改变人的宗教信仰会激怒土著，所以威尔伯福斯在1793年提出准许基督教传教士进入印度的动议在议会未获通过。只是凭借1813年出台的一部特许法案（the Charter Act），福音会教派才赢得了一场大胜利：该法案虽然延长了东印度公司的经营特权，但也同时允许了自由贸易的开展，从而打破了东印度公司的垄断地位，并为传教活动进入印度铺平了道路。福音会教派信奉以教育来变革人性，坚信皈依基督需要一定的学习，所以他们在1813年法案上取得的胜利还包括了每年提供一万英镑来促进对土著的教育。（Stokes，1959年［1989年］: 57页）

然而，早在1797年，查尔斯·格兰特（东印度公司董事之一，且任其主席多年）就向董事会提交了一份私下印刷的论文，主张在印度开展英语教育。[1] 文章题为《关于大不列颠治下亚细亚属民社会状况的几点意见——特别针对道德问题及改进方略》，格兰特在文中认为，"堕落可悲又可鄙的印度人"，身受"邪情淫欲的控制"，且只有一丁点儿"微弱的

---

[1] 格兰特（Grant）的论文在1813年被作为国会文件重新印制，1832年三度印刷。

道德责任感",由于自身宗教的缘故,已经"身陷悲惨之中"了。格兰特从东方学家和传教士翻译的印度文本里旁征博引,来证明自己的论断。他声称惟有英语教育可以把印度人的思想从他们祭司的专横控制下解放出来,使他们得以培养起个人意识。[1] 格兰特料到其反对者要说英语教育会教导印度人来要求英式的自由,于是便坚称开展教育将会最有效地实现英国人来印度的"初衷",即"拓展我们的贸易"。格兰特指出,英国的商品在印度之所以卖不出去,乃是因为印度人民还没有"养成使用它们"的品味;此外,他们也没有能力来购买;这一套说辞我们在威廉·沃德及后来的麦考莱那里都听到了回应。实施英语教育将会唤醒印度人的创造力;他们不仅会"喜欢上"欧洲的精美产品,而且也会在自己的家园里开始进行"种种的改进"。在格兰特看来,一如其后的麦考莱所想的,这乃是"最最崇高的一种征服";"我们或许敢说,我们的原则和语言所到之处,我们的贸易就会跟进。"[2] 在一个被罗摩克里希纳·慕克吉(Ramakrishna Mukherjee)描述成从重商资本主义向英国工业资产阶级霸权过渡的时期里,格兰特的言论似乎特别地相宜[3]。"责任"与"自身利益"的结合将会给英国的贸易带来极大的好处(见 Stokes,1959 年 [1989 年]: 33 页)。

---

[1] 关于克拉彭派"利益"的讨论,见 Stokesn(1959 年 [1989 年]: 30—33 页)。

[2] 格兰特,引自罗摩克里希纳·慕克吉著《东印度公司兴衰史》(Mukherjee 1973 年: 421 页)。

[3] 同上,散见各处。

关于1813年法案拨出的那笔教育经费，是要用于土著的传统教育还是用于西式教育，"东方学家"和"英国语言文学专家"之间激烈争吵了多年[1]。最终，迫于东印度公司管理性质的不断变化，在本汀克任内出台了1835年3月7日的决议案，宣布所供教育经费，"自此而后应作以英语为媒介、向土著传授英国文学及科学知识之用"。[2] 于是，英国人建起了各式学校和学院；英语取代了波斯语成为了这个殖民国家的官方语言和高等法庭上的用语。因此，本汀克推行的行政体制的"西化"，是与推翻康沃利斯的排斥政策而把更多的印度人引入政治集团（英语教育使之成为可能）同步进行的。有鉴于英语有此非常明显之"用处"，公共教育委员会（其主席是麦考莱）遂把重点放在了用英语进行的高等教育上，而对大

---

[1] 关于这一争论的广泛讨论，见Boman-Behram（1942年）。达兰姆帕尔提出，英国人要根除传统教育，可能是因为害怕印度传统教育的文化与宗教内容会对抗拒殖民统治提供一些立足之地（Dharampal 1983年：75页）。查尔斯·特里维廉（Charles Trevelyan）在1838年写道，指望英国人来赞助本土的传统教育是毫无道理的："要我们来把可以激起人性所能有的对我们最为强烈的反抗之情的系统知识加以普及推广，这正是我们的死敌所求之不得的事。"（Trevelyan 1838年：189页）

[2]《印度历史》第2卷第127页。埃里克·斯托克斯认为，早在1813年，东印度公司便无法为其贸易垄断辩护了。印度的"布匹"在欧洲已经有了市场，且随着东印度公司变成为一个"纯粹的军事及行政机构"，它把一切所能得到的税收余额都吃掉了（Stokes 1959年（1989年）37—38页）。英国统治现在在印度所能做的不是去纳贡，而是要为英国商品开辟一个新的市场。此外，1818年马拉地人落败以后，对英国人的最后抵抗也就土崩瓦解了。如何有效地治理东印度公司得来的大片领土便成了主要的任务（同上，第XV页）。英语教育不仅会产生出大批的本土官僚，而且还可开始培养出对欧洲商品的嗜好。

规模的小学教育则不管不问了。

麦考莱并不认为全体印度民众都有学习英语的必要。英式教育的目的是"要塑造可以在我们（英国人）与被我们所统治的百万民众之间充当翻译的一个阶层，这个阶层里的人，其血液和肤色一如印度人的模样，但其品味、意见、道德观和智识却都是英国人的。"[1] 麦考莱是个同威廉·琼斯一样的立法者，也还是印度刑法的制订人。他谈到了印度或许有朝一日会成为独立的国家，到那时，英国人将会留下一个长盛不衰帝国，因为那是"由我们的艺术和道德、我的文学和法律所组建起来的永垂不朽的帝国"。[2]

麦考莱的妹夫——查尔斯·特里维廉曾论及土著精英阶层的影响将如何保障由西式教育所带来的变化"永存下去"："我们的臣民们已经踏上了一条新的改进之路，他们即将获得一种新的品格"（Trevelyan，1838年：181页）。而推动这一变化的媒介将是"英国文学"，它会使印度人谈起英国伟人时同他们的主人一样热情洋溢："受过同样的教育，喜好同样的东西，与我们有着同样的追求，他们的英国味会变得比印度味更浓，"他们会把英国人视为其"天然的庇护人和恩主"，因为他们（印度人）的最大野心就是像我们一样。（同上，189—192页）

麦考莱酷爱穆勒的《历史》，他在1835年关于印度教育

---

[1] 麦考莱（Macaulay）：《印度人的教育》（1835年2月2日备忘录）载Young（1967年：729页）。

[2] 麦考莱：《1833年7月10日演讲》载Young（1967年：717页）。

的备忘录里声称，还没有发现哪个东方学家"可以否认欧洲一间尚好的图书馆里的一架书，其价值可抵印度和阿拉伯半岛的全部本土文学。"[1]特里维廉附和道，后者"比毫无用处还要糟糕"（Trevelyan，1838年：182页）。英国人对英语教育的推广普及，最终的结果便是迫使并怂恿殖民地人民"一起来摧毁他们自己的表达工具"。（Bourdieu，1981年，引自Thnmpson，1984年：45页）

如高里·维斯瓦纳坦（Gauri Viswanathan）所指出的那样，英语教育的引进可以被视作"对历史和政治压力的一个防御性的回应，即是对英国议会和东印度公司之间、议会与传教士之间、东印度公司与土著精英阶层之间的种种紧张关系的回应"（Viswanathan，1987年：24页）。把她的这一论点再推展一步，我想指出，殖民化的翻译实践为通过引入英语教育而具体解决这些紧张关系提供了论述上的条件。本是为西方读者所准备的印度文本的欧洲语言译本，却给"受过教育"的印度人提供了一整套东方学家的意念想象。即便当英国化了的印度人不说英语时，由于英语所能传达的象征权力，"他"也还是会喜欢通过殖民论述里所传播的翻译和历史文本来接触自己的过去。英语教育还使印度人熟悉了逐渐被当作"自然如此"而接受下来的种种观看之道、翻译的技术，或再现的模式。

翻译的哲学素为多种多样的论述打下了根基。这些话语

---

[1] 麦考莱：《备忘录》载Young（1967年：722页）。

不仅是从殖民情境里产生，而且也还反馈到殖民情境中去。翻译为多元决定的产物，殖民统治下的"主体/臣民"也是一样——由多种话语在多个场点之上制造出来，继而引发出多种多样的实践。被殖民者对英语教育的需求，明显不是一个简单的承认"落后"的问题，或只是政治上的一种权宜之计；这是由众多历史因素的盘结交错而产生的一种复杂的需求，一种由殖民翻译所制造并维持的需求。

殖民主体的建构是以皮埃尔·布迪厄（Pierre Bourdieu）所说的"象征型支配"（symbolic domination）为前提的。象征型支配及其暴力通过确认（reconnaissance）与误认（méconnaissance）的结合，有效地再生产出社会秩序；被确认的是占支配地位的语言是合法正当的（我们再次想起了英语在印度的使用），"被误认的则是这种语言……之推行被误认为是支配性的。象征暴力的作用之所以如此不为社会行动者所明见，恰恰是因为它存在的前提，便是受其苦害最为深重之人与其合作共谋"（Thompson，1984年：58页）。布迪厄的分析表明，被殖民者，或甚至后殖民的人们，以其自身对"日常生活之论述实践"的参与，一再地把自己重新加以殖民化；正是这些日常生活中的论述实践，而不是什么自上压下来的强大制度，维持着殖民主义典型的不对等关系。

"土著男童"乞讨英文书的故事里暗含的就是自我殖民化的概念，对此我们可以运用安东尼奥·葛兰西（Antonio Gramsci）的霸权（hegemony）概念作更深入的探讨。葛兰西在国家机器与"市民社会"之间做了一个区别：前者指国家整个强制性的机制，包括军队、警察和立法机关，而后者则包括了学校、家庭、教会和传媒。统治集团凭借国家机器，运用武力或强制手段来实施宰制，而在市民社会中则是凭借意识形态的制造来确保其霸权，通过人们的甘愿（consent）来巩固其权力。[1]

殖民社会是展现霸权文化运作的一个有力的例证。[2]教育、神学、历史编纂学、哲学以及文学翻译等诸多论述渗透了属于殖民统治意识形态结构的霸权机器（hegemonic apparatuses），我们可以再回到葛兰西的著作里，去求助一个摆脱了传统"虚假意识"主张的意识形态概念。[3]在葛兰西看来，意识形态铭刻于种种实践之中（比如，建构殖民主体的实践）；意识形态制造"主体"，因而具有一定的物质性。[4]影

---

[1] 昌达尔·穆菲（Chantal Mouffe）在《葛兰西的统识与意识形态》一文中对葛兰西思想作了很有启发性的讨论。见 Mouffe（1979年）。

[2] 但是请参阅拉纳吉特·古哈在《没有统识的统治及其历史写作》（Guha 1989年）一文中的观点。古哈提出，描述殖民社会，用"宰制（domination）"比"霸权（hegemony）"更为合适，因为"霸权"暗含着所有阶层同意甘愿（consent）之意，而殖民统治只是得到了精英阶层的"认可"（sanction）。在我看来，古哈似乎没有对甚至被麦考莱看出是起着渗透作用的现象给予足够的解释，即殖民统治的不同形态对被殖民者各个部分的弥漫渗透。不过，我得承认，这个概念也许并不适用于所有的被殖民社会。殖民统治可以是霸权性的，如巴巴多斯的情况，但牙买加的就不一样；马提尼克岛是那样，但瓜德罗普岛就不是，如此等等，不一而足。

[3] 认为意识形态是虚假意识是经典马克思主义的观念，意指对"现实"的歪曲再现。葛兰西的概念强调意识形态的"物质性"，对检讨殖民论述的持久性更为有用。

[4] Mouffe（1979年：199页）。阿尔都塞援用葛兰西的意识形态观提出了召唤理论。

响广泛的翻译（比如，18世纪从梵文和波斯文转换成英语的译本）召唤了殖民主体，把某些关于东方的描述加以合法化或权威化，这些描述继而便逐渐获得了"真理"的地位，甚至在"原"著所在的国家里也是如此。西方教育的引进得到了特里维廉所谓的"神学院"的帮助，它们是由政府资助的传教士所开办的一些学校。欧洲的传教团在把殖民地悄然纳入全球经济的过程中，发挥了十分重要的作用；在其他一些殖民地社会里（比如在比利时治下的刚果），传教团常常掌管了整个教育系统。这种在欧洲以外的世界里，不取决于"个人"参与意愿而广泛存在于人类学家、传教士以及殖民行政官员之间的**系统性**合作，乃是霸权性殖民论述运作的典型特征。[1] 因此，在主体化实践的形成过程中，传教士充当的乃是殖民统治的代理人（agents），这不仅见于他们行牧师和教师之责的时候，而且也还体现在他们从事语言学家、语法学家和翻译家的工作过程中。[2]

殖民论述为了遏制的目的而进行翻译（又因为象征型支配与实质型宰制一样重要，也会为了翻译的目的而进行遏制和控制），殖民论述的这种欲望在殖民传教士对"未知"语言之文法的努力编纂上得到了明证体现。欧洲传教士是最早着手为印度的大多数语言准备西式词典的人，他们由此便参与

---

1 我在第2章以较长的篇幅讨论了人类学家与殖民统治之间的关系。关于"系统性"合作（systemic collaboration）的讨论，请参阅 Fabian（1986年）。
2 英国在印度的第一个统治中心是孟加拉，有关传教活动与帝国霸业在这一地区交汇的广泛描述，请参阅 Kopf（1969年）。

了殖民政权赖以为根基的搜集和编纂整理的巨大工程里。像琼斯和哈尔海德这样的行政官员与亚洲学会的成员们,都把撰写出版的语法书籍看作他们十分重要的学术著作:琼斯的波斯语文法出版于1777年,而哈尔海德的孟加拉语文法(第一部使用了孟加拉语书写系统的著作)出版于1778年。哈尔海德在著本书的前言里,抱怨孟加拉语的拼字法"无规律性",很难把欧洲的语法原则用于一个似乎已经丧失"其普遍基本原则"的语言上头去。[1] 加尔各答的威廉堡学院(College of Fort William)同亚洲学会有着密切的联系,并致力于向东印度公司雇员提供"东方的"教育,这家学院的成立对翻译家和语法学家是一个极大的鼓舞。如大卫·考普夫(David Kopf)所说:"到了1805年,学院已经成为一座名副其实的实验室,在这里,欧洲人和亚洲人制订出新的语言转换方案,把口头语规则化成具有准确的语法形式,并用在欧洲还相对不为人知的语言来编写词典"(Kopf, 1969年:67页)。当1812年的一场火灾烧毁了瑟兰波传教士团(威廉·凯里是其中一员,在威廉堡学院授课)的印刷所时,焚毁的手稿里就有一部"囊括了已知的各种东方语言字词"的多语种词典。(同上,78页)

要研究、编纂并"了解"东方——这一欲望所运用的乃是被德里达和德曼这样的后结构主义者加以批判了的,经典的关于再现和真实的观点。与此相关,德里达和德曼等人的

---

[1] 哈尔海德:《孟加拉语文法》引自Kopf(1969年:57页)。

著作也提供了在后殖民脉络下具有重要意义的，对传统历史主义的批判。对历史主义的批判或许有助于我们提出一个复杂的关于**历史性**（historicity）的概念，而文本的"效果史"（effective history）就包含在其间；这一称呼涵盖的是这样的一些问题：是谁使用／解释文本？如何使用？为了什么目的？[1] 对再现的批判和对历史主义的批判都使得后殖民理论家能够对被霍米·巴巴（效法福柯）称之为殖民权力的技术，作出一番分析（Bhabha，1985年：144—165页）。这些批判也还使翻译的问题意识得以重新铭刻：对殖民文本及其"白色神话"（white mythology）的解构，有助于我们看清翻译是如何把种种关于再现和真实的概念制造出来的；这种关于再现和真实的主张不仅支撑着文学批评的论述，也还支撑着西方哲学的奠基概念。

"历史"的问题

萨缪尔·韦伯（Samule Weber）新近撰文，评论弗雷德里克·詹明信（Fredric Jameson）的《政治无意识》，他指责詹明信摆出一副"利用大写历史"（capitalizing History）的姿态来表达"'后结构主义'思想的挑战"（Weber，1987年：40—58页）。"后结构主义"的捍卫者们同指责它否定"历史"的人（包括左右两派）之间的小吵小闹由来已久了，韦伯的

---

[1] 参见《为翻译定位：历史，后结构主义与殖民语境》一书下一节中我对历史性／历史概念的讨论。

批评只是最新发出的一连串炮弹中的一枚。早先由艾伯拉姆斯（M.H. Abrams）以及其他一些人对解构所作的攻击，现在读起来就像是传统文学史家面对凶猛破坏性的尼采主义的攻势，执意要维护他们关于传统、连续性以及历史脉络之种种观念而发出的绝望的喊叫。[1]然而，詹明信却始终不断地力图要与结构主义和后结构主义的思想达成协议，他对历史化的要求乃是源于他给"马克思主义的诠释框架"所赋予的"头等重要的地位"。（Jameson，1981年：10页）

如后结构主义者们（我指的是德里达，尤其是美国的解构主义者）所察觉的，要求他们处理"历史"的呼声日益是来自"左派"，尤其是从那些已经在多种意义上同解构"交手"（杰夫·本宁顿［Geoff Bennington］语）的人（见Attridge, et al., 197页）。虽然关于"历史"的争吵这样厉害，但奇怪的却是，无论是后结构主义者还是对他们采取敌视而又赞赏态度的那些人，竟都对历史意指何物持有非常僵化的观点。如果前者辩难指责历史是"男权逻各斯中心主义"（phallogocentrism），那么后者则指出它是一个"不可超越的视野"（untranscendable horizon）。谁也没有说清道明这里所说的"历史"，是指一种历史写作的模式（对过去的某种构想），还是指"过去"其本身。

我在此所主要关注的不是去细说时下在欧美理论界正在上演着的"历史"大战，而是采取一个策略性的"偏颇"

---

[1] 例如，参阅 Abrams（1977年：425—438页）。

(partial)视角,去问一系列的问题。这便是一个正在崛起的后殖民实践的视角,它一方面愿意得后结构主义的洞见之益,同时在另一方面也要质问历史写作的方式,以便能够理解主体化的运作之道。

鉴于殖民论述的典型步骤之一(如在东方学里)是把殖民主体表现得一成不变且不可改变,历史性——包含变化的观点——便是一个需要认真加以对待的概念。就我的目的来说,历史性是指——不过并非没有带着问题意识——效果史(尼采的"真实历史"[Wirklich Historie]或迦达默尔的"效应历史"[Wirkungsgeschichte]),或者说,仍然在现在起着作用的那部分的过去(Nietzsche,1957年;Gadamer,1975年)。效果史这个概念有助于我们去逆向地解读琼斯在18世纪末所翻译的古老的梵文文本;它还提出了倘若我们在二百年后重译那些文本可能会面对的种种问题。因此,**历史性**一词包含了翻译/重译在过去/现在是如何起作用的,为什么这个文本在过去/现在被移译,以及过去/现在是谁在翻译等这些问题。

我用**历史性**(historicity)一词来避免勾起人们对大写历史(History)的联想,由于我所关注的是"在地的"(local)种种翻译实践(或如福柯所称的微观实践),它们本就无需什么大一统的理论来涵盖。如福柯宣称,"效果史坚信知识乃是一种视角",它也许可以被看作是一种基进的"现时主义"(presentism),我们或许能够以此作为研究的起点(Foucault,1977年:156页)。前面我曾指出,后殖民完全有理由对目的论的历史主义保持一种怀疑的态度,这种历史主义被德里达正确地描绘成是西方形而上学[1]的一个体现。但是,既然"历史"的事实对后殖民来说不可避免,既然对历史的关注在某种意义上是应后殖民情境的**需求**,那么,后殖民理论就不得不在解构策略以外,再提出一种叙事化的策略(narrativizing strategy)。运用历史性/效果史或许可帮助我们绕过线性的形而上学。

我们也许还会发现,路易·阿尔都塞(Louis Althusser)对历史主义的批判能够派上用场;这种批判,按詹明信的话来说,使他提出了"历史是一个没有目的(telos)也无主体的过程",是"对宏大叙述及其孪生的叙述终结(narrative closure)(目的)与人物(历史的主体)这两个范畴的批驳"(Jameson,1981年:29页)。这后一个假定或可被视为是对个人主义主体论的攻击,阿尔都塞自己的主体论就对其进行了解构。詹明信进一步指出,在阿尔都塞看来,历史是一个"虚在的动因"(absent cause),就像雅克·拉康(Jacques Lacan)的"实在"(Real)一样,"我们只能通过文本的形式来接近它"(Jameson,1981年:82页)。历史"只能通过其效应来被理解"(同上,102页)——这一见解对一个试图像福柯的系谱学家那样去理解"支配的运作"和"屈从体系"的理论家来说,是具有直接相关意义的(Foucault,1977年:148页)。福柯论道,系谱学家"需要历史来驱散对于本源的

---

1 德里达运用这个词来指西方哲学的宏伟建构,即建立在至今仍然未被质疑的第一原则或基础之上的一个思想体系。德氏把"解构"这支撑整个西方文化的一套假定视为己任。

种种幻想"（Foucault，1977年：144页）。一种起源于后殖民脉络的理论，当它试图去实践一种反本质主义的历史写作方式时，便需要同对本源与目的（telos）的批判结合起来。在这一课题里，瓦尔特·本雅明的著作提供了另一种支援，他认为，史学家（我们或许也能说翻译家）所掌握的过去景象是与现在融汇成一体的。我们所建构的关于过去的断裂性，也许可以促使我们去讨论翻译之"原因"，以及它是如何展现了一种效果史。[1] 也许，后殖民理论能够显示，我们所需要的是去**翻译**（即扰乱或置换）历史，而不是去解释它（以诠释学的方法）或"阅读"它（以一种墨守文本的方式）。

所谓**本源**其实总是已经包含了多种异质成分，而非什么纯粹、统一的意义之源或历史——这一见解是德里达的著作给后殖民提供的最为深刻的洞见。史学家（historiographers；文学的或其他领域的）若是去指责殖民化的再现"虚假"或"不恰当"，那就会犯下错误；若是据此再去追求恰当之再现，那便会使后殖民的写作陷于一个在场的形而上学之中，陷于德里达称之为时代的"派生问题"（the generative question），即再现的价值问题里去了。[2]

---

[1] 关于对本雅明的翻译与历史观的进一步讨论，见 Niranjana（1992年：第4、5章）。

[2] Derrida（1982b）.把殖民主义的再现视作"虚假"的另一个问题是，殖民主义的"真实"可以说是由殖民者所**生产**出来的，比如，对一个"欺骗的印度人"的再现，暗示着"欺骗"可以构成对殖民统治的一种反抗形式的现实。也许，我们该做的，不是去指责殖民主义再现的虚假，而是要看看其**效应**，说明不同的再现可以导致其他的、能给人更多的可能或力量的效应。

在《言语与现象》里，一篇讨论胡塞尔的文章，德里达写道：

> 当我实际上**有效地**使用字词的时候……我必须从一开始就在一个其基本要素只能是再现性的（representative）重复结构（之内）运作。如果我们用事件来指称一个不可替代又不可回复的经验性独特事例，那么一个符号就决不是个事件。只出现"一次"的符号决不会是个符号……既然这种表现性的结构就是意指（signification）其本身，那么若不从一开始就卷入到无限的再现之中，我便无法进入"有效的"话语里。
>
> （Derrida，1973年：50页）

德里达在此断言的是，不存在什么一个原初的"在场"然后才被"再"现；再现之"再"并不是降临在本源之上的。正是这种再现论压制了差异（而差异乃早已存在于所谓的本源之内），并为整个西方的形而上学奠定了基础。这是一个在场的形而上学，是一个"自我的同一性之绝对接近"（absolute proximity of self-identity）的形而上学（Derrida，1973年：99页），是自我在场（presence to oneself）的形而上学。也许，在场形而上学的最主要的特征就是认为声音和言语优于"书写"（écriture），德里达将其称为语音中心论或逻各斯中心主义；依照此说，书写乃是一种派生形式，摹本之摹本，最终成为对一个遥远的、丢失了的或断裂了的本源的意指。德里达是反对这种说法的,他揭示出任何有关单一、中心或原初的概念,总是已经具备了不可化约或不可超越的多元异质之特征。

在对胡塞尔、海德格尔、索绪尔、列维·施特劳斯以及卢梭的一系列详细解读中,德里达展示出再现——及书写——是如何已经归属于符号和意指(signification)的范畴:"在再现的这番运作下,本源之点变得无从把握了……再没有一个单一本源的存在了"(Derrida,1974年:36页)。至于就欧洲人根深蒂固的关于文明摇篮(亚洲或非洲)的种种历史陈述,以及就后殖民地人民的自我形象而言,这种分散的本源观会产生什么样的冲击,推测一番也是蛮有意思的事。

为了解构逻各斯中心论的形而上学,德里达建议我们按他重新予以铭刻的方式使用书写这个概念。德里达的"书写"是对本源里所存在差异的另一种称谓,它意指"那最最难以对付的差异。它从最接近的亲近处威胁着对活生生言语的欲望追求,它从里面且从一开始就把活生生的言语给**破坏**(breach)了"(Derrida,1974年:56页)。在德里达看来,本源的符号乃是一种书写的书写,它只能表明所谓的本源从一开始就是个翻译(originary translation)。德里达说,形而上学试图要通过再现之恰当性、整体化的表述(totalization),以及历史等这些概念来重新占有在场。笛卡儿—黑格尔式的历史,就像符号的结构,"只能在它所延宕之在场的**基础上**、并在人们想重新占有的被延宕之在场的**视野内**才是可以想象的"(Derrida,1973年:138页)。在这里,德里达指的是历史主义对**本源**和**目的**的关注，及其要构建一个整体化叙述的愿望。"历史"在后结构主义的文本里，是一种抹杀差异的压制性力量，属于那包括意义、真理、在场，以及逻各斯在内的系列中。我们在后面将会看到，瓦尔特·本雅明是如何在对大一统的历史陈述进行的类似批判中，利用唯物主义的史学来作为颠覆之手段的。

由于德里达对再现的批判同时也意味着对传统翻译观的批判，因而对后殖民理论便有了重要的意义。事实上，这两组问题意识在德里达的著作里总是紧密相关的；他不止一次地指出过翻译或许逃出了"再现的轨道"，因而是个"典范性的问题"（Derrida，1982年：298页）。如果说再现代表了对在场的重新占有，那么翻译便是那指代德里达会称之为"播撒"（dissemination）（Derrida，1981年）的符号。然而，我们必须对同属再现、恰当性和真理层面的传统翻译观细加质疑才行。

对于支持了帝国主义的霸业、伴随着对被征服民族之历史性的否定且为了以历史面目出现而压抑历史的种种历史叙述，后殖民理论是会乐于摒弃的；与此同时，它也意识到一直活"在翻译里"的后殖民"主体/臣民"的处境，也需要某种历史观来阐发自身。因为由加尔各答威廉堡学院的学者们所作的从多种印度语言转换成英语的翻译，在构建殖民主体的过程中，给一代代的欧洲人提供了"亚细亚人"（Asiatik）的再现形象。

问题不仅仅是要批评这些刻画描述"不够恰当"或"有失真实"，我们还应该力图去证明这些再现形象与殖民统治之间的共谋关系，以及它们在维系帝国主义的不对等关系里所扮演的角色。后殖民对"历史"的欲望是一种要了解那个"过去"之痕迹的欲望，其所处之情境里至少有一桩事实是无法被化约的：殖民主义及其之后。在这样一种情境下的历史编纂学，就必须提供从过去追回被掩盖了的形象的方法，以解构殖民和新殖民的种种历史叙述。比如在印度，庶民研究（Subaltern Studies）小组就已经开始了这样一种重写历史的计划，现正努力与本质主义和再现的概念问题搏斗。

在一篇讨论庶民研究史学家的文章里，加亚特里·斯皮瓦克（Gayatri Spivak）认为他们的做法与"解构"近似，因为他们提出了一个"变化是符号系统间功能置换场所的理论"，因而这是"一个所可能有的最最广泛意义上的阅读理论"（Spivak，1985年）。斯皮瓦克的文章试图对存在于这些后殖民史学家与后结构主义课题之间的相似之处（以及一些差异之点）作出解释，虽然有点操之过急，但也仍然是有说服力的。斯皮瓦克提供了一个有用的类比，她指出，庶民研究的史学家们所关注的焦点在于"符号功能的置换场所"上，这是"对阅读作为过去与将来之间的积极相互作用（active transaction）的别称"，且这种"相互作用的阅读"（也许我们还可称之为翻译）或可指示出行动的可能性（Spivak，1985年：332页）。

由于翻译的问题意识与历史写作之不可分割的联系是我论点的一部分，我将简要地讨论斯皮瓦克论述庶民研究史学家的主要观点。这些史学家对后结构主义思想的策略性的运用（无论是公开宣称的，还是斯皮瓦克从他们的著作里读出来的），或可有助于我们更加清楚地看到，我所希望予以重新铭刻的历史观和翻译观是如何不仅因后殖民对历史编纂学的批判而得以实现，而且可能会进一步地深化这种批判。

斯皮瓦克所指的后结构主义重要的"主题"，包括对本源的批判、书写与对语音中心论的攻击、对资产阶级自由人文主义的批判、关于"增能性的"话语失败（"enabling" discursive failure）的概念，以及"建设性解构"（affirmative deconstruction）的思想等。庶民研究史学家们所关心的是揭示出一种（殖民或新殖民主义的）历史的论述性（discursivity），而此种历史的论述性乃是经由对历史性的压抑而产生出来的。他们用庶民（subaltern）一词"来称呼南亚社会里普遍的从属性（subordination），无论是体现在阶级、种性、年龄、性别或职务上的，还是表现在其他方面上的"（Guha，1982年：vii页）。精英集团的历史编纂学，通过精心构建暴动庶民的形象，以及一系列持久的错误认识，声称提出了"公正"且"真实"的历史；而后殖民的史学家们则试图去证明这种论述场域（discursive field）是如何建构起来的，以及，按斯皮瓦克的说法，"大写历史之缪斯"是如何与反暴动的势力"串通共谋"的（Spivak，1985年：334页）。或许，历史与翻译在再现、真理和在场的法则之下运作，通过压制差异来制造具有一致性且透明的文本，由此而参与到了殖民支配的过程之中。

按斯皮瓦克的说法，庶民意识的问题在这个小组的工作里是"作为一个形而上学的方法论前提而起作用的",但是这里"总存在着一个对位的暗示",即"庶民意识为精英集团的欲力投入(cathexis)所控,向来无法被完整的复原;它总是从它所获得的能指里歪斜出去;甚至实际上它在被揭示出来的时候也就被抹去了;它是无可复原的论述建构"(Spivak,1985年:339页)。我在本章的第一部分里曾试图指出,由18和19世纪在印度的殖民主义者所作的英语翻译,不仅向"西方",而且也给其(由此召唤的)<u>臣民/主体</u>,提供了权威性的关于东方人自我的描述。1835年以后英语教育的引进以及本土传统教育的式微,保证了后殖民只能在构成殖民论述的翻译和历史里,去寻找他们无法复原的过去。庶民,也只存在于"翻译之中",总是已经被殖民支配所捕获。

斯皮瓦克把庶民史学家对本源的批判挪为己用,这一手法在一些人眼里,或许是一种帝国主义作风的嫌疑:"那些看起来似乎是殖民庶民阶层之历史困境的东西,可以用来转变成**一切**思想、**一切**审慎意识之困境的象征,虽然精英阶层声称不是如此。"(Spivak,1985年:340页,着重号为原文所有)她这里所指的是将庶民创造成为一种"主体—效果"(subject-effect),在一个巨大的"不连续的网络"(discontinuous network)或"文本"里**如主体**般地运作。为了能够像主体般地运作,它被赋予了一个"主权式的且是决定性的"角色;一个实际上是果的东西被说成了因——用了一个置换转喻。斯皮瓦克指出,庶民研究著作里的基本成分

"让人可以作这样一种解读，即把那追回庶民意识的事业看作是要推翻历史编纂学上的一个巨大置换转喻，并给作为庶民的主体之效果加以'定位'的尝试"。（Spivak，1985年：341—342页）

这样，意识这个概念便是策略性地、审慎地且不带怀旧情绪地被用于替"一个认真而可见的政治利益"服务（Spivak，1985年：342页），来指称一种"正在崛起的集体意识"，而不是自由人文主义的主体意识。策略性地运用本质主义的概念是斯皮瓦克和德里达会称之为"建设性解构"的特征标志。德里达在《论文字学》（Of Grammatology）里的一段议论，为了解后殖民理论需要如何给自己定位提供了一条重要的线索：

> 解构行动不是从外部把结构摧毁。解构除非寓居于那些结构之内，否则便不可能、且不会有什么效果，也找不到准确的目标。要以某种方式寓居于结构之内，因为人总是有所寓居的，且当他没有意识到这一点时，更是如此。由于一定要从结构里面入手，从旧的结构里借来一切战略和经济资源以用于颠覆，结构性地借用，也就是说，由于不能把它们的种种元素和原子隔离出来，解构之事业便是在某种程度上为其自身的作业所害了。
>
> （Derrida 1974年：24页）

理论或者翻译，在其所用的概念恰为自己所批判的时候要如何能够避免身陷再现的法则里呢？德里达会说，应该以那种"既留下标记又回头在标记上划过不可判定的一笔"的书写为目标，因为这种"双重的记号逸出了真理的适切性或权威"，在不把它推翻的情况下又将其重新铭写了。这种置换不是一个事件（event），它没有"发生"过；它只是"在写/被写"的东西（Derrida，1981年：193页）。德里达提到的这种双重铭写，与瓦尔特·本雅明的引用策略有类似之处。在本雅明看来，历史唯物主义者（即批判性的历史编纂学家）不加引号地引用，这种手法近似蒙太奇。这是揭示一个过去的年代与现在所形成之星丛聚合（constellation）的一种方式，它不为单一的历史连续性所制约，不为本源和目的的法则所左右。

德里达的双重书写可以有助于我们，对种种殖民化的历史和翻译里明显存在着的"主体化"实践和支配提出挑战。但是，这种挑战将不会是以恢复一个丢失的本质、或一个未遭损坏的自我的名义来展开的。相反，**混杂性**（hybrid）的问题将会贯穿于我们的阅读之中。如巴巴所说：

> 混杂性（Hybridity）是殖民权力生产力的标志，是它的变换力量和永恒固性（shifting force and fixities）；它是对以否定来行支配的过程（即那保证权威之"纯粹"和本源性的歧视性身份的生产）作策略性翻转的别称。混杂性是以重复歧视性的身份效果来对殖民身份之假定

> 所作的重估。它展示的是所有歧视和支配场点的必然形变和移位。

(Bhabha，1985年：154页)

殖民论述虽然替那些被它以权力的凝视所怔住的人制造了身份，但在其权威之源，却是极度暧昧的。混杂性导致的是逃逸了歧视目光的"监视"所造成的差异的扩散。"面对其对象的混杂性"，巴巴说，"权力的**在场**暴露出一副与其识别准则所坚称的不同的面目"(Bhabha，1985年：154页)。当我们开始理解殖民权力是如何最终**生产**了混杂化的时候，"占支配地位的论述条件"便可以被转变成"干预之基础"了(同上，154页)。因此，混杂(主体或脉络)包含着翻译、变形、位移置换。如巴巴所仔细指出的那样，殖民的混杂性不是一个可以用相对主义的方法来加以解决的文化认同的问题；确切地说，它是"殖民化的再现和个体化的一个**问题意识**，这个问题把殖民主义的否定效应翻转过来，以便其他'被排拒的'知识能够进入支配性的论述，并离间其权力之根基"。[1]
(同上，156页)

清楚的是，混杂性这一概念不仅对传统翻译观的批判，而且对庶民研究的历史编纂学批判都有着极其重要的意义；显然，它既"模糊不清而又具有历史的复杂性"(Clifford，1988年：16页)。如果把"混杂性"，或我称之为"活在翻译

---

[1] 关于对混杂的深刻描述，请参阅Ahmad(1986年)。

之中"的框架，仅仅限于后殖民的精英阶层，那便是在否认由殖民和新殖民支配所造成的跨越阶级界限之变革的普遍性，不管其成分是如何的异质。这样说，并不是要提出一个全球同质化的后设叙述，而是要强调，有必要以非本质化的方式重新发明对抗性的文化。因此，我们可以把混杂性视为，在指向一种新的翻译实践的同时又颠覆了本质主义阅读模式的一种后殖民理论的标志。

（翻译：袁伟　校订：许宝强　黄德兴）

为什么文化重要：
重新思考女性主义政治的语言

亚际计划（The Inter-Asia Project），至少像它在IACS（《亚际文化研究》）期刊中所示范的那样，使多种横越亚洲的、富有启发性的对话成为可能。这类处理"亚洲"问题的具有生产性的场所之一，就是女性主义。尽管此区域的许多国家都存在着强而有力的妇女运动，但它们却经常不可避免地专注于当地事务（除非有跨国面向的涉入，就像在性工作者贩卖或移民问题上那样）；为寻找一个切入点来理解不同的女性主义者彼此之间可以如何对话，也并不总是那么容易。为此，我提议可能有必要超越对女性主义政治实时性问题的关注，并代之以对问题发源地进行更仔细的检视。而这种检视，我认为，将不得不聚焦于这样一个问题，即为什么文化对女性主义来说是重要的。在兜了这样一个圈子之后，我的论文将回到当下，对印度女性主义的新发展进行反思。

正如我在最近的一篇文章,《女性主义与亚洲的文化研究》("Feminism and Cultural Studies in Asia")中所表明的那样,(在亚洲)女性主义并没有干扰已经确立的批判的文化研究方式(就像 20 世纪 70 年代在英国发生的那样),相反,它是文化研究这个新领域得以出现的基础(Niranjana,2007年)。它之所以是基础性的,原因就在于女性主义者已经承担了——而且必须承担——非西方社会的文化问题的那种方式。

在亚洲,对女性主义的一个常见的批判来自这样的一项指控,即它脱离了或疏离了"我们的文化"。这种指控,显少加诸于我们任何其他的政治框架,而这些政治框架,也远没有某种清晰可辨的"本土"资源。在别的地方,我已经以较长的篇幅解释了为什么文化的问题——尤其是在前殖民的语境当中——不能与女性如何被定义的问题分离开来。在这篇论文中,我会在一些与印度有关的方面再次详述这个问题。

但首先,我要提及亚际的语境。从 2000 年开始,我通过亚际文化研究会议,获得在亚洲的不同地点参与一系列女性主义讨论的机会。2000 年 12 月于日本福冈举行的第一次女性主义的专家小组讨论,把经常引起争论的女性与国家之间的关系,作为核心问题列入了议程;会上,许多发言人谈到通过既存的、像阶级那样的词汇,来理论化妇女问题和性别问题时的困难。2001 年 10 月在班加罗尔,我本人任职的机构,文化与社会研究中心主办了亚洲女性主义会议,这场会议把亚洲讨论女性与国家(伊朗和新加坡),女性对内战的参与(斯里兰卡),女性主义与宗教认同(印度、马来西亚),文化少数族裔（印度），酷儿公民权（中国台湾地区与中国大陆），女性与法律（孟加拉国、印度）等问题的女性带到了一起。其中，一场重要的、结论性的小组讨论了亚洲女性主义者所制定的批判性语汇，以及从西方语境翻译进来所产生的张力。在许多方面，文化问题是参与此事件的不同流派所关注的核心。此后不久，2001年12月，IACS另类工作坊在班加罗尔为女性主义问题的讨论提供了另一个论坛。这个工作坊在亚洲女性主义会议之后便举行，同时考量到为那些因"9·11"事件后的交通管制而无法参与会议的人提供方便，这个工作坊的目标定于评估我们所立足于其上的政治理论基础。在一场关键的小组讨论中，我们对当前女性主义与当代政治动议相关的难题进行了探讨，并研究了文化实践和女性主义分析的议题。在后来的会议（2005年的首尔会议和2007年的上海会议）中，亚际女性主义者对大众文化、伊斯兰化及其对女性所产生的后果、性工作者运动及其新主体性的生产等议题，进行了理论化的探讨。

再一次地，正如我已经在前面提到的那篇文章中所说过的那样，把女性主义问题带入亚际文化研究的框架，凸显了**文化**问题和亚洲所有的妇女，尤其是女性主义者所进行的具体的协商；开启了如何思考亚洲之**多种现代性**（modernities）的问题；推动了对与社会批判词汇的形成有关的**翻译**问题的探究；促使我们重新思考**政治性**（the political）的议题（政治性不断改变的词汇是什么；政治性是否以过去存在的方式具备可辨识性？）。看起来，在重新思考诸多议题正在发生的亚洲，女性主义是变动最剧烈的领域之一。

也许，对亚洲女性主义来说文化问题的重要性，在以下的一组对照中可以得到说明。西方的女性主义学者已经指出，自然与文化形成了一组二元结构。"（在西方女性主义史上）被提出的、争议不断的一组最常见的术语，就是自然与文化"（John，1998年：203页）。通过分析自然——文化的二元结构，西方女性主义者对知识的组织以及像家庭那样的体制进行了重要的批判。谢利·奥特纳*在她的论文《女性之于男性如同自然之于文化么?》（"Is Female to Male as Nature is to Culture？"）中指出：

> 一切文化都含蓄地承认并主张自然的运作与文化（人类的意识及其产物）的运作之间存在某种区别；而且，文化之特殊性正在于这样一个事实：它在绝大多数情况下能够超越自然条件并以自己的目标因势利导地利用自然条件。这样，文化（也就是说一切文化）在意识的某种层次上都声称自己不但区别于、而且优越于自然，而此种独特性及优越性的意识正依赖于其改变——即"社会化"和"教化"（culturalize）自然——的能力。（Ortner，1974年：72—73页）

---

* 谢利·贝丝·奥特纳（Sherry Ortner，生于1941年9月19日），美国文化人类学家，人类学教授。

在奥特纳看来，正是"身体和女性特有的自然的生殖功能"，造成了这种认为女性更亲近于自然且因而从属于文化的思维传统。然而，在许多非西方社会，女性在历史上被看成是文化的一部分。比如说，印度的女性主义学者已经充分指出，印度之文化观念的表述在许多方面与女性有着十分重要的联系。这把我们的注意力引到殖民统治下文化问题的重要性上。这里，在把文化理解为一种西方殖民关系中的差异及优越性的标记之情况下，我们可以获得一些历史上特定思考印度女性的方式，何以自然化或变得显而易见的洞见。[1]

印度的性别理论中对文化的探讨，植基于对独立前和独立后两个阶段的民族主义计划的批判。女性主义者已考察了反殖民斗争的阶段并检视了一个自我建构的印度认同，是如何在与殖民者对本地人的看法的对立中所诞生的。她们也继续理论化独立之后的阶段，此时人们努力重新想象印度，把印度想象为一个不再臣服于英国统治的独立民族。这种对印度的想象在多个领域内生产出了一系列的再现。在跨越许多学科分际（历史、社会学、文学研究、艺术史、电影研究、和政治科学），多样得令人吃惊的众多著作中，在这些关于印度性（Indianness）与印度文化之形成的讨论语境下，女性主义学者已经对规范性的（normative）女性特质的形成进行了分析。

---

[1] 一份里程碑式的论文集《重铸女性》（Recasting Women；Sangari and Vaid，1989年）收录了阐述这段历史的一些敏锐的文章。

文化问题的浮现

"我们"和"他们"有什么不同？这个问题，作为殖民争论的一部分，在第三世界或者更广泛地说在许多非西方社会中被提出来。所谓的这个问题，我们指的是在殖民者与被殖民者之间发生的、关于他们彼此文化的相对价值的争论。在18世纪末到19世纪初，在西方对印度的猛烈殖民攻势下，被殖民的印度人以主张他们自己文化的优越性来进行回应。如果我们观察用来表示"文化"的术语是如何在现代的印度诸语言中出现的话，我们就会发现，最常用的术语，sanskriti，事实上是英语"文化"（culture）的翻译。

这里的要点，不是说在英国人引进文化的概念之前（印度）就不存在这个概念，而是说，在19世纪之后，我们把不同的意义投进了文化。它变成一切我们独具的特质的场所，并因此而区别于在殖民者的世界所能找到的一切。当我们变成现代印度人，继而变成一个独立民族国家的公民的时候，我们继续坚持那个使我们与他者分离的"我们的文化"的观念。

尽管文化问题是我们现代身份认同之形成的亲密部分，文化在现代性之中却被看作仍是现代之外的某种东西。这意味着，在何为"现代"的讨论/描述中，文化提供了非现代之物、传统的、外在于后来取代现代性的西化进程的东西的对照。文化与现代性之间的这种关系——这种关系植根于殖民语境——可以在何以女性在非西方关于文化的讨论中占据如此核心的位置方面为我们提供一些线索。

印度的语境与其他亚洲社会之间存在着许多类似的地方。库马里·贾亚瓦迪那*的经典著作《第三世界的女性主义与民族主义》(Feminism and Nationalism in the Third World，1986年)已经提到，在非西方这两种运动——女性的权利运动和民族解放运动——共享着某种密切的联系。与之平行，"文化问题"也成了"民族文化问题"，而这，对女性来说有诸多重要的含义。尽管反对殖民者的民族主义运动使女性的政治参与成为可能，但这些运动也在民族的符号象征中为女性创造了一个非常静态的位置。女性越来越被看成是"传统"和"文化"的宝库。

亚洲各地的女性主义者经常面对的一个批评，即她们隔绝或疏离于"我们的文化"，女性主义来自西方，因此女性主义代表的是一组外来的观念。有趣的是，我们的其他政治框架（比如，马克思主义，自由主义）——这些框架也远没有任何显见的本土资源——并没有遭到同样程度的这种指控。那么，女性主义到底为什么受到"是外来的"的指责和攻击呢？女性主义的要求，据称是来自"现代化"的要求，后者看起来意在抹除"我们的"文化并代之以西方的价值观和生活方式。要作出这样的批评是很容易的，而人们也常常这么做，但它却没有把文化的观念本身是如何在我们的语境中成

---

* 库马里·贾亚瓦迪那（Kumari Jayawardena，1931年— ），斯里兰卡著名女性主义学者。

形的纳入考虑范围。

我们的出发点之一是要理解：(a) 民族本质的创造是如何以（我们）与西方的文化差异（"我们"如何区别于"他们"）的主张为基础；(b) 女性何以常被呈现为差异的化身（正是在女人身上，在女性的身体和生命中，差异才得到展示）。当非西方世界的民族主义者发出现代性与文化之间冲突关系的信号的时候，他们所暗示的，也就是女性是文化的，因而是本真的一部分。因此，她们不可能是现代的一部分，或者说，正如更加常见的那样，她们只可能与现代性保持一种高度中介（mediated）的关系。所以，当女性以与现代性相关的方式行事的时候（像是所谓的果敢坚决、个人主义、野心勃勃等这样的词）她们也被看成是在挑战她们在印度文化中的位置，因此也就是在侵蚀这种文化本身。文化，正如我们已经看到的那样，开始同"现代性"对立起来——如果说，二者必须在殖民的印度共存的话，它们就得各自被性别化成女性和男性。在19世纪由城市化和移民所引发的迅速和影响深远的社会变化的语境中，女性成为所有那些被看作习俗和传统的东西的宝库，即便当男人也在殖民社会中工作，并模仿英国人的服饰和举止的时候也是如此。[1]

女性-文化这一对结构于是便形成了在印度所积淀的常识，甚至在妇女运动中仍是一个未得到解决的问题。不时地

---

[1] 关于对此转变以及新兴起的公私领域出现的一个富有影响的描述，参见帕沙·查特吉（Partha Chatterjee）：《民族及其碎片》（The Nation and its Fragments；1993年）。

有惊爆点提醒我们这个悬而未解的问题的存在：2009年初，就出现了这样一个事件。

粉红内裤运动 *

2009年一月末，一个新成立的右翼印度教组织罗摩神之军（Sri Ram Sena, army of the god Rama）在卡纳塔克邦（Karnataka）的沿海城市芒格洛尔（Mangalore）宣布，其成员将把情人节这天约会的青年情侣作为（袭击）目标。罗摩军的头目，普拉莫德·穆塔里克（PramodMuthalik）说："我们的活动分子将于2月14日与僧人、姜黄根和芒加苏特拉**一起出动。如果我们在公共场合遇到情侣相聚并表达他们的爱意的话，我们就会把他们带到最近的神殿，为他们主持婚礼"（《印度教徒》[The Hindu], 2009年）。尽管情人节在印度很大程度上来说只是一个贺卡公司滋生出来的一个节日，最近几年来，它也吸引了广泛注意，甚至在非都市地区、在那些不说英语的人群中也产生了很大的影响。结果，它也引来了右翼政党的攻击，这些政党把情人节谴责为西方文化

---

* The Pink Chaddi Campaign，Chaddi是关于内裤的北印度俚语，这场运动是印度女性主义者发起的，针对极端民族主义组织对印度女性行为管制（主要是进酒吧喝酒）的抗议。
** 芒加苏特拉（mangalsutra）是印度人婚礼的象征，系在妻子的脖颈上；姜黄根一般用来作吉祥的标记。这些用品都出自印度教的婚礼仪式，在婚礼上新郎会将象征婚姻的黄色丝线围在新娘脖子上。有着金色缀饰的丝线在北方叫做芒加苏特拉（mangalsutra），在南方则叫做他利（thali）。金色的缀饰被系在用藏红花粉或姜黄根粉染成的黄色丝带上，然后新娘给丝带打上三个结，分别代表意志、精神和身体。

的堕落表征。在此声明之后，穆塔里克的人袭击了芒格洛尔的一家酒吧，并殴打、驱逐他们在那里所发现的女人。[1]这个事件，在全国范围内的电子和印刷媒体的显著位置上被报道。在卡纳塔克邦，右翼的印度人民党（Bharatiya Janata Party，简称 BJP）掌权，人权组织则声称该党暗地里纵容罗摩军的行动。卡纳塔克邦的整个沿海区域，尤其是在芒格洛尔，数年来已经成为印度教徒、基督徒和穆斯林之间的新的关系紧张的地域，而所有这些信徒几十年来一直在此区域共享着文化和政治的空间。[2]

在芒格洛尔酒吧袭击事件之后，由去酒吧的、开放、前卫的女性组成的社团在社群网站脸书（Facebook）上已经形成。这个社团发起了一场在当年情人节把粉红女式内裤寄给罗摩军的运动。这次抗议运动的风格是印度女性主义政治史上前所未有的。正如这次运动的一个主要组织者提到的那样："我们只是在思考一种使愈来愈大的查迪瓦拉（chaddiwala）显得荒谬的方法"（Susan，2009 年）。这里提到的查迪瓦

---

[1] 这里是一组能够提供一些影像佐证的网络连接：http://www.youtube.com/watch?v-1EbD2aXs-XU（Pub attack）; http://www.youtube.com/watch?v-tnbYYwOvAFo&feature=related（campaign steps）; http://www.youtube.com/watch?v-THITp1E_onU&feature=related（pile of pink chaddis）; http://www.youtube.com/watch?v-Pgrk9YG6Nq0&feature=related（debate on NDTV）; http://www.youtube.com/watch?v-5EQ7NS6jelU&feature=related（latest weapon in culture clashes）。

[2] 对此区域复杂政治的一个简介，参见苏米（Sumi Krishna，2009 年）未出版的著作。

拉，指的是身穿长黄卡其布短裤（在几种印度语言中这种短裤都叫做chaddi）的男子，这是民族志愿卫队（Rashtriya Swayamsevak Sangh, National Volunteers' Organisation），即右翼政党——这些右翼政党合起来被称作同盟家族（Sangh Parivar）——集团的上级组织的制服的一部分。

尼莎·苏珊（Nisha Susan）详细地叙述了这场运动的发展：

> "运动开始的一天内，我们就有了500名非固定的成员。一周内，我们就达到了4万。从波多黎各到新加坡，从钦奈到艾哈迈达巴德，从古瓦哈蒂到阿姆利则，人们给我们写信：怎样寄上我的内裤？但到了那个时候，运动已经走出了网络。老爷爷和老奶奶、学童、中年家庭妇女，来自比哈尔而声音粗哑、不太愿大声说出内裤这个词的大个子男人等等，都给我们打过电话"（Susan，2009年）。

收集中心遍及印度；人们被鼓励着把内裤扔到这些收集中心，以递送给罗摩军在芒格洛尔的总部。虽然有网络之外的活动面向，后来为人所知的粉红内裤运动（Pink Chaddi Campain, PCC）成为也许是第一个印度女性运动的网络运动。（它对网络的依赖）到了这样的程度，以至于当一些城市有组织一系列的街头抗议和游行示威的时候，抗议者的数目远小于抗议侵权事件的集会中通常会出现的人数。即使是3

月8日国际妇女节在芒格洛尔举行的集会,也只有约三百人出席。

对粉红内裤运动的批评有很多:它们来自那些用别的方法承担女性主义进步政治的同侪群体,这些人认为粉红内裤运动是精英主义和轻浮愚蠢的(当然,与女性有关的更严重的问题还有很多);批评也来自印度教主义的群体,他们宣称粉红内裤运动反对印度文化、不尊重印度人的象征体系等等。对抗议者的辱骂性回应不仅来自下层中产阶级的"原教旨主义者",也来自攻击"世俗""进步主义者"的善用互联网的保守主义者,以及男性大学生。这些讨论抛出了一系列相关的概念:世俗的、西方的、现代的(因此也是与"我们的文化"相对立的)——这个联想的链条很容易地被动员起来反对那些认为罗摩军的官方声明是很成问题的女性。绝大多数女性主义团体都支持粉红内裤运动和情人节联盟,甚至那些激烈反对1994年在班加罗尔举行的全球小姐比赛,或在与迪帕·梅塔[*]有关的在《欲火》论证上刻意沉默(这两个实例代表了近来性别——文化——全球化的其他事态)的那些人也不例外(Niranjana and John,1999年)。实际上,有些从未承认或庆祝情人节的人也在2009年2月14日穿上了粉红的衣服。

---

[*] 迪帕·梅塔(Deepa Mehta,1950年1月1日—)印度著名导演,出生于印度,新德里大学哲学学士,曾于乔治卢卡斯制作影片中执导。代表作为三元素(火、土、水)影片系列,这里提到的是序列中的第一部《欲火》(Fire)。

主流媒体对抗议和反抗议的报道显示在这个问题上的两极分化。实际上,线上和网外的抗议都表明,涉及这一事件的人群惊人的多样化。有些人把酒吧袭击解读为一种反全球化的姿态,但这种解读并不能解释家庭暴力、(军队和警察的)监管暴力、以及印度其他针对女性之公共敌意的表现的长期存在。类似地,把粉红内裤运动看作是支持全球化的力量也是不正确的,如同早期的女性运动也不能简单地说是由"西方"所指使的一样。

那些抗议罗摩军袭击的群体之间,似乎也存在另一种有趣的分野。支持情人节的活动吸引了当地群体(包括卡纳达语*民族主义者,一个农民运动组织,和一个前下层社会人物所领导的"世俗"政党)的参与,但同样的这些群体在3月8日妇女节的庆祝活动上却没有出席。当地的群体似乎支持异性恋情人表达自由的权利(就于情人节派遣爱的战车[Love Chariots]巡逻队以保护情人免受罗摩军袭击的威胁而言),但他们对女性主义者所表达的那些妇女权利并无特别的兴趣。

虽然印度的女性主义团体对针对女性的酒吧袭击暴力和后继的个人攻击暴力进行批判,公开谈论粉红内裤运动的人并不是很多。也许是出于对运动的风格有所不安,她们的作风在性方面令人腼腆,却又富有进攻性。为什么粉红内裤是一个有力的浓缩,在一个单一的意象中汇聚了如此广大

---

* 卡纳达语,印度达索尔邦及其附近讲的一种语言。

而多样的趣味性？大众文化的粗俗语言为复杂的 Web 2.0 所用，看起来是这个浓缩能够产生作用的手段之一。对女性主义者来说，若是涉及跨种姓、跨宗教的婚姻或关系的时候，批判"道德安治"（moral policing）一直以来都是相对容易的；在更加明确地涉及性——就像面对情人节的议题或在公园参与 PDA（public display of affection，公共示爱——青年人的一个新术语）的情人——的时候，这种批判就要困难得多。

一些女性主义的博主觉得粉红内裤运动的抗议没什么结果。你寄出内裤，她们寄出粉红色的莎丽。"这取得了什么成就？"她们问道。这种评论看起来并没有考量到，粉红内裤运动现在已经进入了公共词汇，在广告和一般的杂志文章等地方频频出现。在酒吧袭击的例子中，尽管在"受害者群体"中存在的某种凝聚力（这些女性大多数是年轻的城市中产阶级）允许一些人把这场抗议草率地斥责为精英主义的东西，但是，粉红内裤运动很可能标志着印度女性主义政治话语的转变，其中，运动常说的"为被剥夺基本权利的女性说话"的说辞在显然受到了挑战，代表性的问题本身受到了质问。如果女性主义者们不承认粉红内裤运动前所未有的特质，那么，她们就不能看到，这场运动何以决定性地坐落在性以及女性欲望的问题与印度当代政治世界的交叉点上。粉红内裤运动考虑到印度教主义的酒吧袭击的潜台词，及其袭击者的男权主义修辞，并通过公共的展示而让它"公之于众"；它是通过将其嵌入运动的象征体系，而不是通过批判从而将注意力吸引到其潜台词上,来做到这一点的。

把性理论化的兴趣穿越了非西方世界的不同区域,这也许是因为至今的一段时间内,性对女性主义来说一直是一种极限的情况(a limit case)——性是概念介入与政治介入的最模棱两可的领域,无论这涉及权力在异性恋关系中如何分配,还是涉及在另类的性关系中争取一致性的性别行为而斗争。就翻译/词汇的问题而言,性对文化差异论述的展现和表达来说是一个关键的领域,正如其对现代性问题的思考来说一样十分核心那样。通过不止一种的方式把翻译、现代性、文化与政治问题,带入一个单一的、引人注意的、性别化的意象的粉红内裤运动,对我们这些对重塑女性主义语言及其目标与战略有兴趣的人来说,是一个挑战。

(翻译:王立秋)

参考文献:

Chatterjee, Partha. *The Nation and its Fragments*: *Colonial and Postcolonial Histories*, Princeton: Princeton University Press, 1993.

Jayawardena, Kumari. *Feminism and Nationalism in the Third World*, London: Zed Books Ltd, 1986.

John, Mary E. "Feminism in India and the West: recasting a relationship", *Cultural Dynamics* 10(2), July 1998: 197—210.

Krishna, Sumi. "Understanding and responding to the Mangalore assaults", unpublished piece, 11 February 2009, Bangalore.

重新塑造民族主义：
当代南印度电影和女性主义主体*

性别与印度的现代

一个新的民族主义,充溢着浪漫的爱与最亲密的"私人"情感,如今即将成型。印度的流行电影令我们注意到了这一现象。例如,1992年的电影《罗嘉》(Roja)就被称为"一段爱国的爱情故事";在1994年,还有另一部更为成功的电影叫做《爱在烽火云起时》(1942:A Love Story)。这种民族主义出现的前提是新兴中产阶级似乎逐渐脱离了印度独立后的尼赫鲁式国家,该过程导致了人们政治生活中许多核心词汇的意义发生了改变——比如"世俗主义"(secularism)。这就好像民族—现代(national-modern)的逻辑,之前一直隐而不见,现在由于传统力量的新配置,包括"联合家庭"(Sangh

Parivar)[1]的崛起和印度经济的自由化，忽然被揭露了出来。普通商业电影对"主流"角色——平凡的、没什么"英雄色彩"的小人物——的刻画，为我们切入这种复杂的配置打开了一扇门。我将试着揭示出这种民族想象（national imaginary）转向的核心角色——**妇女**。在新现代性的讨论中，妇女不仅仅呈现出被动接受的形象，而且她作为一种行动者（agency）在民族主义的转向里起着关键作用。

印度"妇女"的概念产生于**民族**（想象为自治的主权民族国家）和**现代性**（同时包括民主化、大众传播的扩散等过程，和制造了"传统"与"现代"直接对立的诸种话语）相互交织的时代背景中。然而不同于性别，**种姓**与**社群**（或是宗教身份）都不能够代表与展示现代性或民族地位（这里我指的是低种姓和穆斯林）。不仅如此，种姓与社群往往被表现得**就像是**前现代的、非现代的和反民族的。换言之，向社群和种姓寻求身份的基础，这对于世俗主义者——那些在后独立时期宣称民族为文化霸权的"现代公民"——来说完全不可接受。很奇怪的是，促使民族—现代将种姓与社群抛在身后的正是要求"妇女"获得的现代性与民族性的呼吁。[2] 不过

---

1 Sangh Parivar 的字面意思是"联合家庭"。它指由桑格（Rashtriya Swayamsevak Sangh）领导的一些松散的印度教右翼政治文化组织。它还包括世界印度教徒理事会（Vishwa Hindu Parishad），印度人民党（Bharatiya Janata Party，BJP）和印度青年民兵（Bajrang Dal）等。

2 参见苏西·塔鲁和特贾斯维莉·尼南贾纳的"当代性别理论问题"'Problems for a Contemporary Theory of Gender'，收录于沙希德·阿明（Shahid Amin）和迪佩什·查卡拉巴提编《庶民研究第九期》（德里：牛津大学出版社，1989）

这要求并不完整。加以研究，我们就可能在它对民族想象的构造中发现一些前后不一或错误之处。

妇女对现代性与民族的要求得到了来自她们新身份的支持；在印度后独立时期，妇女在很多领域里（为了她们自己）塑造了这些新身份。到了20世纪90年代，这种身份塑造模式似乎又走上了新方向。流行电影是这种身份构成的主要领域之一，它可能是在电视近期的普及之前最有力的传媒，那些新身份在电影中被叙事化，得到了广泛的展示和探讨，这也是它引起我研究兴趣的原因。这里我们要着重讨论的三部电影——《姬谭伽里》(Geetanjali，1989)，《罗嘉》(1992)和《孟买之恋》(Bombay，1995)——都由曼尼·拉特纳姆（Maniratnam）执导，使用泰米尔语或泰卢固语；后两部电影也成功地制作了印地语配音的版本。[1] 我想要从这些电影中研究的是：一、它们是如何滋养、支持新印度民族主义的，即便是通过电影这种媒介；二、印度独立后的女性主体是如何糅合进新民族主义的塑造过程中的。这里我可能需要说明一下，我不必然认为我的分析能给电影批评做出什么贡献。我把这篇文章当作一种尝试，通过关注某一种文化产品，去理解生成该产品的政治历史背景究竟是如何构造的。所以，我的目的不是从电影的形式手段这些角度来对电影本身进行全面的分析，而是想帮助我们在当下的背景中解释这些电影的

---

[1] 拉特纳姆有时会重新摄制他电影的一些部分，从而能够包容地区或语言差异，所以判断电影重摄何时停止、配音何时开始有时会有点困难。

诉求。

即便从时间上来说,《姬谭伽里》是前曼达尔*时期电影,《罗嘉》是前巴布里骚乱**时期作品(不过他们出现的时间与这两桩重大事件的间隔非常短,分别是 1990 年 9 月至 10 月,以及 1992 年 12 月),我仍然认为,它们所表现的女性身份很有象征性:就前一部电影而言,象征了反曼达尔妇女(anti-Mandal woman);就后一部而言,象征了代表民族的印度教妇女(但并不一定是公开的族群性妇女)。[1] 特别地,《孟买之恋》的女主人公是穆斯林,电影对她的塑造手法多少不同于《姬谭伽里》和《罗嘉》,这一点我稍后会提到。所谓"反曼达尔妇女",指的是一种自我身份:通过否定种姓,她们得以宣称自己是现代的和世俗的。这并不是说"现代和世俗"**等同于**"反曼达尔",这仅仅是一种表现方式,揭示了 20 世纪 90 年代那些正在发生或开始显现的思潮合流。曼达尔委员会当年为了"其他落后种姓"(Other Backward Castes,简称 OBC),建议为他们预留更多政府职位及教育机会,而针对该

---

* 1990 年,印度政府尝试执行"曼达尔委员会"(Mandal Commission)于 1980 年提出的建议,弱化种姓差异,向低种姓民众进行政策倾斜,为他们在政府及学校等预留更多的就业就学机会。结果该预留政策引起了高种姓民众的大规模骚乱,自当年九月底开始造成数百人死亡。
** 巴布里清真寺位于印度教圣城阿约提亚(Ayodhya),曾长期是印度教同伊斯兰教冲突的前线。1992 年 12 月 6 日,"联合家庭"带领大批激进民族主义者强行拆毁了巴布里清真寺。
[1] 也可以再加上一点:就这两个女性形象如何向现代、世俗和民族提出要求,我们也能看出她们的构成非常相似。

建议的骚乱,将现代混同于世俗,又将世俗混同于对种姓差异的超越。[1]

要讨论新民族主义,一个主要问题是,它的词汇看上去似乎和旧的民族主义没什么不同。民族利益、国家安全、民族融合、现代化,这些都是我们从 20 世纪 50 年代起就已经非常熟悉的术语。"世俗化"这个词也一样,它曾经是印度自由派和左翼政治的核心概念。我的论点是,民族主义确实正在转变,但是被这些沿用的术语遮掩了。某种意义上,这种转变令民族—现代的轮廓变得清晰,令它对(低)种姓和(非印度教)社群的排斥合法化。换个可能有点奇怪的表达,我们也想可以称其为"后—民族—现代"(既不是后现代,也不是后民族),用它来描述那些词汇"旧瓶装新酒"的状况。[2]本文中我将聚焦于当代流行电影对这些词汇的使用,以及这些电影所生产的新主体位置(subject-positions)。

一方面,当今有些观点认为政治身份应当根植于种姓和社群,该论断挑战了民族—现代的构成;另一方面,性别的问题却处在非常不同的境地中。[3]即便过去 20 年的妇女运动已

---

[1] 需要注意反曼达尔主义者只讨论"差异",不提"不平等"。

[2] 关于后—民族—现代,以何种方式接触它,如何商讨它、调用它,又如何使用它进行商谈,我们必须意识到这些问题对于不同群体来说一定是不一样的,是由他们的种姓、社群、性别配置以及他们接触的角度的优劣。

[3] 参见苏西·塔鲁和特贾斯维莉·尼南贾纳的"当代性别理论问题"'Problems for a Contemporary Theory of Gender',和维韦克·达勒什瓦尔(Vivek Dhareshwar)的"种性和世俗自我"'Caste and the Secular Self',《艺术与思想》斯刊,1993 年第 25—6 期,115—26 页。

经取得了相当可观的成果，当初女性主义者们提问的形式现在被搬到了一些相去甚远的事情上，包括民族与现代的合并这一女性主义者们正着力批判的概念。自由选择的、自主行动的、主动性强的妇女，都是当今流行电影欣赏的形象。如果仔细研究这些女性（或者我们应该说女性主义者）主体的能动性是如何架构的，例如曼尼·拉特纳姆电影的主人公姬塔（Geeta）*，罗嘉（Roja）和莎伊拉·巴努（Shaila Banu），那么通过对民族-现代的重新审视，我们也许能够从中领会她们蕴藏意义的模式。

反曼达尔妇女

下面这一节，我将尝试在反曼达尔骚乱的背景下研究《姬谭伽里》中的女性主体性。我们都记得，1990年8月，辛格总理（V. P. Singh）宣布执行曼达尔委员会的建议，引发了高种姓青年的大规模暴动；他们绝大多数都来自城市。[1]其中有大量妇女，她们热情参与了反曼达尔委员会论坛（Anti-Mandal Commission Forum，简称AMCF）组织的活动，包括带领学生清扫街道，擦鞋，在火车站搬运行李，以及统筹安排游行队伍和集会等。新闻报道描写道，这些高种姓的青年参与了英雄式的斗争，在混乱的临界点上拯救了他们的民族。他们反对执行曼达尔委员会的建议，认为执行的后果是否认

---

* 姬塔（Geeta）是姬谭伽里（Geetanjali）的昵称。

1 曼达尔委员会建议为低种姓民众在求职和教育机会方面提供额外的预留或配额。

优秀价值,乃至于最终毁灭这个国家。在这场事关"优秀价值"(merit)的战争中,真正爱国的和真正世俗的都是克服并超越了种姓区分的印度人。那些依据种姓而请求执行建议的人都被简单地贴上了种姓主义者的标签。

民族和现代性的形象明显地与关于优秀价值的反曼达尔话语交织在了一起。种姓,或曼达尔委员会的预留政策(该背景下这两个概念可以互相替代),被认为妨碍了国家向更进步高效的方向转变,它用封建主义的残余套牢了印度,阻止这个国家在世界上占据平等的一席。通过公开反对种姓,现代中产阶级主体同时宣告了对自己民族的关怀。

这里,我将稍稍偏离主题,讨论一下我自己的学科——英语——是如何回应曼达尔危机的;我认为这并非不合时宜。19世纪英国人引入了英语文学研究,它在自由人道主义主体——同时也是现代和民族主义——的形成过程中扮演了重要角色。[1] 印度有一批受过英式教育的主体,他们的"世俗主义"使得中产阶级势力有了取代种姓和社群的能力,进而使得种姓和社群成了中产阶级**之外**的东西、中产阶级的**他者**。在反曼达尔骚动中,很多学校英语系的高种姓学生全体参与

---

[1] 关于这些议题的讨论,参见苏西·塔鲁的"政府,捆绑与松绑"(Government, Binding and Unbinding),《英语与外语期刊》(*English and Foreign Languages*)(1991年6月—12月)特刊导论;高里·维斯万纳桑(Gauri Viswanathan),《征服的面具》(*Masks of Conquest*)(伦敦:费伯,1990年);特贾斯维莉·民南贾纳,《为翻译定位:历史,后结构主义和殖民语境》(伯克利:加州大学出版社,1992年)

了抵制运动，要求完全废除预留政策。[1]

毫无疑问，下面这两个现象一定有所关联：一个是曾经代表着民族的中产阶级，他们身上最主要的特点其实是**英国性**（Englished-ness）；另一个是那些"英国化"（Englished）了的中产阶级/高种姓女性学生毅然决然地出现在公共场合，表达对她们所属阶级的愤慨。反曼达尔运动能够被媒体合法化，赢得家长的赞许，这在后独立印度的所有学生运动中都显得非常特殊。很奇怪的是，学生们受到的赞誉有赖于一种想象，即他们的政治行动不但不是政治化的，反而"超越了政治"。[2] 恰恰因为媒体眼中的学生运动非常纯洁、不同于传统反曼达尔分子的政治斗争，学生们的形象才会忽然转变：他们原本礼貌谦和，却长期忍受不公，现在只得怒吼，被迫采取行动挽救自己的民族，阻止它"变成一群狗"。[3] 妇女们出现在街头，公开抗议示威，这景象令媒体回想起了自由斗争的理想主义。在想象中，"妇女"的道德形象纯洁无瑕，故而拯救民族的重任可以放心地托付给她们。和男性一同热情参与反曼达尔骚动的"妇女"没有被简单地当成另一种性别

---

[1] 无论这些要求有时候显得多么合理，从印度行政服务（IAS）官员的公报等例子还是能很明显地看到这些要求针对的是所有预留政策，除了其他落后种姓，也包括为表列种姓（Scheduled Castes，SCs）和表列部落（Scheduled Tribes，STs）制订的预留政策。

[2] 参见维纳·达斯（Veena Das），"信仰的危机"（A Crisis of Faith），《政治家》（1990年9月3日）。

[3] 这是反曼达尔骚乱期间经常听到的口号。另外还有一句名言，当时高等种姓经常用它来表现他们的无私："我关心的不是我自己。没有预留政策，我一样能找到工作。我唯一担心的是这个政策将把我们带向何方。"

的生物，她们也是自由而平等的公民；这意味着，这些自信而雄辩的主体自认为她们是"种姓"（即低种姓）的对立面。于是，属于中产阶级的高种姓"妇女"在后—民族—现代中占据了一席之地；低种姓的人们，无论男女，都不再可见。我们也能看到类似的事情发生在穆斯林身上，无论男女。

然而，我们也不能由此得出结论说，高种姓反曼达尔妇女最主要的特点就是英国性。有趣的是，同样属于民族—现代的南印度的中产阶级妇女，她们看电影的首选是英语或印地语，而不是泰卢固语等。但是现在，她们也成了《姬谭伽里》这种电影和曼尼·拉特纳姆这类"带着乡音"的导演的热心追随者。令拉特纳姆从商业电影中脱颖而出的，是他电影使用的现实主义表现方式、它们技术上的复杂性[1]、演员们看上去的自然和自发性、当然还有对"印度现代性"天衣无缝的塑造。非常重要的是，拉特纳姆的电影在民族空间（nation-space）中插入了地区差异，比如他大胆地把一对泰米尔夫妇放在克什米尔，或者放在孟买，然后为**他们**的性格注入新的民族—现代。谐剧和情节剧的元素是印度语言商业电影的重要方面，然而拉特纳姆抛弃或者弱化了这些元素，让他的电影得以在"现代"空间中成型，也反过来塑造了该空间。所以，他的电影不仅不会让中产阶级印度人觉得尴尬，反而能够让他们骄傲地欣赏。拉特纳姆电影在不同阶级和地

---

[1] 知名电影批评家默罕默德（Khalid Mohammed）在他的评论里说，"拉吉夫·梅农（在《孟买之恋》）的摄影具有国际水准。"（*The Times of India*，9 April 1995）

区受到的欢迎，表明了由音乐电视（MTV）和有线电视节目培养的"世界主义的"品位正在像文化霸权一样显现。[1] 这些电影塑造了新的主体性和女性气质，这可能是它们成功地吸引了年轻女观众的主要原因。电影中的新女性气质成功地坚守了现代性的承诺，它没有让现代性沾上女性主义或女权政治的风险；媒体常常嘲笑，乃至诋毁这种女性主义，认为它是对西方不伦不类的模仿。

今日，拉特纳姆等人的电影生产并传播了女性气质的新定义；新的定义又改变了大众对"现代性"和"传统"这些问题的广泛争执，向它注入了新内容。在我看来，这些争执促使带着侵略性的文化民族主义不断成型，开始借着跨国市场经济的词汇来表达自身，把自己的内容植入这些词汇中。民族想象不断地重构，支持了新的消费经济；而流行电影中女性气质的新塑造，需要与这种新的消费经济联系在一起。它建立在我所谓的"后—民族—现代"概念上，在日常生活的层面——以及商品生活的层面——消解着旧的矛盾，述说着"印度"现代性的建构。

表面上，拉特纳姆部分电影的女主人公不符合我们传统印象中印度好女人的形象。比如，《姬谭伽里》的青年女主角总是说，"Lecchipoddaama（我们要私奔吗）?" 而且还经常

---

[1] 苏尼尔·塞提（Sunil Sethi）这样描写了他在德里与"低层、中产阶级、各族群混合"的观众中观看电影的情形："观众们似乎真诚地喜爱这部电影。我自己极其高兴地发现，哪怕是短暂对话的一点点隐约的细节和微妙的意义，他们都能够成功地捕捉，在所有正确的地方大笑、鼓掌、喘息或者欢呼……"（'Celluloid Metaphor of "Bombay"'，*Newstime*，16 April 1995）

对不同的人说。然而，姬谭伽里的鲁莽和咄咄逼人的性观念，在电影叙事中仅仅是在表现她高昂的精神与幽默。她的"自暴自弃"，某种意义上是被她缺席或者已故的母亲所抛弃，乃至于被生命所抛弃。只有在死亡的边缘，这位女主角的胆识才真正地变得可能。

《姬谭伽里》中，是什么样的叙事轨迹为女性的主张创造了空间？这部电影说的是两个相爱的年轻人，男孩得了白血病，女孩患有心脏病，两人都即将去世。电影把背景设定在戈代加讷尔（Kodaikanal）弥漫的雾气中，渐渐展开了美得令人窒息的风景；在这里，葱郁的绿色（还有女主人公身上缀着各种红与黄的民族服饰）与迫近的死亡故事形成对位，主人公们大概就会在这里死去。有趣的是，电影最明显能够反映死亡的意象是一块墓地上的坟堆和鬼魂，而就在这里，姬塔精心设计了一出恶作剧；她由妹妹帮忙，诱来了几个毫无防备的男人。在女主角看来，死亡仅仅是一个玩笑。坟堆既是"真实"的，又是对恐怖片意象的戏仿。而且，墓地既等待着"无可避免的结局"，又容忍了这个生命依然活着的事实。我们对姬塔的最初印象之一，是她挑了一套鬼魂似的衣服，穿着它，扮恶作剧。直到后面的间歇，观众们才发觉，她原来已病入膏肓。

然而，贯穿电影的叙述，爱情与死亡一直紧紧缠绕在一起，就像依莱亚拉贾（Ilaiyaraja）为电影作的配乐，"Om Namaha"的歌声热情洋溢，伴奏却被放大了的心跳声占据。虽说这部电影在城市外不太流行，在大城市里，来自中产和更低阶级的年轻人还是把它看了一遍又一遍，模仿里面的对话场景,大喊、歌唱或是低语。电影似乎在宣称,人们要活得好像自己明天就会死去一样。为了活在今天,这些新消费者——也就是这部电影的主要观众群体——终于确认了他们的直觉:最重要的事情,是在当下让自己变得好看,是在当下为自己采购时尚服饰(纳加朱纳[*]的牛仔裤和运动衫,吉莉佳[**]的新民族服饰纱丽克米兹和新娘装[***]),因为明天的自己最好也不过是像死了一样。[1] 实际上,迫近的死亡是唯一让"爱情"有意义的语境。正是爱情,被漂亮衣服加固了的爱情,永远不会扰乱观众们的直觉。这爱情不仅没有未来,而且建立在它对差异的完全抹杀之上。

这些主人公明显都是城市人,但又完全脱离了他们日常的背景,甚至与之毫无关联。男主角看上去是印度教徒,女主角是基督徒,可这些都是无关紧要的细节,最多是添加了喜剧成分,比如教堂那场戏里,男主角在弥撒中向上帝投诉他的情人。(《罗嘉》里出现了另一个少数族群身份——穆斯林,这个形象可以被轻易地想象成前现代的和反民族的;在《姬谭伽里》中,女主角身上的印度教形象几乎不可见,她是民族—现代的一部分,这和《罗嘉》里的穆斯林形象形成了

---

[*] 印度男演员,英文名 AkkineniNagarjuna,在《姬谭伽里》中饰演男主角普拉卡什(Prakash)。

[**] 印度女演员,英文名 GirijaShettar,在《姬谭伽里》中饰演女一号姬谭伽里。

[***] 纱丽克米兹(Salwar Kameez)和新娘装(Ghagra Choli)分别是印度传统服饰,前者是由衬衣和宽松的裤子或裙子组成的套装,后者通常是紧身上衣配上褶裙。

1 《姬谭伽里》里的新娘装确实在青年甚至少年女孩中创造了衣着的新时尚。

鲜明对照。)宗教差异在叙事中并不是问题的焦点，毕竟对快要死去的人来说，做什么事都是允许的。《姬谭伽里》这类电影在新消费经济中占据了一个节点（nodal point），新消费经济又构建了一个需要"本真性"的伦理自我。只有那些非本真的、经历着生命中的死亡（death-in-life）的人才会害怕死亡。真正经历过死亡中的生命（life-in-death）的人，他们只生活在当下，他们经历的瞬间只有当生命终点临近时才变得真实，他们并不会害怕死亡。[1]

新消费经济在《姬谭伽里》的中心地位决定了电影绝不会真正地表现**工作**，除了那些为电影增加了一些本地色彩的水果贩子，以及医生、护士等**为**这对情侣工作的人。男主角刚从大学毕业，却由于父母的财力和自己迫近的死亡而免于工作。所以，电影里并没有展现出阶级差异；即便在情节的副线里有个好色的看守，还有他总是眼泪汪汪的妻子，他们的角色都显得谐谑，而且也被叙事的主线吞没了。女主角和她的妹妹们同样不用工作，除了时不时清扫房屋或者精心准备洗油浴。我们甚至完全看不到姬塔学习，因为她生活在颇为"懈怠"的时光里，她需要做的一切就是让自己和他人开心。不同于后来的《罗嘉》和《孟买之恋》，《姬谭伽里》抹去了地区差异；除了剧中人物都操泰卢固语这一点，我们很难看到其他线索，将电影**放置**在任何一个特定的地区。主角们看上去也不会不像是德里、孟买或班加罗尔的

---

[1] 我这个观点来自苏茜·塔鲁。她还让我注意到了电影中"现代性"的对应影像。

大学生。显然，男主人公和那些时髦的城市中产阶级青年都穿着西式服装，但是同样来自城市的女主角在许多南印度电影里都开始穿着北印度的"民族"服饰。电影的女主角不再用穿着来代表地区的特殊性，现在的她，和城市青年妇女一样，因为披上了拉贾斯坦-古吉拉特*装束而变成了"印度的"。在曼尼·拉特纳姆的其他作品里（比如获奖的《寂静交响曲》[Mouna Raagam]），我们能够看到一些频繁出现的幻想序列：将爱情颂歌设置在荒漠中，头巾、刺绣、充足的骆驼、大量的珠宝，等等。这些大众传媒为我们的"私人"幻想提供视觉意象，新印度的图景就这么包含其中。[1]

所以，姬塔是"新女性"，是强健的女主角，既现代又具女性特质。一方面，她随意的衣着和"自发"的举止表明了她"解放"的形象；另一方面，她又同时承载着妇女作为救世主和作为导师的双重负担。姬塔帮助男主角理解了他生命的短暂，也让他向他们俩共同的命运寻求和解。然而，女主角并未免除了责任去保持真正女性的意象。她在她的感情关

---

* 拉贾斯坦和古吉拉特分别为印度西部偏北、同巴基斯坦接壤的两个邦。

[1] 阿西什·拉贾特雅克沙（Ashish Rajadhyaksha）在富有洞察力的论文《给民族的好消息》(Beaming Messages to the Nation, *Journal of Artsand Ideas*, no. 19（1990）, pp.33—52）中探讨了他所谓的土著主义（indigenism）的新定义背后的动机。拉贾特雅克沙认为，由于"地理上定义的地域身份与地理上定义的市场紧密相关"，所以市场的国际化很明显要求构成新的身份。大众传媒，特别是电视和流行电影，从很多方面促进了新土著主义的成像。这个新土著主义吸收了多种被人类学化的民俗传统元素，并将其与本真的、超越时间的"印度"的概念联系在一起。

系中还保有主动性，因为她依然是"印度人"，是**好的**现代性的能指，哪怕她留着及肩的长发。在后独立时期，一系列意象都被城市中产阶级抛入旧传统的范畴，但这部电影依然能有效地在当代重新利用它们（比如准备草药、姬塔和她抹了油的头发、妇女们坐着的大庭院等这些镜头）。能够很明显地看到，这种重新利用再一次的是以妇女为核心。**差的**现代性则由军队少校的好色妻子所代表，由迪斯科·香缇（Disco Shanti）扮演，穿着紧身牛仔裤、迷你裙，或有时只有一条浴巾。这种差的现代性不可避免地和贪得无厌的性欲联系在一起，这一点在迪斯科·香缇色诱看守的"喜剧"桥段里表露无疑。吉莉佳和香缇的角色都有着咄咄逼人的性态度，但前者扮演的姬塔，由于带着死亡的阴影，观众只会同她一起欢笑；而后者的行为到头来只会显得可耻，引发观众的嘲笑。

电影里，姬塔没有母亲，只有一个向她传授"传统"知识的外祖母。她的传统知识通过各种草本化妆品呈现在新消费者的面前。"外祖母的知识"被跨国资本调用，在化学实验室里得到验证并重新制作，从而向"传统"社群开拓新市场。姬塔为什么没有母亲？如果姬塔的母亲属于当代女性主体性叙事化的一部分，她应当会把旧的女性气质传授给姬塔，从而在民族—现代里立足；因为在独立最初几年，我们身上被强加了一些苦难，所以她会因为未来的延续而被好好照料。但是，正因为姬塔没有未来，她才能够挑战传统的女性气质。考虑到她时日无多，她的父亲也容忍了她所有的过分行为。她的鲁莽和放纵都只在死亡的边缘才完全展现，都不可能持续，所以也都能被谅解。

回到我这篇论文的开头，反曼达尔骚乱。《姬谭伽里》预示了一个反曼达尔妇女，她同中产阶级男性占据了平等的空间；在这个空间里，种姓和社群的差异都不再重要，它们都被世俗的主体抛在身后。在朝着后—民族—现代的转向中，这个主体渗入了消费经济的语言，而当下这一时刻因为这部电影得到了定价，更让消费经济显得自然而然。正是消费经济使得不惜一切代价追求效率的要求合法化，而支持预留政策的国家机构和社会福利主义者却无法做到这一点。[1] 缺乏效率的国家机构是电影《罗嘉》的核心主旨，它设定在今日的克什米尔。

民族主义的浪漫曲

《姬谭伽里》把新中产阶级的幻想叙事化，设置在了看似远离日常生活的世界；《罗嘉》则将这个自信而武断的中产阶级的政治戏剧化。这种戏剧化与颇具争议的《孟买之恋》如出一辙。[2]《罗嘉》有些意外地获得了1993年的民族融合奖[*]。拉特

---

[1] 在1990年的反曼达尔骚乱中，中产阶级通常持有的态度是，印度的公共部门已经因为政府的预留政策而变得腐化和低效。

[2] 印度选举委员会首席委员塞珊（T.N.Seshan）在广告牌上公开支持《罗嘉》，表示所有爱国的印度人都应该看这部电影。印度人民党（BJP）的阿德瓦尼（L.K.Advani）坦陈他被男主角抢救国旗的一幕感动了。湿婆神军党（Shiv Sena）的巴尔·塔克雷（Bal Thackeray）获得了电影的部分剪辑，他在访谈中表示《孟买之恋》"好极了"。

[*]《罗嘉》获得的是授予反映民族融合电影的"纳吉斯·杜特奖"（Nargis Dutt Award for Best Feature Film on National Integration）。该奖项不同于另一个"民族融合奖"，即"英迪拉·甘地民族融合奖"（Indira Gandhi Award for National Integration）。

纳姆电影的角色身上没有明显的焦虑（angst），即便拉特纳姆的表现技巧直接继承了20世纪70年代印地语中产阶级趣味电影［要么见于赫里西开什·穆克吉（Hrishikesh Mukherjee）式的沉思模式，要么见于沙依德·米尔扎（Saeed Mirza）的社会批判模式］。拉特纳姆的电影在任何意义上都没有为他的主角们辩解：他颂扬他们的志向与生活方式，而不是批判他们。

《罗嘉》的开篇是一群印度士兵逮捕一名克什米尔军官。这之后跟着另一个开头，描绘了壮美的瀑布、海湾与桑德班普尔（位于印度的某处）村庄明亮碧绿的田野，女主人公罗嘉唱着歌，活蹦乱跳地穿过这片风景。[1] 在这一段像电视剧一样迅速平滑的镜头中，我们看到，罗嘉有时和她的小妹妹一起，开着拖拉机（玩，因为她们不用"工作"），同年长的村民恶作剧，穿上男装，披上学士袍，从妇女们正在插秧的田里跑过。在拉特纳姆的其他电影里，真实的劳动只是一种衬托女主角无忧无虑的背景。接着，我们看到罗嘉和其他女孩赶着一群羊下山（依然不是在工作，还是在玩），穿过公路，拦下男主角的车，在他进村前好好地检查他。罗嘉除了

---

[1] 虽然我对《罗嘉》的泰卢固语版本也很熟悉，但是我还是选择关注它的印地语版本。这个版本是民族的成功，标志着新南印度电影自信地占据了"民族的/全国的"而不仅是"区域的"空间（就政治议程和市场而论）。这部电影的泰米尔语版可能会在不同的轴线上询唤（interpellate）观众，而泰卢固语和印地语版向观众表达的结构都非常相似。但是，印地语版抹去了泰米尔和泰卢固版的一些含混之处，特别是语言的问题。另外，在泰米尔纳德邦的政治语境下，"爱国主义"的问题可能会指向非常不同的论争。由于1991年拉吉夫·甘地（Rajiv Gandhi）在该邦斯里伯鲁布德村遇刺，1992年这部电影最初在泰米尔纳德邦上映时，许多观众被期待去观影，认为这是对泰米尔人因为刺杀事件而感到的集体罪恶的驱魔。

她的"农村"出身不同于姬塔的"城市"背景,其他方面二者非常相似。二者都显得无拘无束,兴致高昂,有些自作主张,从来不会哑口无言。妇女运动为女性创造了空间,让她们以特定的方式变得可见;即便有些女性主义者质疑该空间,认为它被用于恢复妇女的景观化(spectacularization),但无论如何,她们的伶牙俐齿总归受惠于它。有趣的是,罗嘉和姬谭伽里类似的高昂兴致好像都源于她们没有"真实工作"的责任,[1] 所以她们的自负并不是她们在工作场所与他人的交际方式。[2]

瑞希·库马尔(Rishi Kumar),我们彬彬有礼的男主角,来到罗嘉的村子上"探望"罗嘉的姐姐,因为他想要娶一位"农村姑娘"。不仅如此,他还希望他的新娘来自他早已心向往之的美丽村庄("我热爱这里的每一寸土地",他后来说道)。但很清楚的是他不可能随便娶一个人——当他得知罗嘉的姐姐想要嫁给别人、他对她的追求彻底失败之后,他立刻转向了他当时只见过两次的罗嘉。

罗嘉非常漂亮,五官分明,显然来自高种姓。她和什亚姆·贝内格尔(Shyam Benegal)、阿杜尔·戈帕尔克里施纳(Adoor Gopalkrishna)等人的新现实主义"艺术"电影所塑造

---

[1] 早期商业电影也会塑造主人公嬉戏游玩、免于任何劳动等义务的形象。这里我想强调的是,拉特纳姆的电影一方面有着**现实主义**的叙事,让他描写的妇女显得既"真实"又"自然",另一方面他描写的妇女形象又非常不同。
[2] 女主人公免于"劳动"的特点助长了她的自负,让她显得可爱、吸引人、没有威胁性。

的农村妇女非常不同。她管她的父亲叫"爹地"（Daddy），家里有电视机，能轻车熟路地使用电话；还有，她能在城市环境中感到自由自在，可以非常轻松、毫无任何障碍地适应瑞希的上层中产阶级家庭和氛围，除了不懂英文。所以，罗嘉完全不属于老的印地语或印度方言商业电影中的"美丽村妇"那一类。她的旧世界与新生活没有出现互不相容的情况，相反，二者能够无缝对接。鉴于农村的高等阶级/种姓都被卷入了高速的城市化过程，英语已不再是文化差异或者非印度性（non-Indianness）的充分标志。取而代之的是，"英语"可以经由消费主义的训练而掌握；更奇怪的是，英语并不让人联想到非印度的，而是和自信的、民族主义的印度联系在一起——那些显示出瑞希的职业和日常生活的词汇就可以体现这个观点，我稍后还会回来加以解释。

瑞希眼中的农村象征着重新构想的传统主义："民族式（ethnic）"的婚礼，完全不同于酒店或多功能厅里在上层中产阶级看来索然无味的流程；年长的妇女身着五彩的莎丽长袍为新人舞蹈；旁边播放着饶舌歌手巴巴·萨赫佳尔（Baba Sehgal）一类"朴素（rustic）"的婚礼歌曲，它们的歌词在性方面都相当直白。所有这些民族性的内容都没有背离瑞希世界性的现代性（cosmopolitan modernness），相反它们还让这种现代性变得更加自信。除了结婚时穿的民族礼服，瑞希通常身着牛仔裤加衬衫或者毛衣。另一方面，克什米尔军人的着装总能显示出他们是穆斯林。罗嘉和瑞希代表的印度教族群则只是作为印度人之复杂性的一部分。印度教的婚礼仪式已经如此地正常化，以至于我们很少会特别在意它，甚至都不认为它是"宗教的"，就好像我们并不会把电影里罗嘉频繁地向她的偶像祷告这件事看得有多么重要。可那些军人，特别是带头抓捕瑞希的里亚卡特（Liaqat），他们总是在祷告——这行为，加上镜头的切换和配乐，不仅是在强调宗教差异，更显得像威胁或是不祥的预兆。他们的宗教性总是被描绘得冷酷无情，缺乏幽默感；而罗嘉的祈祷就很滑稽讨喜，能够吸引观众分享她的希望和焦虑。

瑞希的职业是"密码破译专家"，这词在电影里是用英语说出的，之后很久都没有解释它的意思，直到他建议罗嘉接受"安全调查"的时候顺便提到了他的工作是处理"机密问题"，包括"加密和解密"（所有这些术语都是用英语说的）。瑞希的镜头，有好几次都是坐在电脑显示器和键盘前面，努力解码一段信息。他在观众看来是一名真正的民族主义者，因为他的工作直接关系到国家的安全利益。而且很有意思，也是我想论证的是，他的民族主义不是反西方的，而是反穆斯林的——即便电影从没这么说过。有些作者宣称，因为尼赫鲁式的民族主义支持西方却不反对穆斯林，所以认定当代民族主义支持西方又倾向于反穆斯林的理论都是站不住脚的。[1]可是对我来说，1950年代的尼赫鲁主义和1990年代的

---

[1] 参见阿伦·库马·帕特奈克（Arun Kumar Patnaik）的"理想主义方程式"（Idealist Equations），《经济和政治周刊》，第29卷32期（1994年8月6日），2108页。

中产阶级新民族主义有着显著的不同。[1]民族地位与现代性交叉的历史背景下，新市民阶层的兴起同时带来了世俗主义，它宣称自身超越了种姓与宗教。所以需要指出的是，尼赫鲁式民族主义并不是简单地不反对穆斯林（它也不是简单地支持西方，但这问题就需要在别的地方慢慢讨论了）。

20世纪50年代"印度人"形成时，它的概念并没有明白地建立在反穆斯林的话语之上，因为市民主体（citizen-subject），除了其他内容，就是被**编码**为是印度教的。如今，在全球化的背景下，印度市民主体隐藏的标记逐渐显露，由高等种姓印度教中产阶级**毫不尴尬**地主张着。因为在后冷战的"新世界秩序"中伊斯兰教被持续地妖魔化，所以他们的不尴尬并不会引起注意。一种显示"差异"的方式——这里，差异是特权而非低人一等——逐渐显现为自由化和全球化的正面议程的一部分。我认为，差异作为特权的标记联结着新中产阶级对于民族空间的广泛要求。这种要求很清楚地反映在了中产阶级对克什米尔"问题"的陈述上。

瑞希的上级本来要去克什米尔协助军队，但是他生了重

---

[1] 为了解释这一点，我们需要仔细研究市民主体在印度的构成。苏茜·塔鲁和我在《当代性别理论问题》（发表于《庶民研究》第九卷）里论证了，19世纪"印度人"概念的兴起总是被高等种姓、中产阶级、印度教徒和男性所标记或**编码**（因为标记并不可见）。有些学者已经显示了，"印度人"的概念同时不平等于殖民者，却主张在特殊领域内优越于殖民者。进而，后独立的印度人宣称，和那些位于帝国核心的自由主义市民来说，他们更加主张平等与福利，并且致力于根除任何形式的"落后"。世俗的印度市民于是把"他"自己表现为超越了种姓和社群的身份，而这种论断与关于解放的主流叙事并不相容。

病,希望瑞希能够代替他。他的问题,"你一定不介意去的,对吧",得到了瑞希这样的答复:"当然不介意。我会去印度的任何地方。克什米尔不是在印度吗?"(观众们响起了热烈的掌声。)虽然罗嘉在电影的开始不理解瑞希,并拒绝了他的求爱,但是婚后的她执意要陪伴丈夫去克什米尔。所以,像很多早期印度电影一样,度蜜月的新婚夫妻来到了"克什米尔"。但正式欢迎他们的场景是,他们被扔到了一个明显没有其他客人的五星级宾馆。他们开车穿过荒芜的街道,罗嘉问道为什么城里看上去这么空空荡荡,瑞希只回了句"宵禁"。罗嘉再问为什么要宵禁,他用上了他最喜欢的字眼:"安全"。从电影创造的观众位置来看,这里不需要其他任何的解释。除了报童和几个兜售纪念品的小贩,电影里几乎没有出现任何寻常克什米尔人。还有两场幻想/唱歌的剧情,我们看到了克什米尔人——要么是女人,要么是小孩,身着精致的戏服。其他的克什米尔人几乎全都是男性军人,只有一个例外。这样的描写,把罗嘉作为女性气质和印度性的承载者——两者都含蓄地带着印度教的印记——同其他人区分了开来。[1]

罗嘉在寺庙祈祷,男主人公去找她,被尾随他的军人

---

[1] 拉维·瓦苏德凡(Ravi Vasudevan)声称"地区身份在妇女的形象中终归显得让它逃避了向民族主义自我理性的转变"(Vasudevan, 'Other Voices: Reading "Roja" Against the Grain', *Seminar* 423, November 1994, pp.43—4)。这个论点很有趣也值得深究。但是,它似乎错过了一个很重要的事实,即拉特纳姆的电影不断地构建"族群"身份而不是特定的"区域"身份。这也许是他的"南印度"语言电影和印地语电影一样取得了非凡成功的原因。

逮捕。那些人要求用瑞希交换他们被捕的首领瓦西姆·汗（Wasim Khan）。罗嘉去警察局报告"raakshasjaiseaadmi"（一群恶鬼般的男人），他们带走了她的丈夫，一个"deshpremi"（爱国者，热爱本民族的人）。国家要拯救它的"好公民"，与武装的"恶鬼"斗争。虽然罗嘉只要找回她的丈夫（"我才不关心这个国家"），但是通过她对她丈夫瑞希和那些军人的描述——前者是爱国者而后者是魔鬼，电影暗示了我们，罗嘉也是一名爱国者。

瑞希被捕期间，有两个非常戏剧化的表演清晰地体现了他对民族的热爱。第一场，逮捕他的军人要他对着录音机说话，叫他亲口提出交换瓦西姆·汗的要求，但是瑞希只是坚定地对录音机说，"Jai Hind"（"印度万岁！"）。甚至在被反复殴打、满面鲜血之后，瑞希依然反复说着这一句话，令观众大声鼓掌叫好。当印度政府拒绝释放瓦西姆的消息传来，一个士兵抓起一块印度国旗，冲到外面，对着它举起了火把要燃烧国旗。瑞希打碎玻璃，跳出窗户，打翻士兵，纵身跳到国旗上，碾灭燃烧的火焰。这举动让观众兴奋异常。他扑灭国旗上的火，站了起来，牛仔裤和毛衫还在燃烧。看上去，他不可思议地像是20世纪90年代经过媒体美化的反曼达尔的鼓动者，那些来自高种姓的人声称他们是真正世俗的，因为他们不相信种姓，只相信优秀价值。如果说在反曼达尔骚动中，种姓差异还只是被编码为缺乏优秀价值，那么《罗嘉》里的宗教和民族差异（尤其是伊斯兰教）就不仅仅是反民族的，还是缺乏人性的。这些经过加密的意象，比如"燃烧"

的瑞希，配合背景音乐的渐强，把民族主义的诗篇融入了胜利的颂歌。这场戏中，镜头的切换让我们看到士兵头领里亚卡特，他在楼里深深地祈祷，完全不顾外面的打斗和燃烧的国旗。

电影快结束时，瑞希还是逃走了。他得到了里亚卡特的妹妹的帮助。后者在电影里一直沉默，由于士兵们虐待俘虏，还有她最小弟弟的阵亡，这都令她饱受惊吓，充满哀伤，不时啜泣。因为她的女性气质和人性，她有责任超越对她自己社群的忠诚，转而效忠国家，最终驱使她帮助那位爱国者，于是她变得世俗化并且——想必是——也具有**印度性**了。即便罗嘉坚持不懈地向军方和一位已经同意释放瓦西姆的官员求情，他们还是没有同克什米尔军人交换战俘；即便瑞希是国家机关的一部分，他也没有仰仗国家让他重获自由。罗嘉是这么对视察驻克什米尔军队的官员说的：我的丈夫不是什么大人物，但"Bharat kip raja to hai"（他毕竟是印度公民），而且我们需要安全。新中产阶级，在宣称对民族国家完全的身份认同时，还要显示出国家并没有满足他们的要求。虽然国家机器看上去依然庞大雄伟，其实它已变得陈旧破败，所以新中产阶级必须展现他们的自给自足。[1] 这个阶级必须将自

---

[1] 虽然我接受斯里尼瓦斯（S.V.Srinivas）的论点（"法律与秩序国度的'罗嘉'"，*EPW*, vol. xxix: 20〔14 May 1994〕, pp.1225—6）和帕特奈克（Arun Patnaik）在《观念论的公式》中对自由化时期国家愈发频繁使用的强制性手段的讨论，但是我想论证的是，这是国家正在**变化**的一个标志，显示了它功能的迁移：随着国家逐渐褪去旧功能，新的要求被加在了国家身上。

己与国家分离，才能体现自己的成熟；我之前已经提到过，因为尼赫鲁式国家被迫要将民主和平等社会主义的幻景写入政策中，所以这一任务可以被看做对尼赫鲁式国家的拒斥（我认为《姬谭伽里》中母亲的缺席是这种拒斥的另一征兆）。新中产阶级会争论道，尼赫鲁式国家的失败政策，克什米尔即是一例，国家已无力掌控克什米尔的局势，只有像瑞希这样的个人才能做出改变。电影的最后，瑞希彻底动摇了里亚卡特，后者手中的步枪还瞄着瑞希，但他居然就这么把男主角放走了。里亚卡特，经历了自己的苦难，见识了瑞希的高尚（也就是爱国主义），他的**人性**终于被点亮。"走吧。"他说，"ugravaadiaansupochegd（军人也会掉眼泪）。"我认为，瑞希的爱国主义或民族主义并不以民族国家为核心；实际上，电影里的国家从各个方面来看都是失败的——它没能击败叛乱，没能救回它的工作人员，没能帮助罗嘉。因为它的失败，中产阶级才能够合理地拒斥它，同时偏向于支持私有化、能够保障更高效率的新经济秩序。[1]

瑞希从很多角度看来都是这部电影的核心角色，不过罗嘉才是他对民族的热爱的必要组成部分。这部电影对女主角的表现方式非常不同于旧式的妇女—即—民族（woman-as-nation）（比如**印度母亲**［Mother India］），在这里妇女不是

---

[1] 这里我不同意查克拉瓦提（Venkatesh Chakravarthy）和潘迪安（M.S.S. Pandian）的论点。他们认为，"电影中，国家明显的无能为力实际上掩盖了它无声却强大的能力。"（See their More on Roja, *EPW*, vol. xxix: 11, 12 March 1994, pp.642—4.）

母亲而是情人。例如，"Roja Jaanemari"这首歌，瑞希在遐想中，看到监牢外的红玫瑰和绿玫瑰幻化成了他新娘的形象（她在电影结尾穿的要么是绿色莎丽袍，要么是橘红色衬衫或红莎丽袍，要么是绿色衬衫）。克什米尔美丽的风景反过来又融入了女主角的美貌，她在这一场歌舞戏中穿着克什米尔服饰，戴着珠宝，还有几个同样穿着克什米尔服装的孩子跟着她。罗嘉在影片开始、结婚之前的那种自立和自负此时都在她的抽泣中消散，她现在只想赢回她丈夫的性命，她个人的能动性此时已逐渐消失。剧终的那场戏，瑞希终于安全了，他冲过桥去，另一边罗嘉也奔向他，摔倒在他脚下，女性—即—民族激动地迎回他，然后他扶起她，拥抱她。

可以看到，浪漫爱情同民族主义交叉的背景为女性和男性提供了不同的空间。对罗嘉而言，婚姻空间的配置和民族空间完全不同；她对丈夫的爱可以表现在她的语言中，比如"我才不关心这个国家，我只要找回我丈夫"。瑞希则不然，他对妻子的爱和对民族的爱汇聚到了一处，比如"Roja Jaanemari"那场歌舞戏，爱情直接被表现为民族主义。现代性真正的主体，在后—民族—现代中，既可以是情人，又可以是公民，所以实际上应该是"作为公民的情人"（lover-as-citizen）。这部电影的叙事逻辑没有允许罗嘉成为这样的欲望主体，因为她的角色必须是被欲望的主体，所以是罗嘉促使了爱情以民族主义的形式显现，电影对她的能动性的呈现与她这种关键的中介作用密切相关。

爱情的世俗主义

《孟买之恋》叙事的核心与《罗嘉》一样，也是好公民代替效率低下的国家机器完成了它无法完成的任务。《孟买之恋》中，浪漫的爱情不仅是现代性的显著标志，还是世俗主义的最高形式。这部电影在印度一些地区成为了激烈争议的焦点。比如海德拉巴（Hyderabad）。

"Bombayi"（《孟买之恋》的泰卢固语版本）于1995年3月10日在安得拉邦（Andhra Pradesh）全境的所有电影院公映。3月14日，电影就在海德拉巴市及其周边的塞康德拉巴德市和兰加雷迪区遭到禁映。[1] 报纸告诉我们，穆斯林团结委员会（Majlis-Ittehadul-Muslimeen）和保卫议会运动（Majlis Bachao Tehreek）*引发了观众针对内政部的暴力活动，导致了电影被禁。报纸还告诉我们，印度学生联合会（Students' Federation of India，简称SFI）和印度民主青年联合会（Democratic Youth Federation of India，简称DYFI）这些左翼组织同右翼的青年印度人阵线（Bharatiya Janata Yuva Morcha，简称BJYM）都反对禁令。SFI和DYFI宣称"这部电影描绘了民族主义情感，并且没有任何涉及族群性（communal）的内容"。[2]

海德拉巴对拉特纳姆电影的反应不能代表整个南印度对

---

1 这部电影删除了三个桥段的版本三周后又重新发行。
* 穆斯林团结委员会和保卫议会运动都是在海德拉巴地区附近非常活跃的穆斯林政党。
2 "新闻时间"（Newstime）的报道（1995年3月15日）。

电影的态度,也不能代表整个安得拉邦。由于海德拉巴非典型的人口分布状况(老城有超过百分之五十的穆斯林,新城也有超过百分之二十),海德拉巴的政治面貌,以及"印度教"和"穆斯林"政党在当地政治生活中的具体议程,都让它在整个南印度显得非常特殊。拉特纳姆早前的电影《罗嘉》,首先上映了泰卢固语版本,然后再上映了印地语版,它不加掩饰的爱国主义和对于克什米尔交战状态的明确谴责让它在海德拉巴得到了大量的赞誉。究竟什么才算作真正的世俗,这对于民族(主义者)来说已经是个常识,在这里它的表述同印度教徒主义(Hindutva)结合在了一起。实际上,与其他当代文化形构一样的是,《罗嘉》中的"世俗主义"很难同"印度教"族群特性的显现所生产的态度区分开来。《孟买之恋》描绘的世俗或印度教元素在许多意义上都与《罗嘉》比较接近。所以,为什么《罗嘉》没有引起少数族群的剧烈反应,而《孟买之恋》收到的反馈截然不同,这很值得我们研究。在我看来,这反馈让我们能够重新思考当今文化政治的一些主要问题,特别是,究竟什么才算作世俗。

这部电影延续了《罗嘉》对影片核心问题——关于民族和关于宗教族群冲突(communalism)——的设计,不过我认为,落到性别的问题上,《孟买之恋》肯定带有一些口吃的痕迹,这在《罗嘉》中不太明显。《罗嘉》所描写的穆斯林几乎完全是恐怖主义的、反印度的;与之相对,《孟买之恋》之所以引起了一些人对电影某些段落的敌意,有部分原因可能是它尝试"(平衡)不同社群之间针锋相对的观点"，[1] 将它多愁善感的世俗主义呈现为"完全不伤害穆斯林感情的东西"。[2] "多么令人悲伤啊，"有记者在《印度教徒报》上写道，"每当人们真诚地努力促进民族融合的时候，一切总是以抗议和暴动终结。"[3] 人们对拉特纳姆的总体观点认为他的确是一位"民族主义"的电影人，这从《罗嘉》获得了1993年的民族融合奖就可见一斑。故而，要求禁映《孟买之恋》的人们所不满的，也许正是民族—现代的构成——正是这一构成让一部分身份变得合法、让另一些身份被边缘化。也是在面对性别这一问题时，我认为，这一构成的断裂变得可见。

但是首先，我会简要介绍一下剧情。谢克哈尔（Shekhar），来自维沙卡区贝埃穆尼帕特纳姆县的高种姓印度教青年，刚刚在孟买完成学业，在一家报社做编辑工作，希望以后能成为新闻记者。一次回乡，他见到了莎伊拉·巴努（Shaila Banu），她是穆斯林制砖工人巴希尔（Basheer）的女儿；谢克哈尔立刻就爱上了她。简短的追求之后，两个家庭都对这桩可能的婚姻充满敌意。谢克哈尔于是回到了孟买，并且安排把莎伊拉·巴努也接到了他的城市。他们在一栋老得快要散架的公寓楼里以租客的身份开始了婚姻生活。后来谢克哈

---

1 纳斯林·苏丹娜（Nasreen Sultana），"解禁'孟买'"（Lift Ban on "Bombay），致编辑的信，"新闻时间"（1995年3月20日）

2 访谈（镜头之眼），"真心话大冒险"栏目，对拉特拉姆导演的访谈《印度时报》（1995年4月2日）

3 巴瓦纳·博玛雅，"'孟买'问题"，《印度教徒报》（1995年3月31日）

尔晋升为记者，莎伊拉·巴努生下一对双胞胎。几年后，巴布里清真寺（Babri Masjid）被毁，谢克哈尔的父亲纳拉亚那穆提（他曾经试着把刻着"Sri Ram"的砖块送往阿约提亚[*]，为他儿子的行为赎罪）担心谢克哈尔一家的安全，特别是得知一对双胞胎名叫卡比尔·纳拉杨（Kabeer Narayan）和卡马尔·巴希尔（Kamal Basheer）[**]之后，他决定去看望他们。莎伊拉·巴努的父母也决定在同样的时间去看女儿。1993年1月，孟买暴乱发生了，前来探望的家长们不幸在一场火灾中遇难；双胞胎也走失了，两位主人公在暴乱的现场寻找他们的孩子。剧末的一场戏，谢克哈尔阻止暴乱分子互相残杀，发表了一段激情澎湃的演讲；孩子们也找回来了。印度教徒和穆斯林们扔下了手中的武器，终于握手言和。这一段简陋的叙述当然无法完全展现拉特纳姆是如何巧妙地实现他所期望的电影效果的。我之后还会提到。

我觉得，之前我说《孟买之恋》带着"口吃"，这需要把它同电影对穆斯林妇女的描写联系起来。电影最初播映时，有些观众一直在问，为什么主角不能是穆斯林男人和印度教女人呢？鉴于拉特纳姆对性别和民族的逻辑，颠倒主角的性别明显是不可能的。例如《罗嘉》中的女主角（印度教徒），

---

[*] 阿约提亚（Ayodhya）是印度北部圣城，据传是史诗《罗摩衍那》的主人公罗摩的出生地。"Sri Ram"意为"圣罗摩"。在印度教中，罗摩不仅是阿逾陀国君，还是主神毗湿奴的第七化身。

[**] "卡比尔"（Kabeer）和"卡马尔"（Kamal）都是源自阿拉伯语的常用人名，意义分别为"伟大的"和"完美的"。

她的形象不完全是世俗的或民族的,因为她不关心民族的安危,只关心她丈夫。所以信仰印度教的男主角就必须承担起责任,点亮穆斯林的"人性",而"人性"在这里也含蓄地代表着世俗和民族。《罗嘉》中,男性军人里亚卡特的人性是被唤醒的,而他的妹妹,通过帮助男主人公出逃,已经展示了她高尚的女性气质——她的人性从未泯灭。她援救主人公的行为让她超越了她的社群身份,在这一过程中,她不再是克什米尔人、武装分裂主义者,而是人性的、印度的。

《孟买之恋》就更含蓄了。莎伊拉·巴努嫁给了信仰印度教的男主人公,一位婆罗门(虽然他身上没有带着种姓或社群的痕迹),但是莎伊拉没有放弃她的宗教信仰,她也没有像南印度的印度教妇女一样穿着,特别是——除了两场歌舞戏——她从不戴吉祥痣*。世俗的男主人公对此自然非常宽容,女主角的这些"差异"某种意义上也吸引着男主角。电影里,一方面男性穆斯林的族群标记(比如礼拜帽或集体朝拜等)都是稍后暴乱的不祥征兆,另一方面女性穆斯林的族群标记——首当其冲的是罩袍——则被魅惑化和情欲化。[1] 谢克哈尔第一次见到莎伊拉·巴努,后者的面纱正巧被风撩了起来;随后两人的多次会面,包

---

* 吉祥痣(bindi)是印度教妇女点在眉心的朱砂,通常表示已婚,并有保存生命能量、抵挡厄运的宗教意义。——译注

[1] 我需要指出,印度人民党和湿婆神军党人在电影中也出现了,他们参与了对印度教神祇带着侵略性的公开朝拜。然而,我认为,这种场景在《孟买之恋》中将穆斯林与印度教的"原教旨主义"混为一谈,这是很有问题的。

括新婚之夜，都将撩拨逗弄作为这种可见性/不可见性的主题。

《罗嘉》的男主角试着去**改变**穆斯林军人的信仰，但不一定了解后者为什么会坚持它；《孟买之恋》的男主角作为世俗的公民还尝试了去**理解**族群的他者，可是他的理解只能通过带着情欲的凝视完成。这个女性他者身上包含着神秘而不可接近的情欲元素，于是在亲昵的行为中强迫对方不断揭开自己的面纱；而对男主角来说，世俗的民族主义者和族裔化（ethnicised）的男性两种身份的关联只可能充满争议。在这些电影的逻辑里，乃至在我们时代占统治地位的文化逻辑里，族裔化的男性都绝不可能是要求民族融合叙事的主角。唯一可能的主角是城市化、西洋化的谢克哈尔，他和《罗嘉》里的瑞希·库马尔一样，都不需要特别地关心自己的种姓或宗教，因为他们对民族主义的支持已经让他们超越了这些身份。[1] 如果我们仔细研究1990年代印度市民主体的构成，印度教女性才是族群的必要载体。所以，融合过程的发起人，或者电影里浪漫恋情的发起人，都只能是个来自主流社群的男人。在这个意义上，《孟买之恋》决不能有穆斯林男主角和印度教女主角。

《孟买之恋》的这种不可能性还与它对性别化了的"世俗"空间作出了明确划分相关。虽然男主角的世俗主义（实

---

[1] 演员斯瓦米（Arvind Swamy）在《罗嘉》中扮演了瑞希·库马尔，又在《孟买之恋》中扮演了谢克哈尔。这并不完全是偶然。

际上是宽容）确实有家庭因素，但是它在家庭环境中仅仅是显得俏皮，比如他让几个小孩子向她的新娘传话——"我得改变宗教信仰吗？"又比如在"Hallagulla"那场歌舞戏里他戴了一下穆斯林的帽子。另一方面，他在公共环境的世俗举止则显得意义重大。比如在暴乱中他痛斥自称"印度教徒"或"穆斯林"的同事，说他们都是"印度人"；再比如在全剧的高潮处，他把汽油泼在自己身上，催促暴乱分子把自己点燃，用这种激将法逼迫他们扔掉了武器。和他相比，莎伊拉·巴努很少在屋外露面，最多就是她和谢克哈尔一起在暴乱中寻找孩子，可她只是被用来展现惊惶与恐惧。这部电影早些地方，女主角用一种让人联想到西方通俗女性主义分析伊斯兰妇女的模式，表达了她的世俗主义：她服从了自己的意志，奔向谢克哈尔，却不小心罩袍被一块锈了的金属钩住（其实那是用旧了的船锚！）；她用力拉扯但还是扯不开，最后（在慢镜头中）她直接抛弃了罩袍，冲向男主角。

这部电影一直用家庭空间与宗教族群冲突（communalism）对位，用家庭里与日俱增的和谐（双胞胎的降生，祖父母们的和解，谢克哈尔想要更多孩子等）同城市里不断积聚的族群性矛盾对比。这部电影好像在建议，融合可以在**家庭内**完成。[1] 家庭空间里谢克哈尔不需要经历任何转变来证明自己的世俗主义。无论如何，他的"宗教信仰"都

---

[1] 在一次访谈中，拉特纳姆说道，"家庭是我们国家最强大的机构。我们的整个生活都取决于我们的家人。"（*Times of India*，2 April 1995.）

不是他身份的核心内容。还有，因为他是家里的经济支柱，他完全不需要挑战男女角色不对称的传统。对电影的叙事来说，这对夫妻拥有孩子是非常重要的一点，因为电影的逻辑提示我们，城市化的核心家庭（nuclear family）有能力解决宗教族群冲突的问题。电影表明，宗教族群冲突的问题只不过是毫无意义的憎恨。这里，就像对印度近期一些事件的分析说的那样，宗教族群冲突被想象成了古代仇恨和原始敌意的复兴。于是，它是**残余**，是非现代的印记，或者是倒退，[1]并且像我之前说的，它是那些反民族的在社群（或者说是种姓）中的表演。所以，世俗主义或者民族主义都表现为宗教族群冲突的"他者"。[2] 然而在1990年代，世俗主义的私有化似乎正在发生，这样的历史空间中，民族主义并不需要成为政治议程的一部分。[3]《罗嘉》已经显示了，中产阶级对自身脱离于国家的尝试，导致了其阶级功能的改动。新市民的努力可以达成国家政策无法完成的任务，而国家实际上只会起反作用。不仅国家的经济企业需要私有化，而且对"文化"问题的解决，比如说宗教族群冲突，也需要私有化。如果这

---

1 这个描述令"现代中产阶级"大规模地参与孟买暴乱这件事变得不可见。

2 关于殖民地时期这一过程更有用的讨论，参见贾南德拉·潘迪（Gyanendra Pandey）的《北印度殖民地时期社群主义的建构》(*The Construction of Communalism in Colonial North India* 德里：牛津大学出版社，1990年），特别是第七章，《民族主义相对于社群主义》(Nationalism versus Communalism)。

3 新民族主义有必要和反帝国主义脱离开来，即便印度人民党和印度民族志工组织对于"抵制洋货运动"（swadeshi campaign）态度不尽相同，所以民族主义成为了纯粹的内部问题，用以反对非印度教徒。我在这里使用"私有化这个词"也指代当前印度经济关于公共部门转型的改变。

些问题被诊断为憎恨,那么解决的办法就一定需要爱。人道主义也就变成了关于好的个人与幸福家庭的问题。就像《孟买之恋》所显示的,爱的现代形式在浪漫的爱情中找到了最崇高、最有典型性的表达,即个人之间的恋爱。进而,我们想问,因为《孟买之恋》伤害了穆斯林的情感而要求的禁映,这能否被简单地看做"原教旨主义"或者是穆斯林父权态度的表现?这是否表明自由主义的分析和解决方案(宗教族群冲突由"恨"而起,能够用"爱"治愈)对于族群性暴力的受害者来说完全不可接受——它不够精确,过于简单,居高临下?[1]这是否在向我们指出,我们有必要重新思考这些问题:世俗主义的主流概念所包含的究竟是谁的宽容,以及"爱"与"宽容"是否能够不加区别地推荐给主流族群和少数族群?

《罗嘉》和《孟买之恋》都带着这些重负:让**人性的、世俗的**和**民族主义的**在当代交汇,以及让那些浓缩到信仰印度教的男主角身上的特征——他们都抛弃了种姓和社群的印记——得到戏剧化。这些电影,通过描写克什米尔问题和孟买暴乱,提出了民族的问题。这两部电影"构架"其问题的模式都把对民族—现代或者后—民族—现代的挑战压缩进了关于宗教身份的简单论断。随着国家的经济主权不断被侵蚀和不断进行的市场整合过程,早前反殖民主义的民族主义此

---

[1] 我使用"居高临下"(patronising)这个词来指代像《孟买之恋》里谢克哈尔这些人的口气,他们因为自己的现代性而认为自己对宗教族群冲突不负任何责任。被化约为恨,宗教族群冲突于是被视为是非现代与非理性的。

时逐渐转变：现在的"敌人"在国内，要么改变它，要么驱逐它。我已经说过，妇女的形象，或者更准确地说是妇女的能动性，在这种新民族主义的形构中占据着中心地位。如果说流行电影真的决定性地中介了当今正在发生的变革，那么姬塔、罗嘉和莎伊拉·巴努这些形象就都是变革的积极中介者。很多拉特纳姆电影的分析者都简单地把妇女看作印度教或穆斯林的父权主义、性别歧视和男性沙文主义的受害者，而本文对妇女的描述能够帮助我们树立一个不太一样的观点。[1]

就我的理解，由那些分析者的方法所酝酿的女权主义政治只能够让妇女参与进某些特定的抗议活动中：在电影描写和电影批评分析奇怪的结合中，莎伊拉·巴努**必须**扔下她的罩袍才能够逃出穆斯林父权，在这过程中重新确认了人们固有印象中那群压迫穆斯林妇女的人，也重新确认了穆斯林社群既是"落后的"又是父权的。罗嘉也一样，不仅仅是父权的受害者，还是使父权重新配置的关键角色。所以我想主张的是，讨论姬塔、罗嘉和莎伊拉·巴努这些角色的叙事功能和浪漫爱情在这些电影中的中心地位，可以为女性主义揭示

---

[1] 查克拉瓦提和潘迪安（More on *Roja*，pp.642—4）认为罗嘉的欲望被瑞希·库马尔和国家机构所代表的印度教父权所压抑。阿依雅（Swaminathan S. AnklesariaAiya）称赞《孟买之恋》是"对人性超越宗派混乱的热烈请愿"，又谴责穆斯林组织要求禁映电影源于他们的"性别歧视"和"男性沙文主义"。他还说道，"妇女作为独立的人的概念，包括选择丈夫、职业和宗教的自由，对这两个传统主义社群来说都是天方夜谭。"('Objecting to "Bombay": Sexism More Than Communalism', *The Times of India*, 15 April 1995）

出新"印度人"的性别化,还可以揭示出"妇女"在排斥种姓和社群、促进市民主体构成的过程中的复杂性。重新思考由拉特纳姆等人的电影提出的一系列问题而激发的女性主义政治,可能需要我们由那些构建了我们日常经验和政治的词汇出发:民族主义、人道主义和世俗主义。

附记:

本文的不同版本曾经在加尔各答、新德里、科伦坡、马德拉斯、海德拉巴和芝加哥发表。我在此感谢所有口头或书面对本文提出意见和建议的人们。

(翻译:周展)

West Heavens: Readers of Current Indian Thought
Series initiated by: Chang Tsong-Zung, Kuan-Hsing Chen, Gao Shiming

Nationalism Refigured
Tejaswini Niranjana

Foreword: Passage to West Heavens

by Chang Tsong-Zung

WEST HEAVENS is an initiative for cultural exchange developed jointly by the Institute of Visual Culture of China Academy of Art and Hanart TZ Gallery, and is supported by the Moonchu Foundation. The aim is to foster closer understanding of India through contemporary art and scholarship, and develop cross-cultural dialogue based on visual culture and notions of Asian modernity. Scholars represented in this series of Readers have been invited to lecture at the 2010 8th Shanghai Biennale and they have specially selected this anthology of representative writings to introduce their thinking to the Chinese public.

Modern India is both near China and far away. Apart from vague generalizations and supposedly Indian-Chinese economic rivalry enthusiastically promoted by Western media, most Chinese people are unaware of India. Of course we are aware of India's rich history, but we are less familiar with its modern culture, in particular the significant role played by Indian thinkers in international academic circles. As China's neighbour and traditional ally, India has long been deserving of China's attention. As a large modern nation, India also has tremendous economic, cultural and technological potentials. But the most important reason for China to connect with India is to enlighten ourselves.

China has been possessed by the demon of modernization for over a century. From revolution to Cold War, and now capitalist globalism, China has been unable to shake off paradigms set by the West. Even Chinese discourse about modernity has so far been trapped by dichotomies of East/West and China/West. No wonder that efforts at developmental self-reliance have only led to increasingly Westernized economic and political institutions and lifestyles. Today the West that China emulates as the model of "advanced civilization" is no longer suitable for guidance, and yet access to China's own historical resource has been blocked by the framework of these models. To establish a position for itself outside the two Western Cold War ideological paradigms, to develop historical resources beyond Western ideals, China must make connections elsewhere. Among Asian countries that have struck off on different paths of modernization, but still successful by the parochial standards of "prosperity", India has much to offer its neighbours.

China's path to modernity has been moulded by a series of

revolutions, having overthrown shackles of the past to create new social forms. The damage of revolution is to become increasingly removed from our historical roots. India has adopted radically alternative ways. India overthrew colonial domination, but has uncharacteristically preserved colonial institutions after liberation. And yet, when China compares its post-revolutionary record with the postcolonial experience of India, we cannot help but be amazed by the prevalence of left wing politics in India. There are currently over forty major parties of Communism in India, engaged in varying forms of revolutionary tactic. At the same time India is also impressively the world's biggest democracy. China's encounter with India inadvertently raises the suspicion: whether China's revolution harbours a latent colonial gene? Conversely, whether the Indian version of postcolonialism is in fact another form of revolution? The singularity of purpose of the Chinese state has achieved the most daunting social engineering tasks in history, but in terms of diversity and richness of historical culture the result is no match for the treasure trove of India, where old and new traditions coexist on the level of daily life. Brahmins and Sadhus of ancient descent are integrated into the fabric of industrial urban life, and indigenous ways are brought into the grammar of modern practices. In the modern encounter of two ancient civlizations, an urgent issue is being raised for China: how do modernity and history coexist?

The modernities of both India and China have been shaped by Western imperialism and capitalist logic, so the modern meeting of India and China cannot but be under the auspices of the West. Asian modernity cannot be understood, no profound inter-Asian exchange is possible, outside of this context. And yet, to go beyond the experience of the modern West, to return to our own histories, a myopic obsession with the past is unrealistic. To truly open up the future, local history and reality must be shown to have global significance. For China this is perhaps the most valuable lesson of our Indian colleagues. The authors collected here are not only well versed in Western academic discourse, their own work have made major contributions worldwide. Indian scholarship in postcolonialism and urban theory, for example, has had major influence on the practice of international contemporary art in recent decades.

West Heavens is not the first effort of the organizers, it is preceded by a series of projects undertaken by the Institute of Visual Culture of China Academy of Art. In 2003, as celebration of the 75th anniversary of the Academy, Director Xu Jiang proposed an investigation into the internal boundaries of "Asia", and I was invited to join Gao Shiming and Wu Meichun in the project. We focused on the cultural political reality of a parallel system of native and Christian calendars at work within Asian countries, and took "Asia's Parallel Time" as the theme for the interdisciplinary investigations and exhibitions brought under the title, *Edges of the Earth: Migration of Contemporary Asian Art and Regional Politics.* In 2008, Gao Shiming, Sarat Maharaj and I co-curated the 3rd Guangzhou Triennial with the project *Farewell To Post-Colonialism*, which reviewed the pros and cons of an East/West bipolar framework. West Heavens is a continuation of this work and it represents an attempt at creating close encounter between Asian cultures. Professor Kuan-Hsing Chen has devoted many years of research to inter-Asian studies, and his participation is crucial for making this intellectual dialogue possible.

In 2010, we launched the first edition of this series to coincide with the opening of the West Heavens forum. This occasion marked the first time several of these important Indian scholars had their works published in Chinese. To meet scholarly demand, we further edited and re-translated six of these books for the second edition in 2012—2013 for Shanghai People's Publishing House. In 2017, with the support of Mr Tang Yunsong, the deputy editor-in-chief of Shanghai Academy of Social Sciences Press, we invited the female authors, preeminent Indian art historian and critic Ms Geeta Kapur and renowned feminist scholar Ms Tejaswini Niranjana, to write new prefaces for their books and to revise the contents in discussion with editor Mr Liang Jie, who also supervised the translations.

For more than a century, challenges of imperialism and

capitalism have forced India and China to develop political strategies that have profoundly transformed both societies. To share this experience is valuable for Indians and Chinese alike. For China, long before the seismic cultural shift towards the West it had experienced one other profound cultural turn. The Buddhist turn did not bring comparable destructive fervour as the past century of revolutions, but its influence was just as far reaching. Buddhist learning took many centuries before it was fully absorbed into Confucian scholarship in the Song dynasty (960—1279). Today, after a century of revolutions, it is important to remember this history of cultural self-transformation. At this age of global change, it is critical for China to remind ourselves that in our imagination of the world there is not just the West, but also the "West Heavens".

August, 2012

Introduction: India as Method
by Kuan-Hsing Chen

It has been a pleasure to be asked by Mr Chang Tsong-zung and Mr Gao Shiming to help organizing *West Heavens: India-China Summit on Social Thought*. They invited me to participate because, in my role as an editor of the journal *Inter-Asia Cultural Studies, Movement* (IACS), over the last twelve years the journal has built a network of critical intellectuals across Asia, including those based in India. Of course, I was more than happy to take up their invitation, and one of the duties assigned to me was to write an introduction for the Readers introducing the distinguished scholars who will be visiting as part of this event. For me, it is a welcome opportunity to explain the driving ideas behind this dialogue between India and China.

When we founded *Inter-Asia Cultural Studies: Movements* twelve or so years ago, we wanted to make our contribution to change the condition of knowledge that existed then and this is still our goal today. We wanted to establish communication and integration among Asian countries, at least within our own circle of intellectuals. The editorial board was made up of over twenty scholars from every part of Asia, and we shared one important understanding of the current condition: throughout the twentieth century, the gaze of Asian thinkers was fixed on Europe and North America. For a hundred years, the basic frame of reference for knowledge revolved around the Euro-American experiences. This framework developed over the course of a century into a highly resilient knowledge structure that created enormous difficulties for Asian thought. It brought about a narrowing of critical perspectives, excluding diverse historical experiences, which should have provided alternative frames of reference. Even more worryingly, Western modes of knowledge became virtually the only paradigm for knowledge production. History has shown that this kind of knowledge is woefully inadequate as we try to comprehend, grasp and explain the living environments in which we exist. At IACS we wanted to generate exchanges between intellectuals from each Asian sub-region, make us see the existence of each other, turn the historical experience of each region into a potential point of reference for other Asian regions. To create new modes of knowledge and better explanations, we must transform and multiply the frames of reference that contain us. This shared understanding has driven us for more than a decade.

Seen retrospectively, we would find that our effort has not been in vain. There may not have been a revolution to radically transform the conditions, but the bonds of knowledge structures mentioned above have been loosened considerably. Changes over the last ten years are bringing about a world moving towards diversity and multiplicity. The shift towards the Left in South America, the forming of ASEAN 10+3, the rise of China and India, sustained economic growth in Africa, the handover from Bush to Obama and the expansion of the EU ... At the end of the 1980s, it felt as though "globalization" meant the collapse of Eastern Europe and the Soviet regime and the unchallengeable hegemony of the United States. But over the past decade the development of multiple political and economic centres seems to have brought an end to the unipolar age. Knowledge systems that were once undeniable and rigid are quickly falling apart, along with their deeply believed values. The highly confident explanatory framework based on the historical experiences of Europe and America faces unprecedented challenges. In this period of transformation, it is time to slow down and take stock, to reconnect with all our intellectual resources rooted in the modern historical experience, to create the pathways we need to new conditions of knowledge. Twelve years is very short. IACS has not yet constructed an alternative mode of knowledge ready for presentation, but we have at least made a start, made an attempt to make out the path of "Asia as method".

In Asia, as in other third world regions, responsibility for the long persistence of "Euro-America as method" must be ascribed to world history. Continually pushed out from the Western centre, China, India and other regions are cast in the permanent role of catch up/overtake (overtaking the UK; struggling to catch up to the US). We learn from Euro-America (including, of course, learning Euro-American values). Intellectual work, academia and the production of knowledge are therefore upheld as the key to the modernization of the nation and its people. Even if we set aside the inherent pitfalls in a knowledge structure predicated on catch up/overtake (does it not conflate normative goals with objective historical explanation?), we must at least start to ask this question: a century on, what exactly has the process of modernization turned these "latecomer" countries into? We learned democracy, we learned science, but what has the application of these concepts brought us? In other words, should we not pause and take a moment to share our experiences of catch up/overtake? Should non-Western regions not hold up a mirror to each other, uncover the routes they have taken to bring themselves to where they stand today? Moving forward depends on our ability to see, understand and fully explain what we have gone through. In this process, we may even find that the road of catch up/overtake has come to an end, and that it is time to change direction.

The goal of knowledge is not some kind of unsupported knowledge for its own sake (presupposing a Truth with a capital T which encompasses the whole world and yet lies outside the existence of history). Knowledge is for explaining the problems and situations of each region, within the context of world history, and from a diverse range of historical experience perspectives. Through a process of comparison and cross reference, we gradually distill knowledge propositions which are relevant to world history. If this is the assumption, then none of the theoretical propositions currently held to be universal are mature. Theories grounded in the reference system of the Euro-American experience can at best explain the histories of Europe and America. Expecting them to explain the historical condition of other regions is absurd. On the contrary: explanations in non-Western regions must be in terms of the region's own historical experiences. One cannot simplistically and improperly apply the Euro-American experience as the standard measurement against which to assess ourselves. I believe this is what subaltern studies scholar Dipesh Chakrabarty means by his project of "provincialising Europe" . It is also very much in the spirit of Professor Mizoguchi Yuzo, who passed away in July 2010, and his notion of "China as method, the world as end".

If the Euro-American historical experience is only one possible reference, and comparing it with the development experiences of latecomer countries, there must be a greater gap, then we must seek to transform our knowledge, by what feminist thinker Tejaswini Niranjana has proposed as the strategy of creating alternative frames of reference for third world regions. Through the change of reference, we can mobilize the differences among us to develop better explanations for our own historical environment. The assumption of the project is that nativist and nationalist tendency to "close off" the outside is unproductive and counter-productive. All they manage to achieve is to indulge in the smug satisfaction of basking in the glory of the past. But even if we are open to other countries, an openness oriented around the catch up/overtake of Euro-American has equally lost its meaning. We must find new reference systems, beyond the nativism (operating within the nation) and cosmopolitanism (hiding its unspoken Euro-America-centrism).

In this context, if "India as method" can be taken seriously, I believe, it would actively contribute to the Chinese intellectual circle to develop new modes of knowledge. However, a precondition for a productive dialogue between China and India to take place is that the "catch up/overtake" sentiment has to be abandoned. "Comparison" between India and China can no longer draw on familiar measures of how backward/advanced they are, on degree of modernization, or on pace of economic growth. To use my own language, we must first set aside normative comparison for the moment and start with analysis of existing realities. When differences emerge, we will then begin to search for explanations immanent in their own history.

India and China are big countries on the world scale and farmers make up the bulk of their populations. The latest data suggests that India is at present the second largest country by population, and by 2026 it will have overtaken China, with 1.5 billion people to China's 1.35 billion. By 2015, the growth rate of India is likely to equal China's. In other words, if historical and cultural issues are left aside, from a sociological point of view, of all the countries in the world, India is the most comparable to China and no other countries match these two.

But there are enormous differences between the two nations. India is a multilingual, multicultural nation, and it has no single unified language-deliberations in Congress are carried out through interpreters. Many important Indian thinkers, including Ashis Nandy, do not believe that India is a nation-state in the European sense at all. Rather, it is a "civilization". In 1947, India was decolonized and freed itself from the status of the colony. Before being taken over by the British Empire, India was not a united political entity. After independence, it struggled (with difficulties) to tell a single national history covering its thousands of years of civilization. It has had to understand its past in a more multiple and complex way. Among many Indians groups, the caste system, remains to be organizing principles, still operates today. The political system must deal with the existence of the caste order, which cannot simply be eradicated. So the polity creates mechanisms by which members of the lower castes can participate in the political process. Because of the many languages, cultural differences intersect with politics. There are "local" political parties and some local politicians (such as provincial governors) even win election by virtue of regional fame and pride, having been stars in films in their local dialects. In this sense, India is the world's largest democracy, and the operation of democracy is based in the local. In order to govern effectively, national political parties must find ways to ally with local political forces.

On my own visits to India over the last decade or so, I always have more questions than I have time to ask my Indian friends. The South Asian experience is very different to the East Asian, and comparing the two, the latter seems more unified because each country has the same national language (be it Mandarin, Korean or Japanese) and the appearance of nation-state seems to be clear; and it does not have a multiple political party system, these interesting differences could be the basis for comparative research. However, most of my Chinese friends, no matter mainland, Hong Kong or Taiwanese, are all stuck in the habit of competitive comparisons via the logic of catch up/overtake: India, they say, was a colony for too long, so China is in a better position (never mind that

Taiwan and Hong Kong were colonies, and Chairman Mao once said China was a "semi-colony", not even a whole colony). India's political system is a product of its colonial past, so China is better, because it was established through the revolutions of Sun Yat-sen and Mao Zedong (again discounting the experience of colonies, and ignoring postwar third-worldism). India has the caste system, so China is better, for having eradicated its feudal systems (but never pursuing how elements of India's past are linked to the contemporary society, or looking back to see how their own society connects with the past and whether China or the Chinese is really no longer feudal). Less frequently, it is claimed that India's problem is its multi-party system, and Taiwanese who raise this point temporarily forget European multi-party systems and try to adopt the USA's two-party system, claiming it to be more progressive (but without the ability to ask the historical question: how did India's multi-party system and its regional political parties came into existence?). Some say that India has cows roaming the streets of its major cities, so it is not as advanced and modern as China, we can't possibly take India as a reference point. For those determined to apply the simple logic of catch up/overtake, the simple logic of modernization as defined by Euro-America, we will wait to see the economy of India overtake China's, for it to achieve global power status, before it is noticed by the Chinese. Until then, the future will tell!

In fact, communication and exchange must be two-way. And there will be many unavoidable misunderstandings along the way. For example, many of my Indian friends are interested in China not because of its economic rise, but for a variety of other reasons: The relationship between China's postwar socialism and its current economic development; the relationship between politics and long-term developments in peasant culture (this is a key concern of research into the working class, exemplified by the work of Partha Chatterjee); women's liberation and the socialist system and their interaction; how China understands the relationship between economic development and capitalist world systems; what new viewpoints China's greatly expanded academia will bring to the world; how China's scholars distil explanations of world history from their own historical practice. Third world scholars have a basic respect for China, and have certain expectations of Chinese intellectuals. Both respect and expectation are very much connected to China's socialist political tradition, not from whether China is now economically more advanced or whether it is modern. However, these issues are neither ones that interested Chinese intellectuals, nor ones on which they are prepared to carry out a dialogue. (Even more frustratingly, as the third world looks forward to establishing a dialogue with China, it often finds that Chiness intellectuals do not return the compliment. For the Chinese counterpart, in their eyes, there are only Euro-American and Chinese themselves. They would say: Don't play at political correctness! Asia does not exist, what value can there be in a dialogue with the third world?)

I hope that I have made clear the assumptions behind "India as Method". Understanding India is a way to understand oneself afresh including, China itself and the world. But our current condition of knowledge is enmeshed in a method of catch up/ overtake that is difficult to escape. Euro-American values permeate intellectual world. Even in socialist mainland China, intellectuals are following and even outdoing postwar Taiwan and Hong Kong in their eagerness to "escape Asia, join Euro-America". The speed at which Chinese thought is embracing Euro-American knowledge systems is shocking, far faster than our economic growth. So don't hold out great hopes for this attempt to start a dialogue between China and India. All we can hope for is that those friends who want to search for alternative mode of knowledge, and can begin to find India as a chance to imagine for the future.

Among the invited scholars, Prasenjit Duara is already familiar to many Chinese readers because the history of China is his field of study, and many of his works have been translated into Chinese. For the other invited friends, whether currently residing in India or not, the formations of their knowledge are rooted in Indian society and history. They represent three generations of Indian scholarship: Ashis Nandy, born in 1937, is already a thinker of global renown in the 1980s; Partha Chatterjee, just retired, widely respected in India and internationally; while cultural theorist Tejaswini Niranjana is in the prime of her career, having made major contributions to post-structural translation theory in the 1990s. The translation of these readers has been a major undertaking. We hope to give Chinese language readers an opportunity to understand the Indian society, history and culture that shaped these thinkers. According to my understanding, this is not the first time some of these scholars has visited mainland of China. Each of them has a level of understanding and insight into China. We hope that their visit will give Chinese intellectual circle the beginning of an equally deep knowledge of India. It will be an opportunity for us to practice the self-transformation.

Finally, I must thank personal friends for agreeing to participate: feminist theorist Tejaswini Niranjana leading art theorist Geeta Kapur, social thinker Ashis Nandy, subaltern studies political theorist Partha Chatterjee, subaltern studies historian Dipesh Chakrabarty, historian Duara Prasenjit who is already so well-known in China, art theorist Sarat Maharaj whom I have not had the pleasure to meet; and world-famous postcolonial theorist Professor Homi K. Bhabha, whom I met on one occasion in Taiwan. We appreciate them for making time to come to China and for granting us translation rights for the essays presented in these eight Readers.

I'd also like to give special thanks for the kind supports by my friends Wang Xiaoming and Wang Anyi, and for the generous help from President Xu Jiang and professor Lu Xinghua, they have been responsible for organizing the dialogues with our visitors. Thanks also to friends from Hong Kong, Taiwan and the mainland who have agreed to be interlocutors for the discussion sessions.

This has been my first opportunity to work with Chang Tsong-zung and Gao Shiming, and it has been a great experience. From them, I have been lucky enough to find linke-minded teammates with a common goal and I have treasured the opportunity. Their boldness, openness and wisdom have proved that so long as we can complement each other's strength and weakness to pool our efforts together, there's always a hope. My thanks to the two of you for yours trust!

August 20, 2010, Chiao Tung University, Hsinchu

Revised in July 2012

Tejaswini Niranjana

Tejaswini Niranjana is currently Professor and Head, Department of Cultural Studies, Lingnan University, Hong Kong. She is also Visiting Professor with the School of Arts and Science at Ahmedabad University, India. She is co-founder of the Centre for the Study of Culture and Society, Bangalore, which offered an innovative inter-disciplinary PhD programme from 2000—2012. During 2012—2016, she headed the Centre for Indian Languages in Higher Education at the Tata Institute of Social Sciences, Mumbai, and was Indian-language advisor to Wikipedia. She is the author of *Siting Translation: History, Post-structuralism and the Colonial Context* (Berkeley, 1992), *Mobilizing India: Women, Music and Migration between India and Trinidad* (Durham, 2006), and a forthcoming monograph on musicophilia in Mumbai. Her most recent edited volume, with Wang Xiaoming, is *Genealogies of the Present: Situating Inter-Asia Cultural Studies* (Delhi, 2015).

Preface to the Second Edition

In early 2016, a premier university in India's capital city, New Delhi, was embroiled in an unexpected political controversy. A meeting was organized by some students on February 9, 2016, at the campus of Jawaharlal Nehru University (JNU) to protest the capital punishment given to two Kashmiri leaders perceived by the Indian government to be separatists. Shortly before the meeting, JNU administrators withdrew permission to hold the event. The students went ahead regardless, and a few masked people, later determined to be outsiders to the campus, allegedly shouted anti-India slogans. The leader of the right-wing Hindu nationalist student body, the Akhila Bharatiya Vidyarthi Parishad (ABVP) had alerted two television channels who were present at the scene and produced footage of the protest meeting. This footage was allegedly 'doctored' and led to 'fake news' being shown on a leading channel, suggesting that the JNU students were terrorists and anti-national. A clash took place between different student groups, and four days later, the JNU Student Union President, a PhD student called Kanhaiya Kumar, was arrested on the charge of sedition and criminal conspiracy under Section 124 of the Indian Penal Code, under a law formulated in 1870 under colonial rule. JNU administration also suspended Kumar and a few other students and debarred them from attending their classes or staying in the university hostel; additionally, they imposed varying amounts of fines on the students.

After nation-wide protests and international criticism of suppression of dissent by the Government of India, and a hunger strike by students, the actions of the university authorities was stayed by the Delhi High Court. But it took nearly a month for Kumar to be released on bail. His first act was to address a huge gathering at JNU calling for 'azaadi' or freedom *within* India— freedom from caste inequalities, from religious intolerance, and from poverty. Leftist leaders like Kumar and his colleague Shehla Rashid took great care to mark their distance from Kashmiri separatists by declaring that although they were not 'anti-national' they did believe in the right to dissent, and supported the need to be critical of social and political measures which tried to curtail freedom of expression. So when they raised the cry of *azaadi* or freedom they were calling not for freedom *from* India (like the

Kashmiri separatists) but freedom *within* India. [1]

The fact that the JNU students and their supporters all over the country stressed the question of freedom created a subterranean link to a 150-year-old history of conceptualising freedom as aspiration, both for the colonized and for all those after Independence who did not see the freedom realized in substance. It's worthy of note that this idea of freedom is tied conceptually to the idea of the nation, which is tasked with making sure freedom can be actualized.

The essays in this volume are drawn from my writings over the last twenty years, and deal with questions of translation, of popular cinema, of the changing language of feminism. Reading through them as I prepare to write this Preface, I am struck by how the idea of the nation continues to inform intellectual debates in India, and wonder if this needs some explanation for a non-Indian audience.

In the seven years that have passed since the first publication of this edited volume of my essays, I have become a little more familiar with the intellectual, political and social context into which the book has made an entry. The West Heavens project which brought me to Shanghai in 2010 has continued its excellent

---

[1] http://www.hindustantimes.com/india/is-this-anti-india-read-full-text-of-jnu-leader-kanhaiya-s-speech/story-rlhVQ9XVALS3Oc5h1UCOmK.html

work of curating conversations of different kinds between Indian and Chinese artists, scholars and even musicians. The Inter-Asia Cultural Studies project, to which I owe my introduction to West Heavens, has spread its ideas through events and publications that have had a transformative impact on scholars and practitioners in the region. I mention these two projects, West Heavens and Inter-Asia, to signpost the changes that have occurred in the milieu or in the Asian circles of thought, and to suggest that my book is now re-entering a space that is already different from that of 2010. I don't know whether the making legible of my concerns in these essays will now find more hospitable ground, because some of the connections that were perhaps new a few years ago are now more obvious.

One of the frustrations I felt during my lecture tour in Shanghai and elsewhere in 2010 was the common one of feeling unable to communicate, not just because of the language issues but because it was difficult to find shared reference points. The post-colonial setting of a good deal of academic work in India was clearly very different from the Chinese context. Let me point to some of the aspects that may not translate well into China, one of which might well be the continual referencing in Indian intellectual debates of the idea of the nation.

Although we in India had a long tradition of nationalist thinkers, both before and after Independence, contemporary critical scholarship in India has involved a critique of the project of nation and nationalism, an interrogation of what I've called 'the political and cultural logic of the national-modern'. To put it simply, the consensus achieved in relation to nation-building, a project led by elite Indians, took precedence over the different struggles of women, Dalits, peasants, tribals and industrial workers. Independence from the British in 1947 seemed to strengthen that consensus, but the political and social power stayed with the elites who ultimately had little interest in redistribution of material or intangible resources.

When speaking to Chinese readers, I always remind myself to emphasize the fact that unlike China, India did not go through a Revolution. What happened in the modern period in India can be more accurately called a process of Reform. In the reform process, a number of changes did take place, but there was no fundamental or radical transformation of society. Thus the social and political structures remained largely what they were, leading to discontent and continued struggles for rights and recognition on the part of many disenfranchised groups. So nearly 70 years after Independence, Kanhaiya Kumar's speech about freedom finds powerful resonance even among people born well after 1947.

What Kanhaiya is demanding is also a new imagination of the nation which draws on its tangible diversity of language, region, and religion, rather than the singular idea of India as belonging to

Hindus who form the majority religion. He also demands that we pay renewed attention to injustices of caste and gender, two key issues that the right-wing nationalism of the present, represented by the government in power in 2017, seeks to underplay. This 21st century ferment in the social domain could be understood in light of the contestations over 'culture' that have marked the birth and expansion of the idea of the nation.

Just a couple of weeks before the JNU incident, on January 17, 2016, Rohith Vemula, a Dalit PhD scholar at the University of Hyderabad in southern India committed suicide, an incident followed by student protests on that campus and the arrest of some teachers and students. The suicide was widely regarded by his fellow students as a mark of protest against an indifferent and oppressive university administration, and against a system that could not provide imaginative opportunities for students from socially under-privileged backgrounds. This failure of the nation's promise to fulfil its own Constitutional obligations has long been a cause for concern for those working towards social change. The Hyderabad student's suicide is one more indication that interventions in the legal domain, which many nation-states including India attempted in the 1950s and 60s, are insufficient to effect a transformation in the cultural. The suicide became a catalyst for many young people across the country, and also in JNU, to argue for the need to create an alliance of the socially marginalized with others attempting their own critique of the nation. Commentators see the swift Government retribution against students in the JNU case as a direct response to this possibility of the formation of a larger critical alliance.

As I write this, members of the ruling party's student wing, the ABVP, which played a central role in getting the JNU students accused of sedition, have attacked and badly beaten up peacefully protesting teachers and students in Ramjas College in Delhi on February 21, 2017. This college, part of Delhi University, had organized a seminar called 'Cultures of Protest' to which one of the invitees was Umar Khalid, JNU student who had been arrested the year before on sedition charges. Anticipating problems, the organisers had already asked Khalid not to take part. But the ABVP disrupted the seminar regardless, with the support of the Delhi Police. And when students and teachers took out a protest march, they were attacked by the ABVP, and several had to be hospitalized with critical injuries. ABVP members claim that anti-national slogans for Kashmir's *azaadi* or independence were heard at Ramjas College. A teacher who was present has clarified that the slogans were for *azaadi* of expression, freedom of speech. Once again, competing ideas of the nation have come to the fore—some arguing that the members of a nation have to hold the same beliefs and perform the same actions at all times; others arguing for a nation that includes multiple expressions and multiple possibilities, including the possibility of criticizing dominant ideas. We could also see these broadly oppositional forces as arguing over definitions of 'Indian culture', such as the contestation we see in the Pink Chaddi Campaign discussed in my essay in this volume, "Why Culture Matters".

Forging a public vocabulary for discussing issues of nation and culture has not been easy partly because of the disciplinary domination of the natural sciences in India, and the expectation that all 'bright students' will aspire to a career in science, leaving the other disciplines to those who could not do well in school. Even amongst those who take up the social sciences, the most confident voices are of the economists. The dominant social science in India has always been economics, whether of the Marxist variety or the neoclassical and developmental strands. State investment in research for seventy years after Independence has focused strongly on institutions that primarily employ economists, and it is rare to find a historian or a sociologist or a cultural theorist amongst them.

However, the work of scholars who have made important contributions to thinking critically about questions of culture and the representation of the nation have gained some circulation. Here I name only a few of them. They include those in the West Heavens series, like political thinkers Ashis Nandy or Partha Chatterjee, or others like cultural theorist Susie Tharu, or historians Romila Thapar and Tanika Sarkar. I see my own arguments as emerging in conversation with the work of these scholars, although I move into areas some of them have not ventured into, like translation theory, South Indian popular cinema, or Caribbean music and culture. In different ways, I see my own work as well as those of the scholars I mention above attempting a critique of the national-modern commonsense of an inherited civilizational essence that was 'Indian'. The critique sustains itself on the ground of translation as practice and philosophy in the colonial period, as I show in the extracts from my book *Siting Translation*. Another way of performing this critique is to create alternate frames of reference that do not take the 'West' as sole point of comparison, an idea I explore in my essay on studying the Caribbean as an Indian scholar. In the essay on South Indian popular cinema's representation of the female protagonist in the period of early globalization in the 1990s, I show how the nation is being refigured in the contemporary moment and how women are being shown as central to that process, often in problematic ways.

The space of the national and its centrality in 20th century academic work has been a significant phenomenon, often taken for granted as the appropriate frame of enquiry. I would say this is true not only for post-colonial societies in south and south-east Asia, but also for post-war Cold War regions, and for post-Civil War and post-Revolution settings like China. The idea of the nation is also acquiring a new popular relevance as the world witnesses unprecedented movements of people, both forced and voluntary, prompting the emergence of new languages of exclusion.

China's astonishing transformations through the 20th century and into the 21st have left many of us in Asia riveted to our seats in anticipation, almost as though we were watching a film on a large screen. As China opens up to the world, not just through carving out new markets but through exploring connections in the intellectual world and in the domains of the visual and performing arts, it would be important for Chinese people to be open to thinking about other histories, other spaces, and to be alert to the significance of difference. It would be important, then, for China not just to understand and engage with the 'West' but to craft new modes of connection with the 'rest', or what Partha Chatterjee calls 'most of the world'. One step in this direction might be to see what significance the ideas of nation and of culture have in Asia, and understand what possibilities are opened up by the critique of these concepts.

Tejaswini Niranjana
March 2017

CONTENTS

179 / Alternative Frames? Questions for Comparative Research in the Third World

209 / Language, a Place of Struggle

279 / Why Culture Matters: Rethinking the Language of Feminist Politics

297 / Nationalism Refigured: Contemporary South Indian Cinema and the Subject of Feminism

Alternative Frames? Questions for Comparative Research in the Third World

[Edouard] Glissant said to me: "I have never met you in Barbados, and you have never met me in Martinique. Why?" And I replied, "Because those journeys were not on our agenda."

George Lamming, *Conversations*

This paper is dedicated to the possibility of creating a critical space for ongoing conversations between intellectuals in different third-world locations. Prompted in part by my own journeys to the West Indies, these reflections will focus on the need for such conversations in our contemporary historical-political context, where the old boundaries are being erased and redrawn, and where the traversing of geographical distance has become, in a sense, both easier and more difficult depending on where one is going.

The project some of my friends and I embarked upon in the late 1980s found immediate resonance in the *Inter-Asia Cultural Studies* field. When I first met Kuan-Hsing Chen and other members of the IACS journal collective, I realized that their questions, although shaped by very different contexts, were uncannily similar to those of myself and my friends in their conceptual and political charge. Therefore, while this paper was not primarily written with this journal's potential audience in mind, there seemed to be a certain appropriateness in placing here the story of "those journeys" that provided the provocations for my questions. In addition, while the IACS collective has chosen to "problematize"—even as it "thematizes"—the notion of "Asia", my own earlier project considered, in very similar ways, the question of the "third world".[1]

This said, I am not unaware of the many difficulties we may encounter in using the term"third world" today, when it is no longer charged with the positive task of forging solidarities based on our common experience of colonialism and our common struggles for self-determination and sovereignty. Clearly, our post Cold War present is configured differently from the 1950s and 1960s—the age of decolonization and the Non-Aligned Movement—when it was possible for the term "third world" to function as an active political category, even though the term itself was coined in the metropolis after the Second World War to endorse the aid and development programmes that took the place of the old imperialism (Singham and Hune 1986). To invoke the term today in an unproblematic anti-imperialist sense might well put one on the side of the ruling elite in one's own nation-state, an elite which has sought to establish connections with other non-

---

[1] The editorial statement of the IACS attempts to interrogate these two terms in conjunction with one another. However, this is not a task I have taken up in the present paper.

metropolitan elites in order to claim back market-space from the Western transnational corporations that are increasingly infiltrating formerly "closed" economies.

The usage I propose, as I hope to demonstrate, is meant to suggest the possibilities of different kinds of solidarities and exchange (than those between ruling groups), both for intellectuals aswell as others engaged in the critique of dominance within their own societies. For my purposes, I shall use the term "third world"[1] to refer to a location formed by the "Bandung project" (the NAM) and its subsequent dismantling. In addition, it will describe a post-colonial political subject—formed by Marxisms and nationalisms of various kinds—who has had to address her/himself in recent years to questions of caste, race, community and gender that had not (indeed could not have) centrally figured in the decolonization debates, and which today seriously undermine the projects of elite nationalism.

To sketch quickly the immediate historical-political context of the contemporary critique of "nation" in the case of India, one might recall that, for radical politics in the 1970s and 1980s (especially those of the Marxist-Leninist groups and the women's movement), the nation-state was a significant addressee. While the critique of the nation was central to radical politics, this critique

---

[1] "Third" also because not first, not even second. In addition, "third" in the historical postwar sense of the term, refers (although in a limited sense, remembering important exceptions like China and Cuba) to "non-aligned" nations with a "mixed" economy, not quite socialist, not quite capitalist.

was, in many ways, still part of the political and cultural logic of the national-modern. The secularism and modernity of the politics depended, as we can now see, on the disavowal of caste, religious identity, ethnicity, regional and linguistic difference. Indeed, the energy and reach of feminism or the Marxist-Leninist (M-L) movement seemed to be made possible by these very disavowals. In the 1990s, however, political events such as the "anti-Mandal agitation", the rise of the Bharatiya Janata Party, the formation of successful regional parties, etc., combined with the drive to privatize and liberalize the Indian economy, have disrupted the narratives of the national-modern, a disruption within which the work of many of us today is situated. For someone like myself, affiliated with the critique of the languages of dominance in her society, a reworking and redeployment of the concept of the "third world" may suggest yet another entry-point into the problem of the universal-modern.

I would want to argue, then, for a "reworlding" of the Third World; for the renewal of our attempt to address seriously the dependency (cultural, political, economic) and the "underdevelopment" of our societies. Given that the nation is still a viable unit for many of us, and given the past use of the term "third world" by ruling elites to claim victimization and "aid", I suggest we reconsider the critical-political uses to which the term can be put within each nation-state. By insistently posing the question as to what being "third world" actually means, and which sections of a society this situation affects most (i.e. for whom is "underdevelopment" a problem?), we can pressurize our ruling groups to clarify their anti-imperialist rhetoric, and force them into political choices that are more accountable and more representative. The assumption of commonality between rulers and ruled underlying the invocation of "third world" in international forums must be called to account, and those who govern made to accept the implications of this assumption. Diverse claims to egality and justice could be strengthened by the availability of successful examples from similarly "third-worlded" regions. What we might want to call for is the deployment of the term "third world" in expanding the theories of what Partha Chatterjee calls "democracy" (his term for a political society, the realm in which political claims are articulated today by various [subaltern] groups), a notion which may well be seen as opposed to "modernity" (a reference to civil society in the third world: a realm that is the exclusive preserve of a few who are eligible to become "citizens") (Chatterjee 1996).

The renewed attention paid to "democracy"[1] should lead also to the revitalization, and democratization, of the academic disciplines in which we work. My own discipline, English Studies,

---

[1] It should be clear by now that Chatterjee's use of the term, which I follow here, is quite different from what is meant by the enforcers of the New World Order.

has, for some time now, been subject to various strands of political questioning. Looking back on what has come to be called "the critique of English Studies in India", one observes certain impasses we have come to recognize, in particular around the problem of relevance. The post-Independence generation of English teachers (R. B. Patankar, Ayyappa Panikkar and U. R. Ananthamurthy, to name just a few figures who were teaching in the 1970s) seemed to resolve the question of the relevance of its profession by doing business as usual in the classroom but engaging actively in the intellectual life of its community primarily in Marathi or Malayalam or Kannada. In the 1980s, however, a few teachers—in Hyderabad, Delhi and Calcutta for example—were beginning to raise different sorts of questions in the English classroom, largely due to their involvement in feminism. In the 1990s, the sharpening of conflicts around issues of nation, community, caste as well as gender, appeared to bring the dissatisfaction and unease of both students and teachers more directly into the classroom, leading to a sustained questioning of received curricula, pedagogical practices and research emphases. Putting it somewhat schematically, we might say that two kinds of work have begun to receive increased attention within English departments: (a) research that seeks to examine Indian languages, literatures and cultural practices, to investigate different kinds of writing (such as writing by women or dalits), or to enlarge the discipline by studying hitherto devalued cultural forms such as popular cinema or children's literature; and (b) research into "common-wealth" or even third-world cultures and literatures. Although the first kind of agenda does seem to require major reorientations in terms of methodologies and politics, the Indian student/teacher is, all said and done, not particularly handicapped in the study of what is in some sense "theirs". (Given the burden of nationalism—clearly visible in their curricula—that the post-Independence social sciences carry in India, and given the necessarily belated relay of this burden to English Studies, the most predictable response I get when I say I teach Caribbean and African texts is: "But why not Indian texts?" There are several possible answers to this question, which for reasons of space I will not go into here.) The second sort of agenda, that of teaching "third-world" literature, is handicapped from the start. Scarce institutional resources can barely be stretched to acquire conventional materials required by the discipline, let alone diverted to the purchase of little-known texts from non-metropolitan places. The teacher's woes are magnified in comparison to those of the researcher, whose access to primary and secondary material is severely limited. Since, in spite of these problems, both teaching and research in these areas continue, I would like to argue here for a re-examination of the implicit premises with which we in India set out to teach and study other third-world contexts, and suggest that the current times call for a critical fashioning of new research agendas that might rethink the assumptions—even as they emphasize the importance—of comparative work.

Indians, Indians everywhere

One of the signs of our times is the spectacular international visibility of the "Indian" (not just beauty queens but also technologists, scientists, artists, economists, historians, or even literary theorists!). As a self-congratulatory cultural nationalism overcomes us, we seldom stop to think about the formation of this "Indian" and his/her deployment by the political economy of global capitalism. An economy that we do not need to emphasize is also an economy of academia and the production of knowledge. In the middle of the 20th century, in the age of Nehruvian socialism and the Non-Aligned Movement, and in the aftermath of the worldwide anti-imperialist struggle, Indians claimed solidarity with other formerly colonized peoples and extended various kinds of support to nations less privileged than they were. At the end of the millennium, however, the Indian is not simply another postcolonial but one who would claim to have attained exceptionality, or special status—an achievement that increasingly sets him or her off from other inhabitants of other postcolonies. Earlier axes of identification are transformed and old solidarities are disavowed as the middle-class Indian, even as she vociferously asserts her cultural difference, becomes a relay in the circuits of multinational capital. Although a good deal of recent critical scholarship has focused on the formation of the Indian citizen—subject and analysed the exclusions (of caste, community and gender, for instance) that underwrite it, the subtle changes occurring in the composition of the "Indian" in transnational spaces have yet to be seriously investigated.

I mention this as a concern arising from my visits to the Caribbean, where I encountered in Jamaica and Trinidad a variety of perceptions regarding "Indians", perceptions often actively fostered, especially by newly immigrant Indian groups, international organizations such as the Vishwa Hindu Parishad (part of the Sangh Parivar "family" which includes the Bharatiya Janata Party) and even the Indian nation-state through its High Commissions. Safe in an Indian university, one can simply read the West Indian text as one among other literary artefacts in a continuum of "newer English" writings; but the Indian researcher working in a Caribbean or African location might well be called upon to make explicit his or her alignments with people of Indian origin who live in those spaces, and explain his or her motives for undertaking comparative research. This demand may be related to the deployment of the notion of "culture" by Indians from India as well as people of Indian origin in the West Indies, their invocation of an ancient past and a glorious civilization as proof of racial superiority. As a Guyanese friend put it, "Indians always say culture is what they have and the black people don't."[1] As I have discussed elsewhere, there is a complex politics to the invocation of Indianness in the Caribbean, the details of which often elude the visiting Indian researcher, partly because of his/her own unexamined notions of what "Indian culture" means (Niranjana 1995).

Teaching the Caribbean

Another profound disorientation I experienced in the Caribbean was that of being in a west that was not the West. Earlier visits outside India had always been to first world spaces, and however different each might have been from the other they were, for me, collectively that which was not Indian, not third world. My encounters with the Caribbean forced me to begin asking other questions about sameness and difference—whether in the realm of the political (with regard to notions of nation and region), the economic (questions of "dependency" and "development") or the cultural (the tradition versus modernity debate) — than those I was accustomed to asking, in relation to India and the West, for example. Not only this, but the encounters had a crucial impact on

---

[1] The situation is further complicated when we have Indians from India studying "East Indian West Indians" . The cultural forms of these diasporic communities are often imaged by Indians as fragmented, deficient or derivative.

the questions I addressed in the classroom, the teaching strategies I adopted, and the texts that I taught.[1]

Some years ago, I wrote a paper—based on a course I had taught in 1989 on Africa and the Caribbean—in which I attempted to explore the implications of teaching non-Western literary texts in Indian Departments of English.[2] For me as well as my students, it had been a first-time exposure to these texts, contexts and histories. Given the dearth of material in our largely Eurocentric libraries, the task of teaching the course was a difficult one, and the engagement with the texts had to be carefully negotiated and re-negotiated at every step.

Clearly our concern was not just one about "content", using new texts in place of the old. I had suggested in the paper that this kind of easy substitution does not question the need for a canon of great texts, a need which brings with it the imperative to teach the canon in particular ways. My argument was that the demand to be included or accommodated within the existing paradigm did not pose a threat to the paradigm itself, "since it never questions the criteria which determine exclusion in the first place" (Niranjana

---

[1] I postpone a detailed discussion of these changes to a later date, only indicating for example that I have had to find ways of introducing students—at least aurally—to the popular culture of the West Indies, simultaneously attempting to initiate a discussion on the politics of language in the Caribbean.

[2] This paper, titled "History, really beginning: compulsions of postcolonial pedagogy", has been subsequently published in Rajan (1992).

1995: 249). Instead, I had suggested, we must look at how we teach/read and examine the expectations we bring to our reading of African and Caribbean texts. I had emphasized the importance of teaching non-metropolitan texts while at the same time resisting "their incorporation into the canon" by not employing "customary ways of reading" (Niranjana 1995: 249).

My contention then was that the non-metropolitan texts posed a radical challenge to the discipline and to conventional literary critical approaches, not because of any intrinsic quality they possessed but because—embedded as they were in histories similar in some ways to that of India—our questions or interests coincided, or came in to a conjuncture with, these Caribbean and African works. The risk, of course, was that in stressing similarities we might ignore real differences between specific third-world societies. All the same, our engagement with these texts "forced our attention away from the aesthetic to the political dimension", "making us seek assonance and dissonance not in poetic form but in the realm of culture, politics and history" (Niranjana 1995: 250). What we managed to accomplish to a certain extent was "to place the text more firmly amidst material and social practices instead of in a purely literary tradition" (Niranjana 1995: 250).

Looking back at these concerns, it seems to me that the emphasis was still on the literary text, with not enough attention being paid either to the discursive networks from which it had emerged, or to other kinds of cultural artefacts. Perhaps this was a problem, simply, of inadequate information. Perhaps it was also the formulation of the question itself—as one of text plus context—that was getting in the way, for in this formulation the text can ultimately be detached from the context, which is imaged as simply surrounding it. The question of how to decide the demarcations of a text's boundaries (or of what constituted a "text" in the first place) was not addressed, except in passing, and consequently one ended up displaying as texts in the classroom precisely those sorts of pieces (a Walcott play, an early Brathwaite poem, a Lamming novel) that the discipline of English Studies would have no difficulty accepting, omitting entirely for example the popular music of the Caribbean, an understanding of which is so central to any attempt at studying West Indian cultural politics.[1]

It seems to me now that the problem was related to our third-worldist attempt to discover cultural artefacts of "our own", which were, to use Kwame Anthony Appiah's words, deserving of dignity. In addition, concepts like the "political" and the "aesthetic" appear in hindsight to have been invoked as though

---

[1] The Walcott, Brathwaite and Lamming texts often become assimilated into literature courses in such a way that their links—both formal and thematic—to popular culture are obscured, leading to their being read like any other modernist text.

their meanings were "given", and the distinction between them too quickly posed, although at the time the terms did perhaps serve as a kind of shorthand for entire methodologies. In 1990, the need for disciplinary transformation was certainly being expressed in different quarters, but for me at least the larger significance of this proposed transformation was, as yet, not adequately thought through. It was only after the dramatic national events of late 1990 (I refer in particular to the anti-Mandal agitation of upper-caste youth seeking to deny affirmative action for the lower castes) that the question of what it meant to challenge "English" in India could be asked in a different form, and the whole terrain on which the dominant "aesthetic" was constructed could be investigated from a different critical perspective. "Mandal", as an event, drew the attention of many middle-class left-oriented secular Indians to the "invisibilizing" of caste in the composition of the citizen-subject. In literary studies, dominated by a modernism congruent in many ways with the secularism of the post-Independence era, it became possible, sometimes by consolidating earlier dalit and feminist initiatives, to confront directly the exclusions that helped form the realm of the aesthetic. Investigating the historical formation of the aesthetic realm, it seems to me, can have important implications for comparative third-world cultural studies, in terms of what we set out to compare and how we go about our task.

The problem of ethnography

One of the tasks of the third-world comparativist is the reconceptualization of third-world spaces that are not her own. Such a task might involve working against the conventional metropolitan characterizations of these spaces, which necessarily presuppose the ethnographic eye, the anthropological attitude.

Although the literary/cultural comparativist often has no formal training in the discipline of anthropology, its modes of argument and its habits of thought are bound to infect any enterprise, like the comparativist's, which undertakes the study of cultural formations other than the one inhabited by the investigator. Predictably, the question of anthropology would never come up when Indian students, for example, study British or American literature. The frameworks and locations that endorse the production of "modern" knowledge ensure that the question only applies to the study of non-Western — or perhaps we should say "Southern" — cultures.[1] However, in the years

---

[1] Interestingly, it is not just the reading of the cultural artefacts of the South that is seen as an anthropological activity. The ethnographic question "sticks" to the production of the artefacts too. For example, a standard literary critical dismissal of African writers like Chinua Achebe is that they are "too anthropological". The same question might sometimes stick to minority literatures in the first world (African-American writing immediately comes to mind) or to Indian dalit writing or women's writing.

after decolonization, anthropology has come under a sustained interrogation of its originating impulses and procedures from several different quarters, noteworthy among them — for our purposes — is the postcolonial-turned-anthropologist (Asad 1973; Scott 1989). Since the project of classical anthropology is to produce a self-understanding of the West through a study of "other" cultures, the anthropological investigator tends to assume the centrality of Western civilization. Given this location provided by the discipline for the investigator, how can the third-world "anthropologist" begin to question this centrality?

When such an anthropologist (and clearly I use this description to name a set of subject-positions, no matter what the disciplinary training of the investigator) ventures into another third-world space, the normalization of her/his location — and thereby subject-position — is opened up to questioning, and the possibility for a critique of the dominant episteme, I would argue, begins to emerge. Such a critique would, of necessity, involve the third-world intellectual — in particular, the Indian intellectual, often by definition upper-class and upper-caste — in an unlearning of his or her privilege (different from the unlearning that takes place in a "national" context) and a recognition of his or her complicity with the institutions and disciplinary frameworks of metropolitan knowledge production.

By now it is fairly well established that the modern

academic disciplines, including of course anthropology, were born simultaneously with a new phase in European expansion, underwriting as well as underwritten by the project of colonial governance (Said 1978; Asad 1973). Whether scholars in the colonial period helped produce stereotypes about the colonized or detailed information about customs and practices, in either case they were constructing a world variously described as non-modern, traditional or primitive, a world thereby rendered amenable to domination by a more "advanced" civilization. It is the scholar's professed expertise (what James Clifford (1983) has so aptly called "ethnographic authority"), certified by metropolitan academic institutions, that continues to endorse the "truth" and factuality of this knowledge.

The ethnographer functions like a translator — indeed, the project of anthropology has been seen as that of translating one culture into terms intelligible to another (Asad 1986; Niranjana 1992). What has only recently come to be addressed within the discipline is the question of how relations of power, such as those under colonial or neo-colonial domination, determine the direction and nature of translation, often simplifying, as Talal Asad has pointed out, towards the stronger language/culture (Asad 1986; Fabian 1986). This also raises once again the question of audience and of the ethnographer's subject-position. Who writes, and for whom? What might be the possible differences between metropolitan and third-world representations of third-world contexts?

Bases of comparative research

Hitherto, the often undeclared bases of comparative study have been a humanism and a universalism that presumed a common human nature: in spite of their superficial differences, all people in the world were thought to be ultimately the same, or in the process of becoming like one another. This was, however, an argument made from above, as it were. The "liberal" Western ethnographer, for instance, could claim the common humanity of the investigator and the objects of study, even if it was on the part of these "objects", that a humanity was to be uncovered through the labour of the ethnographer's translation of their words and deeds into his/her Euro-American language. What could then be compared was the non-Western context with the anthropologist's Westernone.Implicit in this kind of comparison, despite the protestations of human commonality, is what Achille Mbembe, writing about the African context, has called "the perspective of a failed universality":

> *The common unit, the ultimate foundation, **even the intrinsic finality of the comparative project is Western modernity,** understood either as the standard against which*

one measures other societies, or as the final destination toward which they are to move. And each time "African" is introduced into the operation, the comparative act is reduced to an arithmetic relation of "superiority" and "inferiority". Hierarchical figures slip in between these three chimeras of similitude, resemblance, and similarity, establishing orders of value defined in an arbitrary manner, the function of which is to legitimate discrimination and, too often, violence.

(Mbembe 1992: 142—143, emphasis added)

As I have argued in my work on the politics of translation, the very premise of a universal history on which, in comparative study, the unity of human consciousness is predicated allows — as for example in the Hegelian model of world history — the formation of an inner hierarchy that situates third-world cultures below the Euro-American (Niranjana 1992: 69—70).

Consequently, even when third-world intellectuals themselves undertake comparative work, their task becomes one of comparing their cultural products with metropolitan ones — Kalidasa becomes the Shakespeare of India, Tutuola the African Fielding. This is part of the urge to find something in our colonized cultures that, as Kwame Appiah puts it, "lives up to [the label]" (whether it is that of Philosophy or Literature), to find something that is ours which "*deserves* the dignity" (Appiah 1992: 148, emphasis in original). The fact is, says Appiah, taking the case of Africa, that "intellectuals educated in the shadow of the West" are bound "to adopt an essentially comparative perspective" (Appiah 1992: 151). The inherent asymmetry of the comparativist project framed in these terms would be at least displaced (since it cannot simply be done away with) when two different third-world contexts are being compared or studied together by one whose subject-positions and location are in the third world.

Outside metropolitan circuits?

This, then, is an argument about the formation of perspective, about how one's location helps critique one's complicity with metropolitan systems of knowledge and representation. Although it is now acknowledged that the space from which one is speaking, its histories, its questions, crucially configure the perspective of the investigator, the implications of such a configuration for comparative research in the third world have not yet been mapped out. If ethnographic work — always comparativist by definition — has hitherto been embedded both literally as well as figuratively in structures of dominance, we might speculate as to what might happen when the founding impulse is no longer one of greater and more efficient control. If one is not representing, or producing knowledge, in order to govern and regulate, what could be the alternative impulses?

If one of those impulses is the conscious formulation of the political project of dismantling eurocentrism, where would one look for resources (besides of course in one's own local context, which for various reasons may not be adequate) but in other third-world spaces? The project cannot be an isolated one, located only in a single postcolony. While I would certainly not want to deny that colonial and postcolonial trajectories of various regions have been different from each other, arguments for exceptionality in the contemporary context can only weaken the possibilities for the emergence of urgently needed new solidarities.[1] The silence about our common histories mirrors the silence about the possibility of a shared future. There is perhaps, then, some purchase to be gained by positing shared histories at a certain level, since the colonies as well as the disciplinary networks in which they are produced and held have been part of the global enterprise of colonialism/neo-colonialism. As to what the "gain" might be, only the outcome of comparative projects may be able to suggest. Only by risking the formulation of problems in which more than one nationality has similar kinds of stakes can we push for a reconfiguration of our research paradigms.

Just as work on culture in India needs to take into consideration

---

[1] Indians and Brazilians, to give just two examples, often claim such exceptionality in different contexts. Such a claim can only be complicit in the production of the category of the universal.

Orientalist structures of representation (Niranjana1993; Niranjana 1992b), one should undertake similar ground-clearing tasks for other third-world contexts with which one is attempting to engage. As I discovered during my sojourn in the West Indies, my awareness of the ways in which "India" had been produced, in colonialist discourse for example, did not provide a guarantee that I could perceive similar, if different, structures of representation in relation to the Caribbean. Third-world intellectuals who are beginning to think about third-world spaces other than their own, need to address the question of how these different regions have been discursively constructed as objects of knowledge, to examine closely the technologies and theories that have enabled their emergence, and to understand the extent to which our readings of each other in the present are informed by those discursive grids.[1]

Alternative frames

If the disciplines have so far been caught up in these paradigms of domination, what kind of representations of the third world might be produced when this agenda is disrupted? What happens, we may ask, when a West Indian reads the

---

[1] Writing about the African context and using the term "colonial library" coined by V. Y. Mudimbe, Achille Mbembe(1992:141) contends that prior to any contemporary discourse on Africa, there is a "library" an inaugural prejudice that destroys all foundations for valid comparisons.

Nigerian Chinua Achebe? When a South Asian reads the West Indian Kamau Brathwaite? When Lucky Dube in South Africa sings Jamaican-style reggae? What is the significance of these new representations? What sorts of cultural transformations do they signal? Would they function differently from metropolitan cultural products in third-world circuits? What new critical spaces might they help open up in the new locations where they begin to circulate?

More questions: why indeed should we speak to each other across the South? Why should we engage in comparative research across third-world locations? Perhaps the "ends" of the new comparative work are oblique. Perhaps what this kind of work can do is to contribute to the development of alternative frames of reference, so that Western modernity is no longer seen as the sole point of legitimization or comparison. Let me emphasize that I do not intend to suggest that we can eliminate first-world knowledge structures or produce subjectivities entirely unmediated by the "West". My argument is simply that the norming of the comparative axis needs to be questioned. In much of our critical work, as well as our popular cultural conceptions, the two poles that make themselves manifest are "India" and "the West". To recognize that there exist outside our everyday sphere geographical and political spaces other than the West, spaces that have always intersected with our history but by the very logic of colonialism cannot be acknowledged in their mutual imbrication with our past, to arrive at this recognition is a first step towards rewriting our histories as well as envisioning, and enlarging, our futures: together, and anew.[1]

Critical engagements with other third-world spaces might help inaugurate for, and in the South, a new internationalism, different (in its motivations, its desires, its imagined futures) from the aggressive globalization set in motion by the first world. Woven into this paper is an argument about perspective and intellectual/political location. *In* the third world, how do we *read* one another so that we do not appear simply as footnotes to Western history (Mukherjee 1995)? How do we learn to question the epistemological structures through which knowledge about third-world peoples are produced? I quote here the Guyanese scholar-activist Walter Rodney:

When an African abuses an Indian he repeats all that the white men said about Indian indentured"coolies"; and in turn the Indian has borrowed from the whites the stereo type of the "lazy nigger" to apply to the African beside him. It is as though no black

---

[1] As David Scott has remarked, "The issue, of course, is not to erase the West as though to restore to its others some ancient pre-colonial unity, as though, indeed, the West were erasable. The issue…. is rather to establish a reflexively marked practice of dialogical exchange that might enable the postcolonial intellectual to speak to postcolonials elsewhere…through these shared-but-different histories and shared-but-different identities" (Scott 1989: 83—84).

man can see another black man except by looking through a white person. It is time we started seeing through our own eyes. Rodney 1969: 33—34.

What kind of critical awareness ought we bring to our teaching and writing so as to avoid reproducing the stereotypes about black/brown/yellow people that exist in what V. Y. Mudimbe calls the "colonial library" (Mbembe 1992: 142)? How do we learn to ask questions that resonate with the actual concerns of people in other third-world places? What sort of library or archive do we need to construct? What new kinds of literacy do we need to acquire? How can we learn to overcome our multiple amnesia?

This paper has expressed some anxiety about the emergence of the new cosmopolitan Indian who might actively seek identification with the first world rather than the third. In addition, I have tried to suggest why this identification was problematic by focusing on the common problems faced by third-world comparativists, pointing implicitly to the dangers of Indian researchers replicating in relation to other third-world contexts the very manoeuvres and representational modes that had negated and "dehistoricized" their own spaces. In so doing, my intention was not to argue for a simple return to our international politics of the Nehru era, but to urge a rethinking of present possibilities by pointing to forms of solidarity obscured by the growth of the globalized economy.

With the new globalization, the paths to the first world will be more clearly defined than ever before, rendered easier to traverse. Other locations on the map will appear all the more blurred, all the more difficult to reach. Now more than ever a critical perspective on our contemporary political-cultural identities requires that we place those other journeys on our agenda.

Acknowledgements

This paper owes its origins to ongoing conversations in different locations with David Scott, Mary John, Nadi Edwards, Satish Deshpande, Susie Tharu and Vivek Dhareshwar. For comments on an earlier draft of this paper, I am grateful to Uma Maheshwari, Anita Cherian, Rekha Pappu and K. Srilata. My thanks also to the following for critical engagements that have provoked me into reshaping some of my arguments: Craig Calhoun, Ernesto Laclau, Chantal Mouffe, Kumi Naidoo, Luiz Soares and Otavio Velho.

References:

Appiah, Kwame Anthony (1992) "Ethnophilosophy and its critics", in *In My Father's House: Africa in the Philosophy of Culture*, Methuen.

Asad, Talal (ed.) (1973) Anthropology and the Colonial Encounter, Humanities Press.

Asad, Talal (1986) "The concept of cultural translation in British social anthropology", in J. Clifford and G. Marcus (eds.), *Writing Culture: The Poetics and Politics of Ethnography*, University of California Press.

Chatterjee, Partha (1996) "Two poets and death: on civil and political society in the non-Christian world", unpublished paper.

Clifford, James (1983) "On ethnographic authority", *Representations* 1, 118—146.

Fabian, Johannes (1986) *Language and Colonial Power: The Appropriation of Swahili in the Former Belgian Congo, 1880— 1938*, Cambridge University Press.

Mbembe, Achille (1992) "Prosaics of servitude and authoritarian civilities", *Public Culture* 5 (10) : 123—145.

Mukherjee, Meenakshi (1995) A phrasein a talk on "The Caribbean and Us", IACLALS Annual Conference, Mysore: January.

Niranjana, Tejaswini (1992a) *Siting Translation: History, Post-structuralism and the Colonial Context*, University of California Press.

Niranjana, Tejaswini (1992b) "History, really beginning: compulsions of postcolonial pedagogy" in Rajeswari, S. R. (ed.) *The Lie of the Land: English Literary Studies in India*, Oxford University Press.

Niranjana, Tejaswini (ed.) (1993) *Interrogating Modernity*, with P. Sudhir and V. Dhareshwar, Seagull Books.

Niranjana, Tejaswini (1995) "The Indian in me: gender, identity and cultural politics in Trinidad". Paper presented at the International Conference on the Indian Diaspora, Trinidad: University of the West Indies, St. Augustine.

Rajan, Rajeswari Sunder (ed.) (1992) *The Lie of the Land*: *English LiteraryStudies in India*, Oxford University Press.

Rodney, Walter (1969) *The Groundings with my Brothers*, Bogle-l'Ouverture.

Said, Edward (1978) *Orientalism*, Vintage.

Scott, David (1989) "Locating the anthropological subject: postcolonial anthropologists in other places". In J. Clifford and V. Dhareshwar (eds.) *Traveling Theories, Traveling Theorists.* Special Issue of *Inscriptions* (No.5).

Singham, A. W. and Hune, Shirley (1986) *Non-Alignment in an Age of Alignments*, Zed Books.

Language, a Place of Struggle

The passion for English knowledge has penetrated the most obscure, and extended to the most remote parts of India. The steam boats, passing up and down the Ganges, are boarded by native boys, begging, not for money, but for books.... Some gentlemen coming to Calcutta were astonished at the eagerness with which they were pressed for books by a troop of boys, who boarded the steamer from an obscure place, called Comercolly. A Plato was lying on the table, and one of the party asked a boy whether that would serve his purpose. "Oh yes, " he exclaimed, "give me any book; all I want is a book." They gentleman at last hit upon the expedient of cutting up an old *Quarterly Review*, and distributing the articles among them.

Charles Trevelyan, *On the Education of the People of India*

Situating Translation

In apostcolonial context the problematic of *translation* becomes a significant site for raising questions of representation, power and historicity. The context is one of contesting and contested stories attempting to account for, to recount, the asymmetry and inequality of relations between peoples, races, languages. Since the practices of subjection/subjectification implicit in the colonial enterprise operate not merely through the coercive machinery of the imperial state but also through the discourses of philosophy, history, anthropology, philology, linguistics and literary interpretation, the colonial "subject" — constructed through technologies or practices of power/knowledge[1] — is brought into being within multiple discourses and on multiple sites. One such site is translation. Translation as a practice shapes, and takes shape within, the asymmetrical relations of power that operate under colonialism. What is at stake here is the representation of the colonized, who need to be produced in such a manner as to justify colonial domination, and to beg for the English book by themselves. In the colonial context, a certain conceptual economy is created by the set of related questions that is the problematic of translation. Conventionally, translation depends on the Western philosophical notions of reality, representation, and knowledge. Reality is seen as something unproblematic, "out there"; knowledge involves a representation of this reality; and representation provides direct, unmediated access to a transparent reality. Classical philosophical discourse, however, does not simply engender a practice of translation that is then employed for the purposes of colonial domination; I contend that, simultaneously, translation in the colonial context produces and supports a conceptual economy that works into the discourse

---

[1] "[Power] produces knowledge... [they] directly imply one another, " says Foucault *(Discipline and Punish: The Birth of the Prison*, trans. Alan Sheridan, New York: Random House, Vintage Books, 1979, p.27). He further suggests that the "individual" or the subject is "fabricated" by technologies of power or practices of subjectification.

of Western philosophy to function as a philosopheme (a basic unit of philosophical conceptuality). As Jacques Derrida suggests, the concepts of metaphysics are not bound by or produced solely within the "field" of philosophy. Rather, they come out of and circulate through various discourses in several registers, providing a "conceptual network in which philosophy *itself* has been constituted."[1] In forming a certain kind of subject, in presenting particular versions of the colonized, translation brings into being overarching concepts of reality and representation. These concepts, and what they allow us to assume, completely occlude the violence that accompanies the construction of the colonial subject.

Translation thus produces strategies of containment. By employing certain modes of representing the other—which it thereby also brings into being—translation reinforces hegemonic versions of the colonized, helping them acquire the status of what Edward Said calls representations, or objects without history.[2] These become *facts* exerting a force on events in the colony: witness Thomas Babington Macaulay's 1835 dismissal of indigenous Indian learning as outdated and irrelevant, which prepared the way for the introduction of English education.

In creating coherent and transparent texts and subjects, translation participates—across a range of discourses—in the *fixing*

---

1 Derrida, "White Mythology: Metaphor in the Text of Philosophy, " in *Margins of Philosophy*, trans. Alan Bass, Chicago: University of Chicago Press, 1982, p.230.

2 Said, discussion with Eugenio Dona to and others ("An Exchange on Deconstruction and History, " *Boundary* 28, no. 1, Fall 1979, p.65—74).

of colonized cultures, making them seem static and unchanging rather than historically constructed. Translation functions as a transparent presentation of something that already exists, although the "original" is actually brought into being through translation. Paradoxically, translation also provides a place in "history" for the colonized. The Hegelian conception of history that translation helps bring into being endorses a teleological, hierarchical model of civilizations based on the "coming to consciousness" of "Spirit", an event for which the non-Western cultures are unsuited or unprepared. Translation is thus deployed in different kinds of discourses — philosophy, historiography, education, missionary writings, travel — writing — to renew and perpetuate colonial domination.

My concern here is to explore the place of translation in contemporary Euro-American literary theory (using the name of this "discipline" in a broad sense) through a set of interrelated readings. I argue that the deployment of "translation" in the colonial and postcolonial contexts shows us a way of questioning some of the theoretical emphases of poststructuralism.

Chapter 1 outlines the problematic of translation and its relevance to the postcolonial situation. Reading the texts of different kinds of colonial translators, I show how they bring into being hegemonic versions of the non-Western other. Because they are underpinned by the powerful metaphysics of translation, these versions are seen even in the postcolonial context as faithful pictures of the decadence or depravity of "us natives." Through English education, which still legitimizes ruling-class power in formerly colonized countries, the dominant representations put into circulation by translation come to be seen as "natural" and "real." In order to challenge these representations, one must also examine the historicist tenets that endorse them. I will, therefore, discuss the pertinence of the critique of historicism to a world undergoing de-colonization. Given the enduring nature of Hegelian presentations of the non-West and the model of teleological history that authorizes them, a questioning of the model could underwrite a new practice of translation.

In chapter 2, I examine how "translation" works in the traditional discourse of translation studies and in ethnographic writing. Discussing the last two, which are somewhat marginal to literary theory, may nevertheless help us sharpen our critique of translation. Caught in an idiom of fidelity and betrayal that assumes an unproblematic notion of representation, translation studies fail to ask questions about the historicity of translation; ethnography, on the other hand, has recently begun to question both the innocence of representation and the long-standing asymmetries of translation.

In chapters 3, 4, and 5, my main focus is the work of Paul de Man, Jacques Derrida and Walter Benjamin (an earlier critic who is becoming increasingly important to poststructuralist thinkers). My analysis shows how translation functions as a "figure" in all three thinkers, becoming synonymous or associated with a major preoccupation in each: allegory or literature in de Man, the problematics of representation and intentionality in Derrida, and the question of materialist historiography in Benjamin. Pointing out the configurations of translation and history in Benjamin's work, I describe the kind of reading provided by de Man and Derrida of Benjamin's important essay "The Task of the Translator". My argument is that Walter Benjamin's early writings on translation are troped in significant ways into his later essays on the writing of history, a troping that goes unrecognized by both de Man and Derrida. (I use *trope* to indicate a metaphorizing that includes a displacement as well as a re-figuring.) The refusal of these major proponents of deconstruction to address the question of history in Benjamin suggests a critical drawback in their theory and perhaps indicates why deconstruction has never addressed the problem of colonialism.

In the final chapter, with the help of a translation from Kannada, a South Indian language, into English, I discuss the "uses" of poststructuralism in postcolonial space. Throughout the book, my discussion functions in all the registers—philosophical, linguistic, and political—in which translation "works" under colonialism. If at any point I seem to dwell on only one of these, it is for a purely strategic purpose.

This work belongs to the larger context of the "crisis" in "English" that is a consequence of the impact of structuralism and post structuralism on literary studies in a rapidly decolonizing world. The liberal humanist ideology that endorsed and was perpetuated by the civilizing mission of colonialism is still propagated by discourses of "literature" and "criticism" in the tradition of Arnold, Leavis and Eliot. These disciplines repress what Derrida, in the words of Heidegger, calls the logocentric or ontotheological metaphysics by which they are constituted, which involves all the traditional conceptions of representation, translation, reality, unity and knowledge.[1]

There have been few systematic attempts to question "English", or literature, or criticism from a postcolonial perspective, let alone such a perspective that also incorporates insights from contemporary theory.[2] In order to help challenge the complicity of these discourses with colonial and neocolonial

---

1 Post-Romantic literary criticism, for example, relies on a concept of the text as a unified, coherent, symbolic whole that can be re-presented or interpreted by the critic. Derrida would argue that the text is "always already" marked by representation; it was not suddenly brought into being through the "originality" of its "author".

2 See, however, Gauri Viswanathan, "The Beginnings of English Literary Study in British India, " *Oxford Literary Review*, nos. 1—2, 1987, pp.2—26. Viswanathan's book *Masks of Conquest* (New York: Columbia University Press, 1989) provides a finely detailed discussion of the ideological uses of English literature in colonial India. I should also mention here Ngugi wa Thiong'o's famous challenge to Eng. Lit. (Ngugi et al., "On the Abolition of the English Department, " reprinted in Ngugi, *Homecoming*, 1972; reprint, Westport, Conn.: Lawrence Hill, 1983); Chinua Achebe's essays in *Morning Yet on Creation Day* (London: Heinemann, 1975); and Chinweizu, Onwuchekwa Jemie, and Ihechukwu Madubuike, *Toward the Decolonization of African Literature*, vol. 1 (1980; reprint, Washington, D.C.: Howard University Press, 1983).

domination, I propose to make a modest beginning by examining the "uses" of translation. The rethinking of translation becomes an important task in a context where it has been used since the European Enlightenment to underwrite practices of subjectification, especially for colonized peoples. Such a rethinking—a task of great urgency for a postcolonial theory attempting to make sense of "subjects" already living "in translation, " imaged and re-imaged by colonial ways of seeing—seeks to reclaim the notion of translation by deconstructing it and reinscribing its potential as a strategy of resistance.

Given the dispersed nature of its existence, we shall have to approach an understanding of the "postcolonial" through a variety of nodes: the intersection of the present with a history of domination, [1] the formation of colonial "subjects, " the workings of hegemony in civil society, [2] and the task, already under way, of affirmative deconstruction.[3]

---

[1] *History*, like *translation*, is a term under constant interrogation in my text. I shall suggest later some of its relevant uses in the postcolonial situation.

[2] *Hegemony* and *civil society* are terms used by Antonio Gramsci. Definitions will be provided later in the discussion. Gramsci's famous work is the series of fragments collected in *Quaderni del carcere*, available in English as *Selections from the Prison Notebooks*, trans. Quintin Hoare and Geoffrey Nowell Smith (New York: International Publishers, 1971). Autobiographical circumstances determine my examples of "practices of subjectification" , most of which are from colonial and postcolonial India.

[3] See chapter 6 for an example of translation as affirmative deconstruction.

In beginning to describe thepostcolonial, we might reiterate some of the brute facts of colonialism. Starting with the period around the end of the seventeenth century and continuing beyond World War II, Britain and France, and to a lesser extent Spain, Portugal, Germany, Russia, Italy and Holland, dominated—ruled, occupied, exploited—nearly the entire world. By 1918, European powers had colonized 85 percent of the earth's surface.[1] Not until after World War I (referred to by some non-Western writers as the European Civil War) was the process of decolonization initiated. Of course, we cannot speak here of a swift or complete transition to a postcolonial society, for to do so would be to reduce the ruptured complexities of colonial history to insignificance. The term *de-colonization* can refer only crudely to what has, in the language of national liberation struggles, been called the "transfer of power", usually from the reigning colonial power to an indigenous elite.

Although one cannot see as negligible the importance of the transfer, it would be naive to believe it marks the "end" of domination, for the strength of colonial discourse lies in its enormous flexibility. By colonial discourse I mean the body of knowledge, modes of representation, strategies of power, law,

---

[1] For a graphic description of the ambitions of imperial powers, see Edward Said's classic, *Orientalism* (London: Routledge & Kegan Paul, 1978).

discipline, and so on, that are employed in the construction and domination of "colonial subjects". *Discourse* is used here in a sense not incompatible with Michel Foucault's notion; as the rest of this chapter will show, however, my use of the term is not exclusively dependent on the Foucauldian framework. Colonial relations of power have often been reproduced in conditions that can only be called neocolonial, and ex-colonials sometimes hunger for the "English book" as avidly as their ancestors.[1]

The postcolonial (subject, nation, context) is therefore still scored through by an absentee colonialism. In economic and political terms, the former colony continues to be dependent on the ex-rulers or the "West". In the cultural sphere (using *cultural* to encompass not only art and literature but other practices of subjectification as well), in spite of widely employed nationalist rhetoric, decolonization is slowest in making an impact. The persistent force of colonial discourse is one we may understand better, and thereby learn to subvert, I argue, by considering

---

1 Although many critics of imperialism describe contemporary Third World societies as "neocolonial" , I shall use the term *postcolonial* in order not to minimize the forces working against colonial and neocolonial domination in these societies. I have in mind especially the Indian context, from which I draw most of my examples. Also, it is more likely that economists rather than cultural theorists would use *neocolonial.* This is not to posit two separate realms of analysis, but merely to suggest that a term appropriate at one level may not be as accurate at another.

translation.

By now it should be apparent that I use the word *translation* not just to indicate an interlingual process but to name an entire problematic. It is a set of questions, perhaps a "field", charged with the force of all the terms used, even by the traditional discourse on translation, to name the problem, to translate translation. *Translatio* (Latin) and *metapherein* (Greek) at once suggest movement, disruption, displacement. So does *Ubersetzung* (German). The French *traducteur* exists between *interprete* and *truchement*, an indication that we might fashion a translative practice *between* interpretation and reading, carrying a disruptive force much greater than the other two. The thrust of displacement is seen also in other Latin terms such as *transponere, transferre, reddere, vertere*. In my writing, *translation* refers to (a) the problematic of translation that authorizes and is authorized by certain classical notions of representation and reality; and (b) the problematic opened up by the poststructuralist critique of the earlier one, and that makes translation always the "more", or the *supplement*, in Derrida's sense.[1] The double meaning of *supplement* — as

---

[1] In *Positions* (trans. Alan Bass [Chicago: University of Chicago Press, 1981]), Derrida defines *supplement* as an "undecidable", something that cannot any longer "be included within philosophical (binary) opposition", but that resists and disorganizes philosophical binaries "*without* ever constituting a third term . . . ; the *supplement* is neither a plus nor a minus, neither an outside nor the complement of an inside, neither accident nor essence." (p.43).

221

providing both what is missing as well as something "extra"—is glossed by Derrida thus: "The *overabundance* of the signifier, its *supplementary* character, is ... the result of a finitude, that is to say, the result of a lack which must be *supplemented*."[1] Where necessary, however, I shall specify narrower uses of *translation*.

My study of translation does not make any claim to solve the dilemmas of translators. It does not propose yet another way of theorizing translation to enable a more foolproof "method" of "narrowing the gap" between cultures; it seeks rather to think through this gap, this difference, to explore the positioning of the obsessions and desires of translation, and thus to describe the economies within which the sign of translation circulates. My concern is to probe the absence, lack, or repression of an awareness of asymmetry and historicity in several kinds of writing on translation. Although Euro-American literary modernists such as Ezra Pound, Gertrude Stein and Samuel Beckett persistently foregrounded the question of translation, I have not discussed their work, since it has, in any case, been extensively dealt with by mainstream literary critics, and since the focus of my interrogation is not poetics but the discourses of what is today called "theory".

The postcolonial distrust of the liberal-humanist rhetoric

---

[1] Derrida, "Structure, Sign, and Play in the Discourse of the Human Sciences", in *Writing and Difference*, trans. Alan Bass (Chicago: University of Chicago Press, 1978), p.290.

of progress and of universalizing master narratives has obvious affinities with poststructuralism.[1] Derrida's critique of representation, for example, allows us to question the notion of re-presentation and therefore the very notion of an origin or an original that needs to be re-presented. Derrida would argue that the "origin" is itself dispersed, its "identity" undecidable. A representation thus does not re-present an "original"; rather, it re-presents that which is always already represented. The notion can be employed to undo hegemonic "representations" of "the Hindus", like, for example, those put forward by G. W. F. Hegel and James Mill.[2]

Another aspect of poststructuralism that is significant for a rethinking of translation is its critique of historicism, which shows the genetic (searching for an origin) and teleological (positing a certain end) nature of traditional historiography. As I have already suggested, of immediate relevance to our concern with colonial practices of subjectification is the fact that "historicism" really presents as *natural* that which is *historical* (and therefore neither inevitable nor unchangeable). A critique of historicism might show

---

[1] In fact, I use even the terms *post-colonial* and *Third World* with some hesitation, since they too can be made to serve a totalizing narrative that disregards heterogeneity.

[2] Hegel, *The Philosophy of History* (1837), trans. J. Sibree (New York: P. F. Collier, n.d.), pp.203—35, cited henceforth as *PH*; and Mill, *A History of British India* (1817; New Delhi: Associated Publishing House, 1972), cited henceforth as *HBI*.

us a way of deconstructing the "pusillanimous" and "deceitful" Hindus of Mill and Hegel. My concern here is not, of course, with the alleged misrepresentation of the "Hindus". Rather, I am trying to question the withholding of reciprocity and the essentializing of "difference" (what Johannes Fabian calls a denial of coevalness) that permits a stereotypical construction of the other. As Homi Bhabha puts it: "The stereotype is not a simplification because it is a false representation of a given reality. It is a simplification because it is an arrested, fixated form of representation that, in denying the play of difference (that the negation through the Other permits), constitutes a problem for the *representation* of the subject in significations of psychic and social relations." [1]

The "native boys" about whom Charles Trevelyan, an ardent supporter of English education for Indians, wrote in 1838, are "interpellated" or constituted as subjects by the discourses of colonialism. Trevelyan shows, with some pride, how young Indians, without any external compulsion, beg for "English". [2]

---

1 Bhabha, "The Other Question", *Screen* 24, no. 6 (November-December 1983): 27.

2 Under colonial rule, "the *individual is interpellated as a (free) subject in order that he shall submit freely to the commandments of the Subject, i.e. in order that he shall (freely) accept his subjection*," i.e. in order that he shall make the gestures and actions of his subjection "all by himself." (Louis Althusser, "Ideology and Ideological State Apparatuses", in *Lenin and Philosophy, and Other Essays*, trans. Ben Brewster [New York: Monthly Review Press, 1971], p.182; emphasis in original). Interpellation is a term used by Althusser to describe the "constitution" of subjects in language by ideology.

"Free acceptance" of subjection is ensured, in part, by the production of hegemonic texts about the civilization of the colonized by philosophers like Hegel, historians like Mill, Orientalists like Sir William Jones.[1] The "scholarly" discourses, of which literary translation is conceptually emblematic, help maintain the dominance of the colonial rule that endorses them through the interpellation of its "subjects." The colonial subject is constituted through a process of "othering" that involves a teleological notion of history, which views the knowledge and ways of life in the colony as distorted or immature versions of what can be found in "normal" or Western society.[2] Hence the knowledge of the Western orientalist appropriates "the power to represent the Oriental, to translate and explain his (and her) thoughts and acts not only to Europeans and Americans but also to the Orientals themselves."[3]

---

[1] I do not mean to lump together Hegel's idealism, Mill's utilitarianism, and Jones's humanism-romanticism. Their texts are, however, based on remarkably similar premises about India and the Hindus. For a discussion of how these premises led eventually to the introduction of English education in India, see my "Translation, Colonialism and the Rise of English", *Economic and Political Weekly* 25, no. 15 (1990): 773—79. I am grateful to Rajeswari Sunder Rajan for her perceptive criticism of my attempt to relate translation to the beginnings of "English" in India.

[2] Ronald Inden, "Orientalist Constructions of India", *Modem Asian Studies* 20, no. 3 (1986): 401—46.

[3] Ibid., p.408.

Translation as Interpellation

That translation became part of the colonial discourse of Orientalism is obvious from late eighteenth century British efforts to obtain information about the people ruled by the merchants of the East India Company. A. Maconochie, a scholar connected with the University of Edinburgh, urged the British sovereign (in 1783 and again in 1788) to take steps "as may be necessary for discovering, collecting and translating whatever is extant of the ancient works of the Hindoos".[1] Although Maconochie hoped that by these translations European astronomy, "antiquities" and other sciences would be advanced, it became clear in the projects of William Jones—who arrived in India in 1783 to take his place on the bench of the Supreme Court in Calcutta—that translation would serve "to domesticate the Orient and thereby turn it into a province of European learning."[2]

As translator and scholar, Jones was responsible for the most influential introduction of a textualized India to Europe. Within three months of his arrival, the Asiatic Society held its first meeting with Jones as president and Warren Hastings, the governor-general, as patron. It was primarily through the efforts

---

[1] Quoted in Dharampal, *The Beautiful Tree: Indigenous Indian Education in the Eighteenth Century* (New Delhi: Biblia Impex, 1983), p.9.

[2] Said, *Orientalism*, p.78.

of the members of the Asiatic Society, themselves administrators and officials of the East India Company's Indian Government, that translation would help "gather in" and "rope off" the Orient.[1]

In a letter, Jones, whose Persian translations and grammar of Persian had already made him famous as an Orientalist before he came to India, declared that his ambition was "to know *India* better than any other European ever knew it".[2] His translations are said to have been read by almost everyone in the West who was literate in the nineteenth century.[3] His works were carefully studied by the writers of the age, especially the Germans—Goethe, Herder, and others. When Jones's new writings reached Europe, the shorter pieces were eagerly picked up and reprinted immediately by different periodicals. His translation of Kalidasa's *Sakuntala* went through successive reprints; Georg Forster's famous German translation of the translation came out in 1791, after which the play was translated into other European languages as well. As a twentieth-century scholar puts it, "It is not an exaggeration to say that he altered our [i.e. Europe's] whole conception of the Eastern world. If we were compiling a thesis on the influence of Jones we

---

[1] Said, *Orientalism*, p.78.

[2] Letter to Lord Althorp, 2nd Earl Spencer, August 17, 1787, in *The Letters of Sir William Jones*, ed. Garland Cannon (London: Oxford University Press, 1970), 2: 751; emphasis in original. Hereafter abbreviated as *LWJ*.

[3] A. J. Arberry, *Oriental Essays: Portraits of Seven Scholars* (London: George Allen & Unwin, 1960), p.82.

could collect most of our material from footnotes, ranging from Gibbon to Tennyson."[1] Evidence for Jones's lasting impact on generations of scholars writing about India can be found even in the preface of the 1984 Indian edition of his discourses and essays, where the editor, Moni Bagchee, indicates that Indians should "try to preserve accurately and interpret the national heritage by treading the path chalked out by Sir William Jones."[2]

My main concern in examining the texts of Jones is not necessarily to compare his translation of *Sakuntala* or Manu's *Dharmasdstra* with the so-called originals. Rather, what I propose to do is to examine the "outwork" of Jones's translations—the prefaces, the annual discourses to the Asiatic Society, his charges to the Grand Jury at Calcutta, his letters, and his "Oriental" poems—to show how he contributes to a historicist, teleological model of civilization that, coupled with a notion of translation presupposing transparency of representation, helps construct a powerful version of the "Hindu" that later writers of different philosophical and political persuasions incorporated into their texts in an almost seamless fashion.

The most significant nodes of Jones's work are (a) the need for translation by the European, since the natives are unreliable

---

[1] R-M. Hewitt, quoted by ibid., p.76.

[2] Bagchee, foreword to Jones's *Discourses and Essays* (New Delhi: People's Publishing House, 1984), p.xvi.

interpreters of their own laws and culture; (b) the desire to be a lawgiver, to give the Indians their "own" laws; and (c) the desire to "purify" Indian culture and speak on its behalf. The interconnections between these obsessions are extremely complicated. They can be seen, however, as feeding into a larger discourse of improvement and education that interpellates the colonial subject.

In Jones's construction of the "Hindus, " they appear as a submissive, indolent nation unable to appreciate the fruits of freedom, desirous of being ruled by an absolute power, and sunk deeply in the mythology of an ancient religion. In a letter, he points out that the Hindus are "incapable of civil liberty, " for "few of them have an idea of it, and those, who have, do not wish it" *(UN*, p.712). Jones, a good eighteenth-century liberal, deplores the "evil" but recognizes the "necessity" of the Hindus' being "ruled by an absolute power." His "pain" is "much alleviated" by the fact that the natives are much "happier" under the British than under their former rulers. In another letter, Jones bids the Americans, whom he admired, not to be "like the deluded, besotted Indians, among whom I live, who would receive Liberty as a curse instead of a blessing, if it were possible to give it them, and would reject, as a vase of poison, that, which, if they could taste and digest it, would be the water of life" (p.847).

Jones's disgust is continually mitigated by the necessity of British rule and the "impossibility" of giving liberty to the Indians.

He brings up repeatedly the idea of "Orientals" being accustomed to a despotic rule. In his tenth annual discourse to the Asiatic Society, he says that a reader of "history" "could not but remark the constant effect of despotism in benumbing and debasing all those faculties which distinguish men from the herd that grazes; and to that cause he would impute the decided inferiority of most Asiatic nations, ancient and modern".[1] The idea of the "submissive" Indians, their inability to be free, and the native laws that *do not permit* the question of liberty to be raised are thus brought together in the concept of Asian despotism. Such a despotic rule, continued by the British, can only fill the coffers of the East India Company: "In these Indian territories, which providence has thrown into the arms of Britain for their protection and welfare, the religion, manners, and laws of the natives preclude even the idea of political freedom; but … our country derives essential benefit from the diligence of a placid and submissive people" (OAH, pp.99—100).

The glorious past of India, according to Jones, is shrouded in superstition, "marked and bedecked in the fantastic robes of mythology and metaphor" (OAH, p.100), but the now "degenerate" and "abased" Hindus were once "eminent in various knowledge".[2]

---

[1] "On Asiatic History, Civil and Natural, " in *Discourses and Essays*, p.99. Cited hereafter as OAH.

[2] "Third Anniversary Discourse, " in *Discourses and Essays*, pp.7—8. Abbreviated in my text as TAD.

This notion of an Indian Golden Age seems to contradict Jones's insistence on the unchanging nature of Hindu society: "By *Indian* I mean that whole extent of the country in which the primitive religion and languages of the *hindus* prevail at this day with more or less of their ancient purity" (TAD, p.6). He appears to avoid the contradiction, however, by distinguishing, although tenuously, the "religion and languages", which have not changed, from "arts", "government" and "knowledge, " which have become debased (pp.7—8). Jones's distinction seems to sustain the paradoxical movement of colonial discourse in simultaneously "historicizing" (things have *become* debased) as well as "naturalizing" (things have remained unchanged) the degradation of the natives. We shall see the same movement in the historian James Mill, although he dismisses Jones's notion of a previous Golden Age and posits instead an unchanging state of barbarism.

The presentation of the Indians as "naturally" effeminate as well as deceitful often goes hand in hand in Jones's work. In an essay on Oriental poetry, he describes the Persians as characterized by "that *softness*, and *love of pleasure*, that *indolence*, and *effeminacy*, which have made them an easy prey to all the western and northern swarms."[1] Persian poetry is said to greatly

---

[1] Jones, *Translations from Oriental Languages* (Delhi: Pravesh Publications, n.d.), 1: 348. Cited henceforth as *TOL*. The feminization of the "native" is a fascinating trope in colonial discourse but will not be discussed further at this time.

influence the Indians, who are "soft and voluptuous, but artful and insincere".[1] Jones's obsession with the insincerity and unreliability of the natives is a trope that appears in his work — usually in relation to translation — as early as the 1777 *Grammar of the Persian Language*, a copy of which was sent by Samuel Johnson to Warren Hastings. In his preface to the *Grammar*, Jones stresses the need for East India Company officials to learn the languages of Asia. Speaking of the increasing interest in Persian (used as a court language in India), he puts it down to the frustration of the British administrators at receiving letters they could not read: "It was found highly dangerous, " says Jones, "to employ the natives as interpreters, upon whose fidelity they could not depend."[2]

As a Supreme Court judge in India, Jones took on, as one of his most important projects, the task of translating the ancient text of Hindu law, Manu's *Dharmasastra*. In fact, he began to learn Sanskrit primarily so that he could verify the interpretations of Hindu law given by his pandits. In a letter, he wrote of the difficulty of checking and controlling native interpreters of several codes, saying: "Pure Integrity is hardly to be found among the

---

[1] *TOL*, 2: 358.

[2] Jones, preface to *A Grammar of the Persian Language* (1771; 8th ed., London: W. Nicol, 1823), p.vii. The recurring emphasis on *infidelity* suggests the existence of a long, if repressed, tradition of resistance on the part of the colonized. I hope to explore this notion elsewhere.

Pandits [Hindu learned men] and Maulavis [Muslim learned men], few of whom give opinions without a culpable bias" *(LWJ,* p.720). Before embarking on his study of Sanskrit, Jones wrote to Charles Wilkins, who had already translated a third of the *Dharmasastra*: "It is of the utmost importance, that the stream of Hindu law should be pure; for we are entirely at the devotion of the native lawyers, through our ignorance of Shanscrit [sic]" (p.666). Interestingly enough, the famous Orientalist attempt to reveal the former greatness of India often manifests itself as the British or European task of translating and thereby *purifying* the debased native texts. This Romantic Orientalist project slides almost imperceptibly into the Utilitarian Victorian enterprise of "improving" the natives through English education.[1]

Even before coming to India, Jones had formulated a solution

---

1 For a discussion of the shared assumptions of "Orientalists" and "Anglicists" with regard to the practice of *sati*, or widow-burning, see Lata Mani, "Contentious Traditions: The Debate on SATI in Colonial India, " *Cultural Critique* (Fall 1987): 119—56. Viswanathan, "Beginnings of English Literary Study" , suggests that the move to anglicize education for Indians actually draws on the "discoveries" of Orientalism. See also Eric Stokes, *The English Utilitarians and India* (1959; reprint, Delhi: Oxford University Press, 1989) for a finely differentiated comparison of James Mill's attitudes with Thomas Macaulay's. Stokes argues that Mill was no Anglicist, since he did not think English education fulfilled the criterion of "utility, " and since he did not in any case believe in the efficacy of formal education. However, I am concerned here with the larger utilitarian discourse on education that informed the changes in British educational policy in India.

for the problem of the translation of Indian law. Writing to Lord Cornwallis in 1788, he mentions once again the deceiving native lawyers and the unreliability of their opinions. "The obvious remedy for this evil, " he writes, "had occurred to me before I left England" *(LWJ,* p.795). This obvious remedy is, of course, the substitution of British translators for Indian ones. Jones, like his patron Warren Hastings, was a staunch advocate of the idea that Indians should be ruled by their own laws. However, since the "deluded", "besotted" Indians thought of liberty as a curse rather than a blessing, since they certainly could not rule themselves or administer their own laws, these laws had first to be taken away from them and "translated" before they could benefit from them. Another manifestation of the natives' insincerity was what Jones called "the frequency of perjury".[1] The "oath of a low native" had hardly any value at all, for everyone committed perjury "with as little remorse as if it were a proof of ingenuity, or even a merit".[2] Jones hoped to make this perjury "inexpiable" by settling once and for all—in another act of translation—the method of taking "evidence" from Indians (p.682), making them punishable by their own (translated) laws.

It is clear that Jones saw the compilation and translation of

---

[1] Jones, "Charge to the Grand Jury, June 10, 1787, " in *Works*, vol. 7 (1799; reprint, Delhi: Agam Prakashan, 1979).

[2] Ibid., 7: 286.

Manu as "the fruit of [his] Indian Studies, " for he hoped it would become "the standard of justice to eight millions of innocent and useful men" in a kingdom that Fortune threw into Britain's lap while she was asleep (*LWJ*, p.813). The discourse of law functions here in such a way as to make invisible the extensive violence of the colonial encounter. The translated laws would discipline and regulate the lives of "many millions of Hindu subjects, whose well-directed industry would add largely to the wealth of Britain" (p.927). For, according to the translator, "those laws are actually revered, as the word of the Most High, by nations of great importance to the political and commercial interests of Europe."[1] Jones's translation went through four editions and several reprints, the last published in Madras in 1880. Although in the later years of Company rule and under the direct rule of the British Crown Indian law was ostensibly formulated according to Western models, the presence to this day of separate civil codes for different religions suggests that the laws actually derive from Orientalist constructions and translations of "Hindu" and "Muslim" scriptures.

Apart from the fact that giving the Indians their own laws would lead in Jones's logic to greater efficiency and therefore to greater profit for England, there is perhaps also another reason

---

[1] Jones, preface to *Institutes of Hindu Law*, in *Works*, 7: 89.

for employing Indian law. As Jones had pointed out in his tenth anniversary discourse, the "laws of the natives preclude even the idea of political freedom" (*OAH*, p.100). This idea, seen as a reliable (because Western) interpretation of the "original" text, begins to circulate among various styles of discourse, having been set in motion by a concept of translation endorsing, as well as endorsed by, the "transparency" of representation. This kind of deployment of translation, I argue, colludes with or enables the construction of a teleological and hierarchical model of cultures that places Europe at the pinnacle of civilization, and thus also provides a position for the colonized.

As I suggested earlier, William Jones's desire to purify Hindu law, art and philosophy is another version of the British discourse of improvement. Jones, who wished to recover for Indians the glories of their own civilization, describes his task in "A Hymn to Surya" (1786), one of his series of "Indian" hymns, immensely popular in Europe, structured by the figures of the lost Golden Age, the debased and ignorant present, and the translator from a remote land:

And, if they [the gods] ask, "What mortal pours the strain?"
Say: from the bosom of yon silver isle,
"Where skies more softly smile,
"He came; and, lisping our celestial tongue,
"Though not from Brahma sprung,

"Draws Orient knowledge from its fountains pure,

"Through caves obstructed long, and paths too long obscure."[1]

In some poems, like "A Hymn to Ganga" (1785—86), Jones shifts the first-person pronoun away from himself to create a subject-position for the colonized, making the "Hindu" speak in favour of the British, who "preserve our laws, and bid our terror cease" (*TOL*, 2: 333; emphasis mine). Here the discourse of law seems to foreground violence, but only to place it in a pre-colonial time, or, in other words, to suggest that the coming of the British led to the proper implementation of the Indians' own laws and the end of "despotic" violence and "terror."

Two main kinds of translators of Indian literature existed in the late eighteenth and early nineteenth centuries: administrators like William Jones and Christian missionaries like the Serampore Baptists William Carey and William Ward. The latter were among the first to translate Indian religious texts into European languages. Often these were works they had themselves textualized, by preparing "standard versions" based on classical Western notions of unity and coherence. On the evidence of these authoritative translations, missionaries berated Hindus for not

---

[1] TOL, 2: 286; punctuation original.

being true practitioners of Indian religion.[1] Their only salvation, the missionaries would then claim, lay in conversion to the more evolved religion of the West. The missionaries' theology arises from a historicist model that sets up a series of oppositions between traditional and modern, undeveloped and developed. This kind of attempt to impose linear historical narratives on different civilizations obviously legitimizes and extends colonial domination.

William Ward's preface to his three-volume *A View of the History, Literature, and Mythology of the Hindoos*[2] is instructive for the virulence with which it attacks the depravity and immorality of the natives. Their religion, manners, customs and institutions are shown to be characterized, like those of other pagans, by "impurity" and "cruelty", which appear in their most "disgusting" and "horrible" manifestations among the "Hindoos" (*VHL*, p.xxxvii). The author claims, in his obsessive references to "native" sexuality, to have witnessed innumerable scenes of "impurity",

---

[1] For a discussion of the textualization of Indian religion in the context of widow-burning, see Lata Mani, "The Production of an Official Discourse on SATI in Early Nineteenth-Century Bengal, " in *Europe and Its Others*, ed. Francis Barker et al. (Colchester: University of Essex Press, 1985), 1: 107—27.

[2] Ward, *A View of the History, Literature, and Mythology of the Hindoos: Including a Minute Description of their Manners and Customs, and Translations from their Principal Works*, 2nd ed. (London: Kingsbury, Parbury & Allen, 1822). Cited henceforth as *VHL*.

for the Hindu institutions are "hotbeds of impurity", and the very services in the temples present "temptations to impurity" (pp.xxxvi—vii). Unlike William Jones, however, Ward does not see the present state of the Hindus as a falling away from a former Golden Age. Instead, like James Mill, who quotes him approvingly and often, Ward sees the Hindus as corrupt by nature, lacking the means of education and improvement. He suggests that the "mental and moral improvement" of the Hindus is the "high destiny" of the British nation. Once she was made "enlightened and civilized", India, even if she became independent, would "contribute more to the real prosperity of Britain" by "consuming her manufactures to a vast extent". Ward remarks on the "extraordinary fact" that the British goods purchased annually by India "are not sufficient to freight a single vessel from our ports":

> *But let Hindoos then receive that higher civilization she needs, that cultivation of which she is so capable; let European literature be transfused into all her languages, and then the ocean, from the ports of Britain to India, will be covered with our merchant vessels; and from the centre of India moral culture and science will be extended all over Asia, to the Burman empire and Siam, to China, with all her millions, to Persia, and even to Arabia. (VHL, p.liii)*

The entire "Eastern hemisphere" would then become Christian. In the age of the expansion of capitalism, interpretation and translation help create a market for European merchandise. As the missionary texts help us understand, translation comes into being overdetermined by religious, racial, sexual and economic discourses. It is overdetermined not only because multiple forces act on it, but because it gives rise to multiple practices. The strategies of containment initiated by translation are therefore deployed across a range of discourses, allowing us to name translation as a significant technology of colonial domination.

The righteous disgust of Ward's writing is echoed uncannily by the "secular" historiography of James Mill, who constructs a version of "Hindoo nature" from the translations of Ward, Jones, Charles Wilkins, Nathaniel Halhed, Henry Colebrooke and others. Mill's *History of British India*, published in three volumes in 1817, until quite recently served as a model for histories of India.[1] The Indian people, both Hindus and Muslims, were for Mill characterized by their insincerity, mendacity, perfidy and venality. "The Hindu, like the eunuch, " he said, "excels in the qualities of a slave." Like the Chinese, the Hindus were "dissembling, treacherous, mendacious, to an excess which surpasses even the

---

[1] Mill's writings are still used in Indian history classes, often with the barest mention of his racism and with sad approval of the wisdom of his characterizations.

usual measure of uncultivated society." They were also cowardly, unfeeling, conceited and physically unclean (*HBI*, p.486).[1] In defining the Indian, Mill sought to give by contrast a proper picture of the "superior" European civilization. As Edward Said has pointed out, "the Orient has helped to define Europe (or the West) as its contrasting image, idea, personality, experience."[2]

Mill declares that to "ascertain the true state of the Hindus in the scale of civilization" is of the greatest practical importance for the British. The Hindus need to be understood before they can be properly ruled, and to consider them as highly civilized would be a grave mistake (*HBI*, p.456). In order to prove his thesis, Mill sets out to discredit the Orientalists who spoke of a Golden Age, often by a skillful citation of their own works. Mill's strategy is, first, to demolish the idea that India ever had a history, and then, to suggest that the state of the Hindus bears comparison with primitive societies, including that belonging to Britain's own past, that show evidence of the childhood of humankind. The maturity-immaturity, adulthood-childhood opposition feeds right into the discourse of improvement and education perpetuated by the colonial context.

---

[1] The German Indologist Max Muller declared that Mill's History "was responsible for some of the greatest misfortunes that had happened to India" (J. P. Guha's prefatory note to the 1972 reprint of *HBI*, p.xii).

[2] Said, *Orientalism*, pp.1—2.

Framing Mill's *History* is his comment that "rude nations seem to derive a peculiar gratification from pretensions to a remote antiquity. As a boastful and turgid vanity distinguishes remarkably the oriental nations they have in most instances carried their claims extravagantly high" (*HBI*, p.24). Throughout the book, Mill again and again uses the adjectives wild, barbaric, savage and rude in connection with the "Hindus", thus forming by sheer force of repetition a counterdiscourse to the Orientalist hypothesis of an ancient civilization.

The same descriptions provided by the Orientalists as evidence of the high civilization of the Hindus are declared by Mill to be "fallacious proof". The "feminine softness" and gentleness of the Hindus, for example, was taken to be the mark of a civilized community. Mill, on the other hand, suggests that the beginnings of civilization are compatible with "great violence" as well as "great gentleness" of manners. As in the "savages" of North America and the islanders of the South Seas, mildness and the "rudest condition of human life" often go together (*HBI*, pp.287—88). As for the austerities prescribed by Hinduism, they tend to coexist with the encouragement of the "loosest morality" in the religion of a rude people (p.205). Where an Orientalist might remark on the rough tools but neat and capable execution of tasks by the Hindu, Mill comments that "a dexterity in the use of its own imperfect tools is a common attribute of a rude society" (p.335).

Should anyone suggest that the Hindus possess beautiful poetry, Mill comes back with the remark that poetry points to the first stage of human literature, where the literature of the Hindus seems to have remained (p.365).

Drawing on what he calls his knowledge of human nature, which appears in a variety of guises but displays an "astonishing uniformity" with regard to the different stages of society (*HBI*, p.107), Mill further consolidates his teleological model of world history. The trial by ordeal prescribed by Hindu law, for example, was common "in the institutions of our barbaric ancestors" (p.108). Mill seems to pick up the theories of, say, William Jones, about the Indo-Aryan origins of European civilization and employ them in a way that actually clarifies their ideological underpinnings for us. Both the Orientalist and the Utilitarian discourses end up producing the same historicist model and constructing the colonial subject in a very similar fashion. Mill actually draws directly on Jones's view of Hindu law when he says that the account of creation in Manu is "all vagueness and darkness, incoherence, inconsistency and confusion" (p.163) and the religious ideas of the Hindus are also "loose, vague, wavering, obscure, and inconsistent". The "wild mythology" and "chain of unmeaning panegyric which distinguishes the religion of ignorant men" (p.182) is characteristic of the rude mind's propensity to create that which is extravagant, "fantastic and senseless" (p.163). Compare this with Jones's description in the preface to his translation of Manu of the system created by "description and priestcraft", "filled with strange conceits in metaphysicks and natural philosophy, with idle superstitions.... it abounds with minute and childish formalities, with ceremonies generally absurd and often ridiculous" (p.88).

Nearly half of the twenty-eight footnotes in chapter 1 of Mill's *History* mention William Jones, while the footnotes of chapter 2 are divided primarily between Halhed's translation of the *Code of Gentoo Laws*[1] and Jones's translation of Manu's *Institutes*. Quoting judiciously from these two texts (as well as from Colebrooke's *Digest of Hindu Law on Contracts and Successions*),[2] Mill manages to establish that the Hindu laws are both absurd and unjust. He quotes from Halhed's preface to the *Code of Gentoo Laws* to the effect that Hindu morals are as gross as Hindu laws, the latter grossness being a result of the former (*HBI*, p.125 n.90). From Charles Wilkins's translation of the *Hitopadesa* (a collection of fables),[3] Mill obtains a picture of the

---

[1] Nathaniel Halhed, *Code of Gentoo Laws, or, Ordinations of the Pundits, from a Persian Language translation made from the original writings in the Shanscrit Language* (London: n.p., 1777).

[2] Henry Colebrooke and Jagannatha Tarakapanchanana, *Digest of Hindu Law*, 3d ed. (Madras: Higginbotham, 1864).

[3] See the collated version by Henry Colebrooke, *Hitopadesa* (Serampore: Mission Press, 1804).

"abject", "grovelling" Hindus, whose self-abasement provides him with proof of the despotic Hindu state; and from William Ward, of course, Mill procures "superabundant evidence of the immoral influence of the Hindu religion" and the "deep depravity" produced by it.

Translations of inscriptions on monuments are used selectively by Mill (*HBI*, p.469; p.504 n. 30). Claims of nobility or antiquity are immediately dismissed as wild fabrications, while anything that shows the depravity of the Hindus is considered legitimate evidence. Mill trashes the *Puranas* (mythological tales) as false history, but is willing to accept evidence from the play *Sākuntala* regarding the political arrangements and laws of the age (pp.133, 473). History is dismissed as fiction, but fiction — translated — is admissible as history. Mill embeds in his text several quotations from Captain Wilford's writings (Wilford is also one of Hegel's authorities) in *Asiatic Researches*, saying: "The Hindu system of geography, chronology, and history, are all equally monstrous and absurd" (p.40). The whole stock of Hindu historical knowledge could thus be contained in a few quarto pages of print (p.423). The language is remarkably similar to that Macaulay was to use barely a decade later to denounce Indian education. As the historian Ranajit Guha has pointed out, Mill begins his *History* with a chapter on the ancient history of the Hindus, and then interrupts the text with nearly five hundred pages (or nine chapters) on the "nature" of the Hindus (that is, their religion, customs, manners, etc.).[1] These nine chapters, predominantly in the present tense, perform the function of dehistoricizing the situation of the Hindus, thereby establishing their eternal and unchanging nature, as well as fixing their place in a hierarchy of civilizations. Not only do secular historiography and philosophy of history participate in colonial discourse, Western metaphysics itself (and the "historicism" that is emblematic of it) seems to emerge in a certain age from colonial translation. The concept of representation put into circulation by eighteenth and nineteenth-century translators of non-Western texts grounds, for example, the Hegelian theory of world history.

Whether we acknowledge it or not, whether we know it or not, says Paul de Man, we are all "orthodox Hegelians."[2] De Man's concern is to perform a critique of the kind of traditional historicism that is suggested by Hegel's teleological scheme of the coming to consciousness of Spirit. In India, says Hegel, "Absolute Being is presented.... as in the ecstatic state of a dreaming condition"; and since "the generic principle of Hindoo Nature" is

---

1 Ranajit Guha, "Remarks on Power and Culture in Colonial India" (MS), p.59.

2 De Man, "Sign and Symbol in Hegel's Aesthetics, " *Critical Inquiry* 8, no. 4 (Summer 1982): 761—75. For discussing this and other related points in chapter 1 with me, I am grateful to Sanjay Palshikar.

this "character of Spirit in a state of Dream", the Indian has not attained to "self" or to "consciousness". [1]Because "History" for Hegel refers to the "development of Spirit", and because Indians are not "individuals" capable of action, the "diffusion of Indian culture" is "pre-historical", "a dumb, deedless expansion" (*PH*, p.206) ; hence "it is the necessary fate of Asiatic Empires to be subjected to Europeans" (p.207).

While Hegel is willing to grant that Indian literature depicts its people as mild, tender and sentimental, he emphasizes that these qualities often go hand in hand with absolute lack of "freedom of soul" and "consciousness of individual right" (*PH*, p.225). The idea of the "pusillanimous", "effeminate" Hindus with their despotic Asian rulers, and their inevitable conquest by the West, is part of a Hegelian philosophy of history that not only interpellates colonial subjects but is authorized by colonial translations. Hegel's condemnation of the Hindu as cunning and deceitful, habituated to "cheating, stealing, robbing, murdering", echoes the writings of James Mill, and the translations of Colebrooke, Wilkins, and other Orientalists.

Mill's model of history participates, as I have pointed out, in the British discourse of improvement that found such enthusiastic adherents in Macaulay and Trevelyan. The ideologists of "utility"

---

1 *PH*, pp.204—25.

and "efficiency" used the opposition between traditional and modern, created in part by Orientalist projects of translation, to make feasible the dismissal of indigenous education and the introduction of Western education.

As examiner or chief executive officer of the East India Company in London from 1830 on, James Mill influenced a number of modifications in Company policy. His son J. S. Mill wrote in his *Autobiography* that his father's despatches to India, "following his History, did more than had ever been done before to promote the improvement of India, and teach Indian officials to understand their business."[1] When William Bentinck became governor-general in 1828, he acknowledged his indebtedness to and discipleship of James Mill. Although Mill was skeptical about the efficacy of formal education, [2] in his passion for "useful knowledge" he supported Bentinck's attempts to introduce educational reforms. For Bentinck, "the British language" was "the key to all improvements" and "general education" would lead to "the regeneration of India."[3]

The radical or utilitarian discourse was supplemented by the Evangelicals, whose horror of Jacobin atheism spurred

---

[1] J. S. Mill, *Autobiography*, cited in Stokes, *English Utilitarians and India*, p.49.

[2] See Stokes, *English Utilitarians and India*, p.57.

[3] Bentinck, quoted in Percival Spear, *A History of India* (Harmondsworth: Penguin Books, 1970), 2: 126.

them to propagate missionary activity in all parts of the rapidly consolidating British empire. Evangelicals such as William Wilberforce and Charles Grant (members of the Clapham Sect) and their supporters held positions of great power in government, as well as in the East India Company. However, Wilberforce's 1793 motion to allow Christian missionaries into India was defeated in Parliament because of British fears that proselytizing would enrage the natives. It was only with the Charter Act of 1813 that the Evangelicals won a major victory: although the act renewed the Company's charter for operations, it also broke the Company's monopoly by allowing free trade and cleared the way for missionary work in India. Given the Evangelicals' belief in the transformation of human character through education, and their conviction that conversion to Christianity required some amount of learning, their victory with the 1813 Act included the provision of an annual sum of £10, 000 for the promotion of education for the natives.[1]

As early as 1797, however, Charles Grant, a director of the Company and its chairman for many years, presented to the Court of Directors a privately printed treatise in which he advocated English education in India.[2] Entitled *Observations on the State of*

---

1 Stokes, *English Utilitarians and India*, p.30.

2 Grant's treatise was reprinted as a Parliamentary Paper in 1813 and again in 1832.

Society among the Asiatic Subjects of Great Britain, Particularly with Respect to Morals; and on the Means of Improving It, Grant's treatise argued that the "lamentably degenerate and base Hindus", "governed by malevolent and licentious passions" and possessed of only a "feeble sense of moral obligation", were "sunk in misery" owing to their religion. Supporting his allegations with copious quotations from Orientalist and missionary translations of Indian texts, Grant contended that only education in English would free the minds of the Hindus from their priests' tyranny and allow them to develop individual consciences.[1] Anticipating his opponents' argument that English education would teach the Indians to desire English liberty, Grant asserted that "the original design" with which the British had come to India—that is, "the extension of our commerce"—would best be served by the spread of education. In phrases we hear echoed by William Ward and later by Macaulay, Grant points out that British goods cannot be sold in India because the taste of the people has not been "formed to the use of them"; besides, they have not the means to buy them. English education would awaken invention among the Indians; they would initiate "improvements" at home as well as "acquire a relish" for the ingenious manufactures of Europe. For Grant, as for

---

[1] For a discussion of the Clapham's Sect's "interests," see Stokes, *English Utilitarians and India*, pp.30—33.

Macaulay after him, this was "the noblest species of conquest": "Wherever, we may venture to say, our principles and language are introduced, our commerce will follow."[1] In a phase described by Ramakrishna Mukherjee as the period of transition from mercantile capitalism to the hegemony of the British industrial bourgeoisie, Grant's arguments seemed especially appropriate.[2] British commerce would benefit substantially from the coinciding of "duty" and "self-interest."[3]

For years a controversy raged between "Orientalists" and "Anglicists" as to whether the money set aside for education by the act of 1813 was to be used for indigenous education or Western education.[4] Finally, the compulsions of the changing nature of Company rule enabled, during Bentinck's tenure, the Resolution

---

[1] Grant, quoted in Ramakrishna Mukherjee, *The Rise and Fall of the East India Company* (1955; rev. ed., Bombay: Popular Prakashan, 1973), p.421.

[2] Ibid., passim.

[3] See Stokes, *English Utilitarians and India*, p.33.

[4] For an extensive discussion of this debate, see B. K. Boman-Behram, *Educational Controversies of India: The Cultural Conquest of India under British Imperialism* (Bombay: Taraporevala Sons, 1942). Dharampal suggests that the uprooting of indigenous education could have been prompted by the British fear that the cultural and religious content of Indian education would provide grounds for resistance to colonial hegemony (Dharampal, *Beautiful Tree*, p.75). Charles Trevelyan wrote in 1838 that it was unreasonable to expect the British to sponsor indigenous education: "Our bitterest enemies could not desire more than that we should propagate systems of learning which excite the strongest feelings of human nature against ourselves" (Trevelyan, *On the Education of the People of India* [London: Longman, Orme, Brown, Green & Longmans, 1838], p.189).

of March 7, 1835, which declared that the funds provided should "be henceforth employed in imparting to the Native population knowledge of English literature and science through the medium of the English language."[1] Schools and colleges were set up by the British; Persian gave way to English as the official language of the colonial state and the medium of the higher courts of law. Bentinck's "Westernization" of the administrative system went hand in hand, therefore, with a reversal of Cornwallis's exclusionary policies and induction of more and more Indians into the hierarchy, a move enabled by English education. Given this rather obvious "use" of English, the Committee on Public Instruction, of which Macaulay was president, emphasized higher education in English and disregarded large-scale primary schooling.

Macaulay did not think it necessary for the entire Indian

---

[1] *History of India*, 2: 127. Eric Stokes argues that as early as 1813 the East India Company could not justify its trade monopoly. Indian "piece-goods" no longer had a market in Europe, and with the Company becoming a "purely military and administrative power, " it absorbed all available revenue surpluses (Stokes, *English Utilitarians and India*, pp.37—38). What British rule could now do in India was not to extract tribute but to create a new market for British goods. Besides, after the defeat of the Marathas in 1818, the last resistance to the British crumbled, and the main task became one of effectively administering the large territories acquired by the Company (ibid., p.xv). English education would produce not only large numbers of native bureaucrats but also begin to create the taste for European commodities.

populace to learn English: the function of anglicized education was "to form a class who may be interpreters between us (the British) and the millions whom we govern; a class of persons, Indian in blood and colour, but English in taste, in opinions, in morals, and in intellect."[1] A lawgiver like William Jones, Macaulay, who also formulated the Indian Penal Code, spoke of the time when India might become independent, when the British would leave behind an empire that would never decay, because it would be "the imperishable empire of our arts and our morals, our literature and our laws."[2]

Macaulay's brother-in-law, Charles Trevelyan, wrote about how the influence of the indigenous elite would secure the "permanence" of the change wrought by Western education: "Our subjects have set out on a new career of improvement: they are about to have a new character imprinted on them."[3] The agent of this change would be "English literature", which would lead to Indians speaking of great Englishmen with the same enthusiasm as their rulers: "Educated in the same way, interested in the same objects, engaged in the same pursuits with ourselves, they become

---

[1] Macaulay, "Indian Education" (Minute of the 2nd of February, 1835), in *Prose and Poetry*, ed. G. M. Young (Cambridge, Mass.: Harvard University Press, 1967), p.729.

[2] Macaulay, "Speech of 10 July 1833, " in *Prose and Poetry*, p.717.

[3] Trevelyan, *Education of the People of India*, p.181.

more English than Hindus" and look upon the British as their "natural protectors and benefactors", for "the summit of their [the Indians'] ambition is, to resemble us."[1]

In his 1835 minute on Indian education, Macaulay, who was an avid reader of Mill's *History*, claimed he had not found a single Orientalist "who could deny that a single shelf of a good European library was worth the whole native literature of India and Arabia", [2] and Trevelyan agreed that the latter was "worse than useless".[3] The British propagation of English education resulted ultimately in people being compelled and encouraged "to collaborate in the destruction of their instruments of expression".[4]

As Gauri Viswanathan has pointed out, the introduction of English education can be seen as "an embattled response to historical and political pressures: to tensions between the English Parliament and the East India Company, between Parliament and the missionaries, between the East India Company and the native elite classes."[5] Extending her argument, I would like to suggest that the specific resolution of these tensions through the

---

[1] Trevelyan, *Education of the People of India*, pp.189—92.

[2] Macaulay, "Minute, " in *Prose and Poetry*, p.722.

[3] Trevelyan, *Education of the People of India*, p.182.

[4] Pierre Bourdieu, *Ce aue parler veut dire*: *L'Economie des echanges linguistiques* (Paris: Fayard, 1981), cited by John Thompson in *Studies in the Theory of Ideology* (Berkeley and Los Angeles: University of California Press, 1984), P. 45.

[5] Viswanathan, "Beginnings of English Literary Study, " p.24.

introduction of English education was enabled discursively by the colonial practice of translation. European translations of Indian texts prepared for a Western audience provided the "educated" Indian with a whole range of Orientalist images. Even when the anglicized Indian spoke a language other than English, "he" would have preferred, because of the symbolic power conveyed by English, to gain access to his own past through the translations and histories circulating through colonial discourse. English education also familiarized the Indian with ways of seeing, techniques of translation, or modes of representation that came to be accepted as "natural".

The philosopheme of translation grounds a multiplicity of discourses, which feed into, as well as emerge out of, the colonial context. And just as translation is overdetermined, so is the "subject" under colonialism, overdetermined in the sense that it is produced by multiple discourses on multiple sites, and gives rise to a multiplicity of practices. The demand for English education on the part of the colonized is clearly not a simple recognition of "backwardness" or mere political expedience, but a complex need arising from the braiding of a host of historical factors, a need produced and sustained by colonial translation.

The construction of the colonial subject presupposes what Pierre Bourdieu has called "symbolic domination". Symbolic domination, and its violence, effectively reproduce the social order through a combination of recognition and misrecognition (*reconnaissance* and *méconnaissance*) — recognition that the dominant language is legitimate (one thinks again of the use of English in India) and "a misrecognition of the fact that this language... is imposed as dominant. The exercise of symbolic violence is so invisible to social actors precisely because it presupposes the complicity of those who suffer most from its effects."[1] Bourdieu's analysis suggests that the colonized — or even the postcolonial — recolonizes him/herself again and again through her/his participation in "the discursive practices of everyday life", which, rather than any powerful system imposed from above, maintain the asymmetrical relations characteristic of colonialism.

The notion of autocolonization implicit in the story about the "native boys" begging for English books could be explored in greater depth through Antonio Gramsci's concept of hegemony. Gramsci makes a distinction between the state apparatus and "civil society": the first includes the entire coercive mechanism of the state, including army, police, and legislature, while the second includes the school, the family, the church, and the media. The dominant group exercises domination through the state apparatus, with the use of force or coercion, and ensures its hegemony

---

[1] Thompson, *Studies in the Theory of Ideology*, p.58.

through the production of ideology in civil society, where it secures its power through consent.[1]

Colonial society presents a good example of the workings of a hegemonic culture.[2] The discourses of education, theology, historiography, philosophy and literary translation inform the hegemonic apparatuses that belong to the ideological structure of colonial rule. We may turn again to Gramsci's work for a conception of ideology that breaks away from the traditional notion of "false consciousness".[3] Ideology, which for Gramsci is inscribed in practices (for example, colonial practices of

---

[1] For an illuminating discussion of Gramsci's ideas, see Chantal Mouffe, "Hegemony and Ideology in Gramsci," in *Gramsci and Marxist Theory*, ed. Mouffe (London: Routledge & Kegan Paul, 1979).

[2] But see Ranajit Guha's argument in "Dominance without Hegemony and Its Historiography," in *Subaltern Studies VI: Writings on South Asian History and Society*, ed. Guha (Delhi: Oxford University Press, 1989). Guha suggests that domination more appropriately describes colonial society than hegemony, because hegemony implies the consent of all classes, whereas colonial rule had the "sanction" only of the elites. It seems to me that Guha does not sufficiently account for what even Macaulay saw as the filtration effect—that is, the gradual pervading by different forms of colonial rule of all sections of the colonized. This notion, I should admit, however, may not apply to all colonized societies; colonialism may be hegemonic, for example, in Barbados, but not in Jamaica; in Martinique, but not in Guadeloupe, and so on.

[3] Ideology as false consciousness, a classical Marxist notion, suggests a distorted representation of "reality." Gramsci's conception, which stresses the "material nature" of ideology, is more useful in examining the persistence of colonial discourse.

subjectification), produces "subjects" and has therefore a certain materiality.[1] Influential translations (from Sanskrit and Persian into English in the eighteenth century, for example) interpellated colonial subjects, legitimizing or authorizing certain versions of the Oriental, versions that then came to acquire the status of "truths" even in the countries in which the "original" works were produced. The introduction of Western education was facilitated by what Trevelyan calls "seminaries", missionary-run schools sponsored by the government. European missions, which played an important role in easing colonies into the global economy, often ran the entire education system in other colonial societies, such as the Belgian Congo, for example. The systemic collaboration of anthropologists, missionaries and colonial administrators in the non-European world, in being independent of the willing participation of "individuals, " is characteristic of the workings of hegemonic colonial discourse [2]. Missionaries, therefore, functioned as colonial agents in the formation of practices of subjectification, not only in their roles as priests and teachers but also in the capacity of linguists, grammarians and

---

[1] Mouffe, "Hegemony and Ideology, " p.199. Althusser draws on Gramsci's notion of ideology in formulating the theory of interpellation.

[2] I discuss the relationship between anthropologists and colonial rule at greater length in chapter 2. For a discussion of "systemic" collaboration, see Johannes Fabian, *Language and Colonial Power* (Cambridge: Cambridge University Press, 1986).

translators.[1]

The desire of colonial discourse to translate in order to contain (and to contain and control in order to translate, since symbolic domination is as crucial as physical domination) is evidenced in colonial-missionary efforts to compile grammars of "unknown" languages. European missionaries were the first to prepare Western-style dictionaries for most of the Indian languages, participating thereby in the enormous project of collection and codification on which colonial power was based. Administrators and Asiatic Society members like Jones and Halhed published grammars as their first major works of scholarship: Jones's Persian grammar came out in 1777, and Halhed's Bengali grammar, the first one to use Bengali script, in 1778. Halhed complained in the preface to his work about the "unsettled" orthography of Bengali, and the difficulty of applying European principles of grammar to a language that seemed to have lost "its general underlying principles".[2] The establishment of the College of Fort William in Calcutta, closely associated with the Asiatic Society and devoted to the "Oriental" education of East India

---

[1] For a comprehensive description of the convergence of missionary and imperial efforts in Bengal, the first center of British government in India, see David Kopf, *British Orientalism and the Bengal Renaissance* (Berkeley and Los Angeles: University of California Press, 1969).

[2] Halhed, *A Grammar of the Bengali Language* (Hooghly: n.p., 1778), cited in Kopf, *British Orientalism and the Bengal Renaissance*, p.57.

Company employees, provided a major impetus to translators and grammarians. As David Kopf puts it, "By 1805 the college had become a veritable laboratory where Europeans and Asians worked out new transliteration schemes, regularized spoken languages into precise grammatical forms, and compiled dictionaries in languages relatively unknown in Europe."[1] When a fire in 1812 destroyed the printing shop of the Serampore missionaries, one of whom — William Carey — taught in the college, among the manuscripts destroyed was that of a polyglot dictionary "containing words of every known oriental tongue."[2]

The drive to study, to codify and to "know" the Orient employs the classical notions of representation and reality criticized by poststructuralists like Derrida and de Man. Their work offers a related critique of traditional historicism that is of great relevance in a postcolonial context. The critique of historicism may help us formulate a complex notion of historicity, which would include the "effective history" of the text; this phrase encompasses questions such as: who uses/ interprets the text? How is it used, and for what?[3] Both the critique of representation and the critique of historicism empower the postcolonial theorist to undertake an

---

[1] Kopf, *British Orientalism and the Bengal Renaissance*, p.67.

[2] Ibid., p.78.

[3] See the next section of this chapter for my discussion of the notion of historicity/history.

analysis of what Homi Bhabha (following Foucault) has called technologies of colonial power.[1] These critiques also enable the reinscription of the problematic of translation: the deconstruction of colonial texts and their "white mythology" helps us to see how translation brings into being notions of representation and reality that endorse the founding concepts of Western philosophy as well as the discourse of literary criticism.

The Question of "History"

In a recent essay on Fredric Jameson's *The Political Unconscious*, Samuel Weber charges Jameson with using the gesture of "capitalizing History" to address the "challenge of 'post-structuralist' thought".[2] Weber's is one of the latest salvoes in the prolonged skirmishing between the defenders of "poststructuralism" and those (on the right as well as the left) who accuse it of denying "history". The early attacks on deconstruction by M. H. Abrams and others now read like the despairing cries of traditional literary historians intent on preserving their notions of tradition, continuity and historical context against the onslaught

---

[1] Bhabha, "Signs Taken for Wonders: Questions of Ambivalence and Authority under a Tree outside Delhi, May 1817, " *Critical Inquiry* 12, no. 1 (Autumn 1985): 144—65; cited henceforth as SW.

[2] Samuel Weber, "Capitalizing History: The Political Unconscious, " in *Institution and Interpretation* (Minneapolis: University of Minnesota Press, 1987), pp.40—58.

of a violent, disruptive Nietzscheanism.[1] Jameson, however, has consistently attempted to come to terms with structuralist and poststructuralist thought, and his imperative to historicize derives from the "priority" he gives to "a Marxian interpretive framework".[2]

As the poststructuralists (I have in mind Derrida and the American deconstructionists in particular) perceive it, the demand that they address "history" comes increasingly from the "left", especially from those who have "taken on" (the phrase is Geoff Bennington's) deconstruction in more senses than one.[3] With all the quibbling about "history", it is curious that both the poststructuralists and those who maintain an antagonistic, but admiring, stance toward them should have such a monolithic view of what history means. If the former polemicize against history as "phallogocentrism", the latter argue that is an "untranscendable horizon". Neither specify whether the "history" in question refers to a mode of writing history (a certain conception of the past) or to the "past" itself.

---

[1] See, e.g., Abrams, "The Deconstructive Angel, " *Critical Inquiry* 3, no. 3 (Spring 1977): 425—38.

[2] Jameson, *The Political Unconscious* (Ithaca, N.Y.: Cornell University Press, 1981), p.10; cited henceforth as *PU*.

[3] See the recent anthology *Post-Structuralism and the Question of History*, ed. Derek Attridge, Geoff Bennington, and Robert Young (New York: Cambridge University Press, 1987).

My central concern here is not to elaborate on the battle for "history" now being staged in Euro-American theory but to ask a series of questions from a strategically "partial" perspective — that of an emergent postcolonial practice willing to profit from the insights of poststructuralism, while at the same time demanding ways of writing history in order to make sense of how subjectification operates.

Since one of the classic moves of colonial discourse (as, for example, in Orientalism) is to present the colonial subject as unchanging and immutable, historicity — which includes the idea of change — is a notion that needs to be taken seriously. For my purposes, I take historicity to mean — although not unproblematically — effective history (Nietzsche's *wirkliche Historie* or Gadamer's *Wirkungsgeschichte*), or that part of the past that is still operative in the present.[1] The notion of effective history helps us read against the grain Jones's late eighteenth century translations of ancient Sanskrit texts; it also suggests the kinds of questions one might work with in re-translating those texts two hundred years later. The term historicity thus incorporates questions about how the translation/re-translation worked/works, why the text was/is translated, and who did/does the translating.

---

1 Nietzsche, *The Use and Abuse of History*, trans. Adrian Collins (Indianapolis: Bobbs-Merrill, 1957), 2d ed.; Hans-Georg Gadamer, *Truth and Method*, trans. Garrett Barden and John Cumming (1975; reprint, New York: Crossroad, 1985).

I use the word historicity to avoid invoking History with a capital H, my concern being with "local" practices (or micropractices as Foucault calls them) of translation that require no overarching theory to contain them. As Foucault declares, "effective history affirms knowledge as perspective"; it may be seen as a radical kind of "presentism", which we may be able to work from.[1] I indicated earlier that postcolonials have good reason to be suspicious of teleological historicism, which Derrida has rightly characterized as a manifestation of Western metaphysics.[2] But since the facts of "history" are inescapable for the postcolonial, since attention to history is in a sense demanded by the postcolonial situation, postcolonial theory has to formulate a narrativizing strategy in addition to a deconstructive one. The use of historicity/effective history may help us sidestep the metaphysics of linearity.

We may also find useful Louis Althusser's critique of historicism, which leads him, in Jameson's words, to formulate the notion that "history is a process without a telos or a subject", "a repudiation of... master narratives and their twin categories

---

[1] Foucault, "Nietzsche, Genealogy, History, " in *Language, Counter-Memory, Practice*, ed. Donald Bouchard (Ithaca, N.Y.: Cornell University Press, 1977), p.156.

[2] Derrida uses this term to refer to the edifice of Western philosophy, a system of thought built on a first principle or foundation that remains unquestioned. He sees his task as one of "deconstructing" this body of assumptions that underwrites the whole of Western culture.

of narrative closure (telos) and of character (subject of history)" (*PU*, p.29). The latter assumption may be seen as an attack on the individualist idea of the subject, which Althusser's own notion of subject deconstructs. Jameson further suggests that history for Althusser is an "absent cause", that it is like Jacques Lacan's "Real", "inaccessible to us except in textual form" (*PU*, p.82). The notion that history can be "apprehended only through its effects" (p.102) is directly relevant to a theorist seeking, like Foucault's genealogist, to understand the "play of dominations" and "systems of subjection" (*LCP*, p.148). The genealogist, says Foucault, "needs history to dispel the chimeras of the origin" (*LCP*, p.144). A theory emerging from the postcolonial context needs to ally itself with the critique of origin and telos as it tries to practice a way of writing history that is anti-essentialist. In this project, another source of support is the work of Walter Benjamin, who sees the historian (or we may even say the translator) seizing the past image that comes into a constellation with the present. The discontinuity of the past we construct may provoke us to discuss the "why" of a translation and how it manifests effective history [1]. Perhaps postcolonial theory can show that we need to translate (that is, disturb or displace) history rather than to interpret it (hermeneutically) or

---

1 For an extended discussion of Benjamin's notions of translation and history, see chapters 4 and 5.

"read" it (in a textualizing move).

The most profound insight Derrida's work has afforded topostcolonials is the notion that origin is always already heterogeneous, that it is not some pure, unified source of meaning or history. It would be a mistake for historiographers (literary or otherwise) to challenge colonial representations as "false" or "inadequate"; the striving for adequacy based on such a challenge would trap postcolonial writing in a metaphysics of presence, in what Derrida has called "the generative question" of the age, the question of the value of representation.[1]

In "Speech and Phenomena, " his essay on Husserl, Derrida says:

When in fact I effectively use words.... I must from the outset operate (within) a structure of repetition whose basic element can only be representative. A sign is never an event, if by event we mean an irreplaceable and irreversible

---

[1] Derrida, "Sending: On Representation," trans. Peter and Mary Ann Caws, *Social Research* 49, no. 2 (Summer 1982): 294-326. Another problem with seeing colonial representations as "false" is that the colonial "reality" can be said to be produced by the colonizer. The representation of a "cheating Hindoo," for example, implies the production of a reality in which "cheating" can be a form of resistance to colonial domination. Instead of challenging the colonial representation as false, perhaps we should look at its effects, arguing that different representations can produce other, more enabling or empowering effects.

empirical particular. A sign which would take place but "once" would not be a sign.... Since this representative structure is signification itself, I cannot enter into an "effective" discourse without being from the start involved in unlimited representation.[1]

What Derrida is claiming is that there is no primordial "presence" that is then re-presented. The "re-" does not befall the original. It is the concept of representation that suppresses the difference that is already there in the so-called origin and grounds the whole of Western metaphysics. This is a metaphysics of presence, of the "absolute proximity of self-identity" (*SP*, p.99) and of presence to oneself. Perhaps the predominant characteristic of the metaphysics of presence is the privileging of voice and speech over "writing" (*écriture*) that Derrida calls phonocentrism or logocentrism, wherein writing, as a derived form, the copy of a copy, comes to signify a distant, lost or broken origin, a notion Derrida contests by revealing that any notion of the simple, the centre or the primordial is always already characterized by an irreducible or untranscendable heterogeneity.

In a series of detailed readings of Husserl, Heidegger,

---

[1] Derrida, *Speech and Phenomena*, trans. David B. Allison (Evanston: Northwestern University Press, 1973), p. 50. Cited henceforth as *SP*.

Saussure, Levi-Strauss and Rousseau, Derrida demonstrates how representation—and writing—already belong to the sign and to signification: "In this play of representation, the point of origin becomes ungraspable.... There is no longer a simple origin."[1] It is interesting to speculate what impact this notion of a dispersed origin might have on deep-rooted European histories of the cradle of civilization (Asia or Africa) and on postcolonial peoples' images of themselves.

To deconstruct logocentric metaphysics, Derrida proposes we use the notion of writing as he has reinscribed it. Derrida's "writing" is another name for difference at the origin; it signifies "the most formidable difference. It threatened the desire for living speech from the closest proximity, it breached living speech from within and from the very beginning" (*OG*, p.56). The sign of origin, for Derrida, is a writing of a writing that can only state that the origin is originary translation. Metaphysics tries to reappropriate presence, says Derrida, through notions of adequacy of representation, of totalization, of history. Cartesian-Hegelian history, like the structure of the sign, "is conceivable only on the basis of the presence that it defers and in view of the deferred presence one intends to reappropriate" (*SP*, p.138). Here Derrida

---

[1] Derrida, *Of Grammatology*, trans. Gayatri C. Spivak (Baltimore: Johns Hopkins University Press, 1974), p. 36. Cited henceforth as *OG*.

points to historicism's concern with origin and telos and its desire to construct a totalizing narrative. "History", in the texts of poststructuralism, is a repressive force that obliterates difference and belongs in a chain that includes meaning, truth, presence, and logos. We shall see later how Walter Benjamin, in a similar critique of monolithic histories, instead uses materialist historiography as a means of destabilization.

Derrida's critique of representation is important for postcolonial theory because it suggests a critique of the traditional notion of translation as well. In fact, the two problematics have always been intertwined in Derrida's work. He has indicated more than once that translation perhaps escapes "the orbit of representation" and is therefore an "exemplary question".[1] If representation stands for the reappropriation of presence, translation emerges as the sign for what Derrida would call "dissemination".[2] We must, however, carefully interrogate the conventional concept of translation that belongs to the order of representation, adequacy and truth.

While postcolonial theory would willingly dispense with the historical narratives that have underwritten the imperialistic enterprise, that come into being with the denial of historicity to

---

[1] Derrida, "Sending: On Representation," p.298.

[2] *Derrida, Dissemination, trans.* Barbara Johnson (Chicago: University of Chicago Press, 1981).

conquered peoples, and that suppress history in order to appear as history, it is aware that the situation of the postcolonial "subject", who lives always already "in translation", requires for its articulation some notion of what history is. The translations by Calcutta's Fort William College scholars from Indian languages into English, in constructing the colonial subject, provided representations of the "Asiatik" to generations of Europeans.

The point is not just to criticize these characterizations as "inadequate" or "untrue"; one should attempt to show the complicity of the representations with colonial rule and their part in maintaining the asymmetries of imperialism. The postcolonial desire for "history" is a desire to understand the traces of the "past" in a situation where at least one fact is singularly irreducible: colonialism and what came after. Historiography in such a situation must provide ways of recovering occluded images from the past to deconstruct colonial and neocolonial histories. In India, for example, the Subaltern Studies group, which has initiated such a project of rewriting history, is grappling with the conceptual problems of essentialism and representation.

In an essay on the Subaltern Studies historians, Gayatri Spivak argues that their practice is akin to "deconstruction", since they put forward a "theory of change as the site of displacement of function between sign-systems" and this is "a theory of reading in the strongest possible general sense".[1] Spivak's essay is a persuasive, if somewhat anxious, attempt to account for the similarities (and a few of the differences) between these postcolonial historiographers and the projects of poststructuralism. She provides a useful parallel when she suggests that the Subaltern Studies historians focus on the "site of displacement of the function of signs, " which is "the name of reading as active transaction between past and future, " and that this "transactional reading"—perhaps we can also call it translation—may indicate the possibility of action (*DH*, p.332).

Since it is part of my argument that the problematics of translation and the writing of history are inextricably bound together, I shall briefly go over Spivak's main points regarding the Subaltern historians. Their strategic use of poststructuralist ideas (whether self-declared or emerging from Spivak's reading of their work) may help us see more clearly how the notions of history and translation I wish to reinscribe are not only enabled by the postcolonial critique of historiography but might also further strengthen that critique.

The significant poststructuralist "themes" Spivak refers to are

---

[1] Spivak, "Subaltern Studies: Deconstructing Historiography," in *Subaltern Studies IV: Writings on South Asian History and Society* (Delhi: Oxford University Press, 1985). Cited henceforth as *DH*.

the critique of origins, writing and the attack on phonocentrism, the critique of bourgeois liberal humanism, the notion of the "enabling" discursive failure and the notion of "affirmative deconstruction". The Subaltern historians are concerned with revealing the discursivity of a history (colonial or neocolonial) that has come into being through a suppression of historicity. They use the term subaltern "as a name for the general attribute of subordination in South Asian society whether this is expressed in terms of class, caste, age, gender and office or in any other way".[1] Through elaborate construction of the figure of the insurgent subaltern and a series of sustained miscognitions, elite historiography presents a history that purports to be "disinterested" and "true". The postcolonial historian tries to show how this discursive field is constituted, and how, as Spivak puts it, the "Muse of History" and counterinsurgency are "complicit" (*DH*, p.334). History and translation function, perhaps, under the same order of representation, truth, and presence, creating coherent and transparent texts through the repression of difference, and participating thereby in the process of colonial domination.

The problem of subaltern consciousness, according to Spivak, "operates as a metaphysical methodological presupposition" in the

---

[1] Ranajit Guha, preface to *Subaltern Studies I: Writings on South Asian History and Society* (Delhi: Oxford University Press, 1982), p.vii.

group's work, but "there is always a counterpointing suggestion" that "subaltern consciousness is subject to the cathexis of the elite, that it is never fully recoverable, that it is always askew from its received signifiers, indeed that it is effaced even as it is disclosed, that it is irreducibly discursive" (*DH*, p.339). As I tried to suggest in the first section of this chapter, translations into English by colonialists in India in the eighteenth and nineteenth centuries offered authoritative versions of the Eastern self not only to the "West" but to their (thereby interpellated) subjects. The introduction of English education after 1835 and the decline of indigenous learning ensured that postcolonials would seek their unrecoverable past in the translations and histories constituting colonial discourse. The subaltern, too, exists only "in translation, " always already cathected by colonial domination.

In a move that some may see as imperialistic in its own way, Spivak appropriates the Subaltern historians' critique of origins: "What had seemed the historical predicament of the colonial subaltern can be made to become the allegory of the predicament of all thought, all deliberative consciousness, though the elite profess otherwise" (*DH*, p.340, emphasis in original). What she refers to is the creation of the subaltern as a "subject-effect", its operation as subject in an enormous "discontinuous network" or "text". In order to function as subject, it is assigned a "sovereign and determining" role; what is really an effect is presented as a cause—a metalepsis is posited. Spivak indicates that elements in the work of Subaltern Studies "warrant a reading of the project to retrieve the subaltern consciousness as the attempt to undo a massive historiographical metalepsis and 'situate' the effect of the subject as subaltern" (*DH*, pp.341—42).

The notion of consciousness, then, is used strategically, deliberately, unnostalgically, in the service of "a scrupulously visible political interest" (*DH*, p.342), to refer to an "emergent collective consciousness" rather than that of the liberal humanist subject. The strategic use of essentialist concepts marks what Spivak, and Derrida, would call "affirmative deconstruction". A comment of Derrida's from *Of Grammatology* offers an important clue to the way in which postcolonial theory will have to situate itself:

> *The movements of deconstruction do not destroy structures from the outside. They are not possible and effective, nor can they take accurate aim, except by inhabiting those structures. Inhabiting them in a certain way, because one always inhabits, and all the more when one does not suspect it. Operating necessarily from the inside, borrowing all the strategic and economic resources of subversion from the old structure, borrowing them structurally, that is to say without being able to isolate their*

elements and atoms, the enterprise of deconstruction always in a certain way falls prey to its own work. (OG, p.24)

How can theory, or translation, avoid being trapped in the order of representation when it uses the very concepts it criticizes? Derrida would say that it should aim to be the kind of writing that "both marks and goes back over its mark with an undecidable stroke", for this "double mark escapes the pertinence or authority of truth", reinscribing it without overturning it. This displacement is not an event; it has not "taken place". It is what "writes / is written".[1] The double inscription Derrida mentions has a parallel in Walter Benjamin's strategy of citation or quotation. For Benjamin, the historical materialist (the critical historiographer) quotes without quotation marks in a method akin to montage. It is one way of revealing the constellation a past age forms with the present without submitting to a simple historical continuum, to an order of origin and telos.

Derrida's double writing can help us challenge the practices of "subjectification" and domination evident in colonial histories and translations. The challenge will not, however, be made in the name of recovering a lost essence or an undamaged self. Instead, the question of the hybrid will inform our reading. As Bhabha

---

1 Derrida, *Dissemination*, p.193.

puts it:

> *Hybridity is the sign of the productivity of colonial power, its shifting forces and fixities; it is the name for the strategic reversal of the process of domination through disavowal (that is, the production of discriminatory identities that secure the "pure" and original identity of authority). Hybridity is the revaluation of the assumption of colonial identity through the repetition of discriminatory identity effects. It displays the necessary deformation and displacement of all sites of discrimination and domination. (SW, p.154)*

Colonial discourse, although it creates identities for those it transfixes by its gaze of power, is profoundly ambivalent at the source of its authority. Hybridity leads to proliferating differences that escape the "surveillance" of the discriminatory eye. "Faced with the hybridity of its objects, " says Bhabha, "the presence of power is revealed as something other than what its rules of recognition assert" (*SW*, p.154). When we begin to understand how colonial power ends up producing hybridization, "the discursive conditions of dominance" can be turned into "the grounds of intervention" (p.154). The hybrid (subject or context), therefore, involves translation, deformation, displacement. As Bhabha is careful to point out, colonial hybridity is not a problem of cultural identity that can be resolved by a relativistic approach; it is, rather, "a problematic of colonial representation and individuation that reverses the effects of the colonialist disavowal, so that other 'denied' knowledges enter upon the dominant discourse and estrange the basis of its authority"[1] (p.156).

Clearly, the notion of hybridity, which is of great importance for a Subaltern critique of historiography as well as for a critique of traditional notions of translation, is both "ambiguous and historically complex".[2] To restrict "hybridity", or what I call "living in translation", to a postcolonial elite is to deny the pervasiveness, however heterogeneous, of the transformations wrought across class boundaries by colonial and neocolonial domination. This is not to present a metanarrative of global homogenization, but to emphasize the need to reinvent oppositional cultures in nonessentializing ways. Hybridity can be seen, therefore, as the sign of a postcolonial theory that subverts essentialist models of reading while it points toward a new practice of translation.

---

[1] For a forceful description of the hybrid, see Aijaz Ahmad, "Jameson's Rhetoric of Otherness and the 'National Allegory,' " *Social Text* 15 (Fall 1986): 325.

[2] James Clifford, *The Predicament of Culture* (Cambridge, Mass.: Harvard University Press, 1988), p.16.

Why Culture Matters:
Rethinking the Language of Feminist Politics

The Inter-Asia Project, not least as it is exemplified in the IACS Journal, has enabled a variety of stimulating conversations across Asia. One such productive site of engagement with "Asian" questions has been feminism. Although there are strong women's movements in many countries in the region, they often deal by necessity with local issues (unless there are cross-border aspects involved, as in the case of sex-trafficking or migrants), and it is not always easy to find a point of access for understanding how different feminisms may speak to one another. I suggest that it may be necessary to go beyond looking at the real-time questions of feminist politics, and instead examine more closely the locations from where the questions originate. Such an examination, I propose, will have to focus on why culture matters to feminism. Having taken this detour, my essay will come back to the present to reflect on a new development in Indian feminism. As I show in my recent article, "Feminism and Cultural Studies in Asia", instead of feminism being an interruption of already established ways of studying culture critically (as in 1970s England for example), it is foundational to the emergence of the new area of cultural studies (Niranjana 2007). It is foundational because of the way in which feminists have taken on—have had to take on—the culture question in non-Western societies.

A standard criticism of feminism across Asia derives from a charge that it is disconnected or alienated from "our culture". This is a charge that is seldom made against any of our other political frameworks which are far from having a clearly identifiable "indigenous" source. Elsewhere, I have explained at some length why the question of culture — especially in formerly colonial contexts — cannot be separated from the question of how women come to be defined. In the course of this essay, I will elaborate on this issue with reference to India.

But first, a referencing of the inter-Asia context. Starting in 2000, I had the opportunity to be part of a series of feminist discussions in different Asian locations through the Inter-Asia Cultural Studies conferences. The first feminist panel discussion at Fukuoka in December 2000 tabled as a central question the often contentious relationship of women with the state, and many of the speakers talked about the difficulty of theorizing the question of women and that of gender through already settled vocabularies like that of class. In Bangalore in October 2001, my institution, CSCS, hosted the Feminisms in Asia conference, which brought together Asian women who discussed women and the state (in Iran and Singapore), women's engagement with civil war (in Sri Lanka), feminism and religious identities (India, Malaysia), cultural minorities (India), queer citizenship (in Taiwan and China), women and the law (Bangladesh, India). An important concluding panel explored the critical vocabularies formulated by feminisms in Asia, and the tensions of translation from Western contexts. In many ways, the culture question was central to the different strands of this event. Shortly afterwards, in December 2001, the IACS Alternatives Workshop in Bangalore provided another forum for discussion of feminist questions. Coming in the wake of the Feminisms in Asia conference, and focusing on accommodating those who could not make it to the conference because of travel advisories after the 9/11 events, this workshop aimed at an assessment of the political-theoretical ground on which we stand. In a key panel, we explored the current dilemmas of feminists regarding contemporary political initiatives, and investigated issues of cultural practice and feminist analysis. In later meetings (Seoul 2005, Shanghai 2007), inter-Asian feminists have theorized popular culture, Islamization and its consequences for women, the sex-workers' movement and its production of new subjectivities.

Again as I've said in the article I referred to above, bringing feminist issues into an inter-Asia cultural studies frame has foregrounded the *culture* question and the specific negotiations all women in Asia and feminists in particular undertake; opened up the question of how to think about Asian *modernities*; prompted an investigation into the problems of *translation* in relation to the formation of the vocabularies of social criticism; urged us to re-think the *political* (what are the changing vocabularies of the political; is the political recognizable in the ways that it used to be?). Feminism appears to be one of the most volatile domains in Asia where the rethinking is taking place.

The culture question's importance for feminism in Asia might be illustrated by the following contrast. Feminist scholars in the West have suggested that nature and culture formed a binary. "[In Western feminist history] the most common pair of terms to be evoked and fought over are nature and culture" (John 1998: 203). By analyzing the nature-culture binary, Western feminists produced important critiques of organization of knowledge as well as institutions like family. Sherry Ortner, in her essay "Is Female to Male as Nature is to Culture?" argues that:

Every culture implicitly recognizes and asserts a distinction between the operation of nature and the operation of culture (human consciousness and its products); and further, that the distinctiveness of culture rests precisely on the fact that it can under most circumstances transcend natural conditions and turn them to its purposes. Thus culture (i.e. every culture) at some level of awareness asserts itself to be not only distinct from but superior to nature, and that sense of distinctiveness and superiority rests precisely on the ability to transform—to "socialize" and "culturalize" nature. (Ortner 1974: 72—73)

According to her, it is the "the body and the natural procreative functions specific to women" which have brought about this convention of regarding women as closer to nature, and hence subordinate to culture. However, in non-Western societies, women were historically seen as part of Culture. Feminist scholarship in India, for example, has been able to show that the formulation of notions of culture in India is crucially related to women in a variety of ways. This draws our attention to the significance of the culture question under colonial rule. With culture understood here as a mark of difference as well as superiority in relation to the colonizing West, we can gain insights into how a historically specific way of thinking about Indian women came to be naturalized or rendered obvious.[1]

The discussions about culture in gender theory in India are based on critiques of the nationalist project in both pre-and post-Independence phases. Feminists have looked at the time of the anti-colonial struggles and how a self-constructed Indian identity was born in opposition to the view the colonizers had of the natives. They have also gone on to theorize the post-Independence

---

[1] The landmark anthology *Recasting Women* (Sangari and Vaid 1989) has several incisive articles elaborating this history.

period, when efforts were underway to imagine India anew, as an independent nation that was no longer subject to British rule. This imagination of India gave rise to a range of representations within various fields. In an astonishingly diverse set of writings spanning a range of disciplinary locations (history, sociology, literary studies, art history, film studies, political science) feminist scholars have analyzed the formation of normative femininity as it takes shape in the context of discussions about Indianness and Indian culture.

Emergence of the Culture Question

How are "we" different from "them"? This question is posed in the third world or more broadly non-Western societies as part of a colonial contestation. By this we mean a contest between colonizer and colonized on the relative merits of their cultures. With the onslaught of the colonizing West in India in the late eighteenth to early ninteenth century, colonized Indians responded by asserting the superiority of their own culture. If we look at how the term for "culture" emerged in modern Indian languages, we notice that the most commonly used term, *sanskriti*, is actually a translation of the English word "culture". The point being made here is not that there was no concept of culture before the English introduced it, but that after the ninteenth century we invest different meanings in culture. It becomes the location of everything that is uniquely ours, and therefore different from anything that can be found in the world of the colonizer. As we become modern Indians, and then go on to become citizens of an independent nation, we hold on to the idea of "our culture" as setting us apart from others.

Although the culture question is an intimate part of the formation of our modern identity, culture in modernity is seen as something that remains the other of that which is modern. This means that in discussions on/descriptions of what is "modern", culture provides the contrast case of that which is not-modern, that which is traditional and is outside the processes of Westernization that then come to stand in for modernity. This relationship between culture and modernity, a relationship that has its roots in the colonial context, may give us some indication as to why women occupy such a central place in discussions about culture in the non-West.

There are many similarities between the Indian context and other societies across Asia. Kumari Jayawardena's classic work *Feminism and Nationalism in the Third World* (1986) had argued that in the non-West these two movements — movement for women's rights and the movement for national liberation — share a close relationship. Parallelly, the "culture question" also becomes a "national culture question", with significant implications for women. Although nationalist movements fighting against the colonizer enable women's political participation, they also create for them a position in national symbolism that is remarkably static. Women come to be increasingly seen as the repositories of "tradition" and "culture".

A criticism routinely faced by feminists across Asia is that they are deracinated or alienated from "our culture", that feminism comes from the West and therefore represents an alien set of ideas. Interestingly, this is not a charge levelled against any of our other political frameworks (e.g. Marxism, liberalism), which may also be far from having any obvious indigenous source. Why then does feminism come under fire for being alien? Feminist demands are allegedly demands arising from "modernization", which is seen to erase "our" culture and replace it with Western values and ways of life. This criticism is easily and frequently made, but it does not take into account how the notion of culture itself has been put together in our context.

One of our starting points would be to understand (a) how the creation of the national essence was based on the assertion of cultural difference from the West (how "we" are different from "them"), and (b) how women were frequently represented as the embodiment of that difference (that it is in women, their bodies and lives, that this difference is displayed). When nationalists in the non-Western world signal a relationship of conflict between modernity and culture, what is being implied is that women are part of that which is cultural and therefore authentic. They cannot therefore be part of the modern, or, as is more common, can only have a highly mediated relationship to modernity. So when women behave in ways associated with modernity (read assertive, individualistic, ambitious...), they are seen as challenging their place in Indian culture and therefore undermining that culture itself. Culture, as we have seen, came to be opposed to "modernity"—if both had to co-exist in colonial India, they had to be gendered female and male respectively. In a context of rapid and far-reaching social changes caused by urbanization and migration in the ninteenth century, women became the repositories of all that was seen as part of custom and tradition even as men went to work in colonial society and imitated the dress and manners of the English.[1]

The women-and-culture pair thus forms part of a sedimented commonsense in India, and has always been an unresolved issue even in the women's movement. From time to time, flashpoints remind us of this unresolved problem: one such incident occurred in early 2009.

The Pink Chaddi Campaign

In late January 2009 a newly-formed right-wing Hindu group called the Sri Ram Sene (army of the god Rama) in the coastal

---

[1] For an influential account of this shift and of the emergence of a new sense of public and private spheres, see Partha Chatterjee, *The Nation and its Fragments* (1993).

town of Mangalore in Karnataka announced that its members would target young couples found together on Valentine's Day. The Ram Sene's leader, Pramod Muthalik, said: "Our activists will go around with a priest, a turmeric stub and a *mangalsutra* on February 14. If we come across couples being together in public and expressing their love, we will take them to the nearest temple and conduct their marriage" (*The Hindu* 2009).[1] Although Valentine's Day in India is largely a celebration generated by greetingcard companies, over the last several years it has attracted widespread attention even in non-metropolitan areas and amongst those who don't speak English. It has also consequently attracted attacks from right-wing political parties who have condemned it as a manifestation of the depravity of Western culture. Following this announcement, Muthalik's men attacked a pub in Mangalore and beat up and drove out the women they found there.[2] This event featured prominently in the electronic and print media across the entire country. In the state of Karnataka, the right-wing

---

[1] The *mangalsutra* is a Hindu symbol of marriage worn around the neck by a wife; the turmeric stub is used to make auspicious marks.

[2] Here is a short list of URLs which offer some visual references: http: //www.youtube. com/watch?v=lEbD2aXs-XU (pub attack); http: //www.youtube.com/watch?v=tnbYYwOvAFo&feature=related (campaign steps); http: //www.youtube.com/watch?v=THITp1E_onU&feature=related (pile of pink chaddis); http: //www.youtube.com/watch?v=Pgrk9YG6Nq0&feature=related (debate on NDTV); http: //www.youtube.com/watch?v=5EQ7NS6jelU&feature=related (latest weapon in culture clashes).

Bharatiya Janata Party (BJP) is in power and human rights groups claimed that the party was tacitly condoning the actions of the Sri Ram Sene. The entire coastal area of Karnataka and Mangalore in particular had already for some years become the site for new tensions between Hindus, Christians and Muslims, all of whom for decades have shared cultural and political space in the region.[1]

A few days after the Mangalore pub attack, the Consortium of Pub-going, Loose and Forward Women was formed on the social networking site Facebook. This consortium launched a campaign to send pink panties to the Sri Ram Sene on Valentine's Day that year. The idiom of this protest was unprecedented in the history of Indian feminist politics. As one of the key organizers of the campaign wrote: "[W]e were only thinking of a way to render absurd the ever-bigger chaddiwala" (Susan 2009). The chaddiwala referred to is a man who wears the long khaki shorts (*chaddi* in several Indian languages) which are part of the uniform of the Rashtriya Swayamsevak Sangh (National Volunteers' Organisation), the parent organization of the group of right-wing parties collectively known as the Sangh Parivar or family of organizations.

Nisha Susan recounts the growth of the campaign: "Within a day of starting the campaign we had 500 odd members. In a week

---

[1] For a succint introduction to the complex politics of the region, see the unpublished piece by Sumi Krishna (2009).

we hit 40, 000. From Puerto Rico to Singapore, from Chennai to Ahmedabad, from Guwahati to Amritsar, people wrote to us, how do I send my chaddis? But by then the campaign had gone offline. Elderly men and women, schoolchildren, middle-aged housewives, gravelly-voiced big men from Bihar who did not quite want to say the word chaddi aloud called us" (Susan 2009). Collection centres sprang up across India; people were encouraged to drop off panties at these points to be couriered to the Sri Ram Sene headquarters in Mangalore. While there were offline aspects to this protest, the Pink Chaddi Campaign (PCC) as it came to be known was perhaps the first internet campaign of the women's movement in India. So much so that when a series of street processions and demonstrations were organized in a few cities, the protesters numbered far fewer than those who usually showed up for rights-violation agitations. Even the March 8th International Women's Day rally held in Bangalore had only about 300 people.

Criticisms of the PCC were many: they came from peer groups who would otherwise have shared in the progressive politics of feminists who called the PCC elitist and frivolous (surely there were far more serious issues to be dealt with in relation to women) ; and from Hindutva groups who claimed the PCC was against Hindu culture, disrespectful of Hindu symbolism, and so on. The abusive responses to the protesters also came not just from lower middle class "fundamentalists", but from internet-savvy conservatives attacking "secular" "progressives" and from male university students. The discussions threw up a chain of related concepts: secular, Western, modern (and therefore against "our culture") — this chain of association was mobilized with ease against women who find the Sri Ram Sene's assertions problematic. Most feminist groups have supported the PCC and Valentine's Day rallies, even those who agitated against the Miss World beauty contest in Bangalore in 1994 or maintained a studied silence on the Fire controversy involving Deepa Mehta's film (these two representing other recent conjunctures of gender-culture-globalization) (Niranjana and John 1999). In fact, people who had never recognized or celebrated Valentine's Day were seen wearing pink on February 14, 2009.

Mainstream media representations of the protests and counter-protests suggested a class polarization over the issue. In actuality, both online and offline protests indicate that an astonishingly diverse set of people were involved. Some have read the pub attack as an anti-globalization gesture, but this reading does not account for the long history of domestic violence, custodial violence (by the army and the police), and other displays of public hostility towards women in India. Similarly, it would not be correct to see the PCC as an assertion of pro-globalization forces, just as earlier campaigns of the women's movement cannot simply be dismissed as "Western" inspired.

Another interesting divide seems to exist between the groups of those protesting against the Sri Ram Sene's attacks. The Valentine's Day support campaign drew on the participation of local groups (including Kannada linguistic nationalists, a farmers' movement, and a "secular" political party led by a former underworld figure), but the same groups did not show up on March 8th to celebrate Women's Day. The local groups seemed to support heterosexual lovers' right to freedom of expression (to the extent of sending out patrolling Love Chariots on Valentine's Day to protect lovers against the threatened attacks of the Sri Ram Sene), but was not particularly interested in women's rights as articulated by feminists.

While feminist groups in India have criticized the violence against women evident in the pub attack and in the individual attacks that followed, not many have spoken openly about the PCC. Perhaps there is a discomfort with the idiom of the campaign, which is both sexually coy and aggressive at the same time. Why is the Pink Chaddi a powerful condensation, a range of varied interests converging on one image? The vulgarity of popular culture harnessed to the sophistication of Web 2.0 is one of the means by which this condensation seems to work. It has been relatively simpler for feminists to criticize "moral policing" when it is associated with inter-caste and inter-religion marriage or relationships; and harder when it is seen as relating more explicitly to sexuality, as in Valentine's Day or lovers in parks engaging in PDA (public display of affection—a new term in the youth lexicon).

Some feminists bloggers have felt that the PCC protest has not been productive. You sent chaddis, they sent pink saris. What has been achieved? They ask. This comment does not seem to take into account the fact that the PCC has now entered the popular vocabulary, showing up in advertisements and general journalistic articles alike. While there was a certain cohesiveness to the "victim group" in this instance of the pub attacks (the women being mostly young, urban and middle class) which may allow some to dismiss the protest as elitist, the PCC may well mark a shift in the language of feminist politics in India, where the comfort of "speaking for" underprivileged women that the movement has always had is being challenged, and the question of representation itself is being interrogated. If feminists don't recognize the unprecedented nature of the PCC, they will not be able to see how it is crucially situated at the intersection of questions of sexuality and female desire with the worlds of contemporary politics in India. The PCC took on board the sexual sub-text of the Hindutva pub attack and of the masculinist rhetoric of its perpetrators, and "outed" it through a public display; it did so not by criticizing and therefore drawing attention to that sub-text but by embedding it in the symbolism of the campaign.

The interest in theorizing sexuality has cut across different regions in the non-Western world, perhaps since sexuality has for some time now been a limit case for feminism—the most ambiguous area of conceptual and political engagement, whether it is in relation to how power gets distributed in heterosexual relationships, or in relation to the striving for coherent gendered behaviour even in alternatively sexual relationships. For the translation/vocabulary question, sexuality is a key area for the playing out of arguments over cultural difference, just as it is central to thinking about questions relating to modernity. In more ways than one, the PCC which brought together in one arresting and sexualized image the issues of translation, of modernity, of culture and of the political is a challenge to those of us interested in reshaping both the language of feminism as well its objectives and strategies.

References:

Chatterjee, Partha. *The Nation and its Fragments: Colonial and Postcolonial Histories*, Princeton: Princeton University Press, 1993.

Jayawardena, Kumari. *Feminism and Nationalism in the Third World*, London: Zed Books Ltd, 1986.

John, Mary E. "Feminism in India and the West: recasting a relationship", *Cultural Dynamics* 10 (2), July 1998: 197—210.

Krishna, Sumi. "Understanding and responding to the Mangalore assaults", unpublished piece, 11 February 2009, Bangalore.

Nationalism Refigured: Contemporary South Indian Cinema and the Subject of Feminism*

---

* Versions of this paper have been presented to audiences in Calcutta, New Delhi, Colombo, Madras, Hyderabad and Chicago. My thanks to all of those who have taken issue with me both orally and in print.

Gender and the Indian Modern

A New Nationalism is in the air today, a nationalism suffused with romantic love, with the most intimate and "private" of emotions. Popular cinema in India draws our attention to this phenomenon: *Roja (1992)*, for example, is advertised as "a patriotic love story", and one of the more successful films of 1994 was called *1942: A Love Story*. This nationalism appears to be premised on a detaching of the new middle class from the Nehruvian state of the post-Independence years, a process that has led to changes in the meaning of some of the key terms in our political life, such as "secularism", for example. It is almost as if the hitherto hidden logic of the national-modern is now acquiring visibility owing to a new configuration of forces which include the rise of the Sangh Parivar[1] and the liberalization of the Indian economy. The portrayal of "mainstream" characters—unexceptional, not particularly "heroic"—in commercial cinema provides one point of access to this complex configuration. Central to the shift in the national imaginary, as I shall show, is the figure of *woman*. In this negotiation of the new modernity, the woman is

---

1 The term Sangh Parivar literally means the Sangh family. The reference is to the loose group of Hindu right-wing political and cultural organisations headed by the Rashtriya Swayamsevak Sangh, and including rhe Vishwa Hindu Parishad, the Bharatiya Janata Party and the Bajrang Dal.

not presented as just a passive counter; rather, her agency is shown as crucial for the shifts that are taking place.

The Indian "woman" is produced at a particular conjuncture between Nation (imaged as an autonomous, sovereign, nation-state) and Modernity (including both processes such as democratization or the spread of mass communication, and discourses such as those which produce the very distinctions between "tradition" and "modern"). Unlike gender, however, *caste* and *community* (or religious identity) are not privileged sites for the representation or staging of modernity and nationhood. (I refer here to lower caste-class and Muslim.) Quite the contrary. The pre-modern or non-modern, as well as the anti-national, is often staged *w caste and community. To put it differently, invoking identities based on community and caste would be unacceptable to the secularist, the "modern citizen", who has laid hegemonic claim to the nation in the post-Independence period. The leaving behind of caste/*community by the national-modern, curiously enough, is facilitated* by the claim of "woman" to modernity and the nation.[1] The claim, however, is incomplete, and an analysis of it might well point to multiple fault lines and incoherences in the formation of the national imaginary.

---

[1] See Susie Tharu and Tejaswini Niranjana, "Problems for a Contemporary Theory of Gender", in Shahid Amin and Dipesh Chakrabarty (eds), Subaltern Studies IX (Delhi: Oxford University Press, 1989).

This claim of women to entitlement is supported by the new identities fashioned by/for them in the post-Independence period on a host of different sites, a fashioning that seems to have taken new directions in the 1990s. My interest in popular cinema as a major site for such identity formation derives from the fact that it is perhaps the single most powerful medium, until the fairly recent coming of television, in which identities have been publicly displayed, negotiated and narrativized. The three films discussed here at some length, *Geetanjali (1989)*, *Roja* (1992) and *Bombay* (1995), all directed by Maniratnam, were produced in Tamil and Telugu, the second and third having been successfully dubbed into Hindi as well.[1] What I intend to investigate in these films is: (a) how they feed into, and endorse, even as they produce in the cinematic medium, the new Indian nationalism; and (b) how the post-Independence feminist subject is imbricated in the fashioning of this new nationalism. Perhaps I should clarify here that I do not necessarily think of my analysis as a contribution to film criticism. Instead, I see it as an attempt to understand how a historical political conjuncture is structured by focusing on one kind of cultural artefact produced in it. My aim, therefore, is not to present a complete account of the films in terms of their formal devices,

---

[1] Maniratnam sometimes re-shoots parts of his films to incorporate regional or linguistic differences. It becomes a little difficult therefore to say where the reshooting stops and trie dubbing begins.

but to suggest how we might be able to account for the films' appeal in the present conjuncture.

Although chronologically speaking *Geetanjali* is a pre-Mandal film and *Roja* a pre-Babri Masjid one (they are, however, uncannily close to the two events—September-October 1990 and December 1992—named here), I would like to suggest that their representations of feminine identities are emblematic, in the first case, of the anti-Mandal woman, and in the second of the (Hindu) woman who stands for the nation (but is not necessarily the openly communal woman).[1] Primarily because she is Muslim, the central woman character in *Bombay* is portrayed somewhat differently from the heroines of *Geetanjali* and *Roja*, as I shall demonstrate later. I use the term "anti-Mandal woman" to designate the self-identity of those who, by disavowing caste, are able to lay claim simultaneously to both the modern and the secular. This is not to suggest that "modern and secular" is *the same as* "anti-Mandal"; it is merely one way of indicating the convergences that occurred, or became evident, in the 1990s. The agitations in 1990 against the recommendations of the Mandal Commission for reservation of government jobs and educational opportunities for the Other Backward Castes had framed the modern *as the* secular, and the

---

[1] One could also add that the structuring of these two feminine figures is similar, in terms of haw they make a claim on the modern, the secular and the national.

302

secular as that which transcended caste differences.[1]

One of the major conceptual difficulties in talking of the new nationalism is that its vocabulary does not seem so very different from that of the older nationalism. National interest, national security, national integration and modernization are terms familiar to us since the 1950s. So is the term secularism, which has been central to liberal and left politics in India. My contention is that the continuity of terms obscures the real shifts that are taking place. In some ways, the process is one in which the contours of the national-modern are made evident, its exclusions of caste (the lower castes) and community (the non-Hindu) legitimized. Using a rather awkward term, we should perhaps speak of the "post-national-modern" (not the postmodern, not the postnational) to describe this situation in which old terms are acquiring new significations.[2] I focus here on the mobilization of these terms in contemporary popular cinema and the new subject-positions which are being produced in the films.

Today, while the composition of the national-modern is being centrally challenged by the assertion of political identities based

---

[1] Note that the anti-Mandalites talked of "differences", not "inequalities".

[2] The modes of access to, the negotiation of and with, and the deployments of this post-national-modern would have to be understood as necessarily different for different kinds of groups, depending on their caste/community/gender configuration and the position of relative advantage or disadvantage from which they access it.

on caste and community, the question of gender occupies a very different position.[1] In spite of the considerable gains made by the women's movement over the last twenty years, the idiom in which feminist questions were raised is being mobilized today in very different kinds of initiatives, including the consolidation of the national-modern that feminists set out to criticize. The woman who chooses, the woman who acts independently, who takes the initiative, are today admired figures in popular cinema. If we examine closely the structuring of the agency of these female (or should we say feminist) subjects, like for example Maniratnam's protagonists Geeta, Roja and Shaila Banu, we might begin to perceive the modes of their implication in the refiguring of the national-modern.

The Anti-Mandal Woman

In this section I attempt an analysis of female subjectivity in *Geetanjali* in the light of the anti-Mandal agitation. The announcement in August 1990 of the implementation of the Mandal Commission recommendations by Prime Minister V. P. Singh, as we all remember, set off large-scale rioting by upper-

---

[1] See Susie Tharu and Tejaswini Niranjana, "Problems for a Contemporary Theory of Gender", and Vivek Dhareshwar, "Caste and the Secular Self", *Journal of Arts and Ideas*, nos 25—6 (1993), pp.115—26.

caste youth who were, by and large, urban.[1] Many of these young people were women who took part enthusiastically in the activities of the Anti-Mandal Commission Forum (AMCF), which included organising batches of students to sweep the streets, polish shoes, carry luggage at railway stations, and orchestrate processions and rallies. The press represented such uppercaste youth as engaged in a heroic struggle to save the nation from impending chaos, supporting the idea that implementing reservations would lead to a derecognition of merit and a consequent destruction of the country. In the battle for "merit", the truly patriotic and truly secular Indian was the one who rose above caste divisions; anyone who asked for reservations on the basis of caste was simply being casteist.

Prominently woven into the anti-Mandal discourse on merit was the figure of the Nation, and that of Modernity. Caste or the reservations policy (used interchangeably in this context) was described as that which had trapped India in a residual feudalism, preventing the country from achieving the progress and efficiency which would allow it to take its equal place in the world. By decrying caste, the modern middle-class subject also proclaimed its concern for the nation.

To take a slight detour into my own discipline, English,

---

[1] The Mandal Commission recommended additional reservations or quotas for Backward Castes in job and educational opportunities.

and see how it responded to the Mandal crisis, may not be-inappropriate here. The study of English Literature, introduced in the nineteenth century by the British, had played a significant part in the formation of the liberal humanist subject who would be both modern and nationalist.[1] In India, the "secularism" of the English-educated subject enabled a displacement of both caste and community from the middle-class sphere, so that these got marked as what lay *outside*, was *other* than, the middle class. During the anti-Mandal agitation, upper-caste English Department students in many universities boycotted classes *enmasse* to demand the abolition of reservations altogether.[2]

There are connections, no doubt, between the fact that the (old) middle class which used to stand in for the nation is marked, above all, by its *Englished-ness*, and the phenomenon of middle-class/uppercaste female "Englished" students emerging so decisively into the public realm to express the outrage of their class. Of all

---

[1] For a discussion of some of these issues, see Susie Tharu, "Government, Binding and Unbinding", Introduction to the Special Issue of the *Journal of English and Foreign Languages* (June-December 1991); Gauri Viswanathan, *Masks of Conquest* (London: Faber, 1990); Tejaswini Niranjana, *Siting Translation: History, Post-structuralism and the Colonial Context* (Berkeley: University of California Press, 1992).

[2] However qualified the demand sometimes appeared, it was evident for instance from the proclamation of the national association of IAS officers that reservations in general (even for Scheduled Castes and Scheduled Tribes [SCs] and [STs]) were being targeted, and not only the new Other Backward Castes (OBC) reservations.

student agitations in post-Independence India, the anti-Mandal one was surely unique in its legmmization by the media and in the fond parental approval it generated. The acclamation, curiously enough, was related to the imaging of this student politicization as being "above politics".[1] Precisely because of what was seen by the media as the purity and distance from conventional politics of the anti-Mandalites, their protest became the rage of the righteous who had suffered far too long because of their innate courtesy and politeness, who were now forced to take action to prevent the nation from "going to the dogs".[2] The fact of women appearing on the streets in public protest made the media recall the idealism of the freedom struggle. "Women" were imaged as morally pure, and thereby entrusted with the task of saving the nation. The enthusiastic participation of "women" in the anti-Mandal agitation along with their men, not as sexed beings but as free and equal citizens, suggests that these articulate and assertive subjects define themselves against "caste" (read lower castes). As middle class, upper-caste "women" thus claim a space in the post-national-modern, both men as well as women of the lower castes become

---

[1] See Veena Das, "A Crisis of Faith", in *Statesman* (3 September 1990).

[2] A phrase heard constantly during the anti-Mandal agitation. Another common remark of the time framed the upper-caste speaker in a discourse of Selflessness: "I'm not concerned for myself. I can always get a job in spite of reservations. I'm only worried as to where this is taking us."

invisible. A parallel process can be seen with regard to Muslim men and women.

It would be inaccurate, however, to think that the upper-caste anti-Mandal women were marked primarily by their Englishedness. Interestingly, South Indian women of this class—positioned within the national-modern—would not, for example, have watched popular Telugu films, their first choices being English and Hindi movies. But today they are ardent admirers of films like Geetanjali, and "vernacular" directors like Maniratnam. What makes Maniratnam's films unique in commercial cinema is their use of realistic modes of representation, their technical sophistication, [1] and the seeming naturalness and spontaneity of his actors, as well as the careful shaping of a seamless "Indian modernity". Importantly, Maniratnam's films mark the insertion of regional difference into the nation-space; witness the audacity with which the filmmaker puts a Tamil couple in Kashmir, or in Bombay, and claims for them the characteristics of the new nationalmodern. The films produce as well as take shape within a "modern" space, having either discarded or de-emphasized the elements of farce and melodrama that are staple aspects of Indian-language commercial films. They make themselves available, therefore, to be celebrated

---

[1] "Rajiv Menon's cinematography [in *Bombay*] is of an international calibre", says well-known film critic Khalid Mohammed in his review in *The Times of India* (9 April 1995).

without embarrassment, even with a certain pride, by the middle-class Indian. The growing popularity of Maniratnam's films across class and region, in fact, indicate the near-hegemonic emergence of a "cosmopolitan" taste, mediated by MTV and cable television programming.[1] In these films new subjectivities, and a new femininity, are being fashioned, this being perhaps a key element in their successful appeal to younger women. This new femininity holds out the promise of a modernity without the perils of feminism or feminist politics, which are frequently ridiculed in the media, and sometimes vilified, as imitative of Western aberrations.

The redefinitions of femininity produced and circulated today in films like Maniratnam's feedatmanylevels into, and reinflect, popular debates around questions of "modernity" and "tradition". These debates, it seems to me, are helping to constitute an aggressive cultural nationalism which is beginning to articulate itself alongside and into the vocabulary of the multinational market economy. The re-figuring of femininity in popular cinema is linked to the emergence of a new consumer economy supported by the ongoing reconstitution of the national imaginary. It is premised on

---

[1] Sunil Sethi writes of the "lower middle-class ethnically mixed" Delhi audience he watched *Bombay* with: "Film-goers seemed genuinely appreciative of the movie. I myself was greatly cheered to notice that not the subtlest nuance or bits of passing dialogue was lost on the audience, which laughed and clapped and gasped and cheered in all the right places..." ("Celluloid Metaphor of 'Bombay' ," *Newstime*, 16 April 1995).

what I have been calling the idea of a post-national-modern, an idea that articulates at the level of everyday life—and in the life of commodities—the construction of an "Indian" modernity which has resolved the older contradictions.

On the surface, some of Maniratnam's heroines don't match our conventional notions about good Indian women. The teenaged heroine of Geetanjali, for instance, is constantly saying, "Lecchipoddaama, shall we elope?", and not always to the same person. However, Geetanjali's daring and her sexual aggressiveness are presented in the narrative merely as a manifestation of her high spirits and sense of humour. Her "abandon" in some sense comes from being abandoned, by an absent or dead mother, and by Life. The boldness of the heroine becomes literally possible only on the verge of death.

What is the narrative trajectory that creates the space of feminine assertion in the film? Geetanjali is the story of two young lovers, both dying of incurable illnesses, the boy from leukaemia and the girl from heart disease. Set amidst the swirling mists of Kodaikanal, where the protagonists seem to have gone to die, the film unfolds into breathtaking landscapes whose lush greenness (and the yellows and reds of the heroine's "ethnic" clothes) counterpoint the tale of imminent death. Interestingly, the only images of death foregrounded in the film are the tombs and ghosts of the graveyard where Geeta, as she is called, lures unsuspecting men in order to play an elaborate practical joke on them with the help of her young siblings. Death, as far as the female protagonist is concerned, is just a joke. The tombs are simultaneously "real" as well as parodic images out of a horror film. The graveyard is therefore what awaits "the inevitable end", as well as what sanctions a life lived in the present continuous tense. One of our first impressions of Geeta is of a prankster in ghost-like attire who has adopted the dress for fun and out of choice, for it is not until the intermission that the audience finds out about her incurable disease.

Throughout the narrative, however, love and death are closely intertwined, as for example in the lyrical Ilaiyaraja composition "Om Namaha" with its background music dominated by a magnified heartbeat. Although the film was not well received in non-urban areas, middle-and lower-middle-class young people in large cities saw it again and again, shouting, chanting or whispering, according to context, every crucial piece of dialogue. What the film seems to reaffirm is that one should live as though one will die tomorrow. In living for today, the new consumers who form the bulk of the audience confirm their intuition that what is important is to look wonderful now, to buy their fashionable clothes (Nagarjuna's jeans and sweatshirts, Girija's neo-ethnic salwar-kameez and ghagra-choli) now, for tomorrow they will be as good as dead.[1] In fact, impending death is the only context

---

1 The *Geetanjali* version of *ghagra-choli* did indeed create a new line of clothing for teenagers as well as little girls.

311

in which "love" begins to make sense, for it is a love that is reinforced by the pretty clothes, a love that never disturbs the assumptions of the audience because not only does it have no future, it rests on the almost complete erasure of differences.

The protagonists are obviously metropolitan, but they are totally distant from, and uninvolved with, their normal context. The hero seems to be Hindu and the heroine Christian, but this is a trivial detail, used mostly for comic effect, as in the church scene where the boy calls out to God during Mass to complain about his lover. (Contrast this with Roja, in which another minority identity—Muslim—imaged effortlessly as both pre-modern and anti-national, is counterpointed to that which is invisibly Hindu and part of the national-modern.) Nowhere in the narrative is religious difference a point of contention, for everything is permitted to those who are about to die. The new consumer economy in which films like Geetanjali occupy a nodal position constitutes a new ethical self, a self premised on the need for "authenticity". Only the inauthentic, those who experience death-inlife, are afraid of death. Not the ones who truly experience life-indeath, whose moments, lived solely in the present, are authenticated by the imminence of their end.[1]

The centrality to Geetanjali of the new consumer ensures that work is never really represented in the film, except for the fruit-

---

[1] I owe this point to Susie Tharu, who also drew my attention to the counterpointed images of "modernity" in the film.

sellers who function as local colour, and the doctor and nurse who in any case are working for the lovers. The hero, although recently graduated from college, is exempt from work partly because of his parents' affluence and partly because of his impending death. Class differences, therefore, are not represented here, except for the lecherous caretaker and his weepy wife in the parodic subplot, and they too are subsumed in the general movement of the narrative. The heroine and her sisters again don't work, except to clean the house now and then or prepare elaborately for oil baths. Geeta is not even shown studying, for she lives in a kind of "slack" time where all she has to do is entertain herself, and others. This film, unlike the later Roja and Bombay, erases regional 'Versions of this paper have been presented to audiences in Calcutta, New Delhi, Colombo, Madras, Hyderabad and Chicago. My thanks to all of those who have taken issue with me both orally and in print.1 The term Sangh Parivar literally means the Sangh family. The reference is to the loose group of Hindu right-wing political and cultural organisations headed by the Rashtriya Swayamsevak Sangh, and including rhe Vishwa Hindu Parishad, the Bharatiya Janata Party and the Bajrang Dal. differences, except only in as much as the language spoken by the characters is Telugu; there is no other marker to place the film in any specific region. The look of the protagonists is not unlike those of college students from Delhi or Bombay or Bangalore. Obviously, the hero is dressed in

Western clothes like other fashionable urban, middle-class youth; but the urban heroine in many South Indian films is increasingly dressed in North Indian "ethnic" clothes. Instead of being through her clothes (langa-daavni or sari) the bearer of regional specificity, the film-heroine is now marked as "Indian", like present day urban young women themselves, through her Rajasthani-Gujarati apparel. In other films by Maniratnam (for example, the awardwinning Mouna Raagam), we find obligatory fantasy sequences with a love song set in the desert, replete with camels, turbans, mirrorwork, and chunky jewellery. The visual imagery provided by mass media for our "private" fantasies thus includes pictures of the new Indian.[1]

Geeta, then, is the "new woman", the strong heroine, both modern as well as feminine. While her casual clothes and "spontaneous" gestures represent her as "liberated", she simultaneously carries a double burden—the burden of woman as saviour and teacher. Geeta helps the hero understand his mortality

---

[1] In a perceptive essay, "Beaming Messages to the Nation", *Journal of Artsandldeas*, no.19 (1990), pp.33—52, Ashish Rajadhyaksha discusses the impulses behind what he calls the new definitions of indigenism. Rajadhyaksha suggests that since "geographically defined regionalist identities are closely linked to geographically defined markets", the internationalization of markets obviously demands the formation of new identities. Mass media, especially TV and popular cinema, have contributed in important ways to the imaging of the new indigenism, an indigenism that takes up elements from diverse and anthropologized folk traditions and combines them into the authentically and timelessly Indian'.

and reconciles him to the fate she also shares. The heroine is not thereby exempt from sustaining the image of the truly feminine. She is allowed to take the initiative in the relationship because, in spite of her shoulder-length hair, she is "Indian", and a signifier of the good modernity. The film deploys a series of images which suggests a contemporary reappropriation of that which had, for the urban middle class, been relegated in the post-Independence period to the realm of tradition (shots of herbal preparations, Geeta with oil in her hair, the large courtyard where the women sit). This reappropriation, it must be obvious, is once again centred around the woman. The bad kind of modernity is signified by the army major's lusty wife, played by Disco Shanti, dressed in tight jeans or miniskirts or sometimes only a bath-towel. This bad modernity is inevitably associated with an insatiable sexual appetite, portrayed in the "comic" scenes of Disco Shanti's seduction of the caretaker. Both women are sexually aggressive, but whereas Geeta's actions are sanctioned by death and the audience only laughs with her, the other woman's actions are ultimately presented as reprehensible, or as something to be laughed at.

Geeta has no mother in the film, only a grandmother, who passes on to her "traditional" knowledge, imaged for the new consumer through herbal cosmetics. This "grandmother's knowledge", mobilized by multinational capital, is authenticated and refashioned in the chemical laboratory in order to create new markets in "traditional" societies. And why doesn't Geeta have a mother? If she had been part of this narrativization of contemporary female subjectivity, Geeta would have had to be schooled by her into the older femininity, to claim a place in the national-modern; she would have to be groomed fora future continuous, for the kind of austerity enjoined on us by the years just after Independence. Geeta, however, can challenge conventional models of femininity precisely because she is presented as having no future. Her father tolerates all her transgressions in the light of her imminent death. Her daring, her abandon, are permissible because they will not last, since they find full expression only on the verge of dying.

To come back to the anti-Mandal agitation with which I began this section of my essay: the anti-Mandal woman is prefigured in Geetanjali with regard to her occupation of an equal space with middle-class men, a space where differences of caste or community do not matter because rhey have been left behind by the secular subject. In its transition to the post-national-modern, this subject is articulated into the consumer economy, an economy naturalized by the film in its valorization of the present moment. And it is the consumer economy that legitimizes the demand for efficiency at all costs that a welfarist, pro-reservation state cannot provide.[1] This inefficient state is centrally thematized in Roja, which is set in present-day Kashmir.

The Romance of Nationalism

Whereas Geetanjali narrativizes the fantasies of the new middle class in a setting seemingly distant from the everyday world, Roja, which incidentally won the National Integration Award for 1993, dramatizes—as does the controversial Bombay (1995) —the politics of this assertive and self-confident class.[2] Although Maniratnam's representative technique has as its immediate ancestor the Hindi middle-brow film of the 1970s (either in its wistful Hrishikesh Mukherjee mode or the social-critique mode of Saeed Mirza), there is no angst apparent in his characters. Unapologetic about their protagonists in every way, Maniratnam's films celebrate rather than critique their aspirations and lifestyles.

The opening sequence of Roja shows a Kashmiri militant

---

[1] During the anti-Mandal agitation of 1990, the commonly held middle-class perception was that India's public sector had become corrupt and inefficient because of the reservations policy followed by the government.

[2] *Rojav/as* publicly endorsed on hoardings by Chief Election Commissioner T.N. Seshan as a film every patriotic Indian must see. The BJP's L.K. Advani confessed to having been moved by the scene of the hero saving the burning Indian flag. In an interview, the Shiv Sena's Bal Thackeray, who asked for and got certain cuts in the film, acclaims *Bombay AS* "a damn good film".

leader being captured by soldiers of the Iffdian army. This is followed by another beginning, which depicts the splendid waterfalls and coves and shining green fields of the village of Sunder Bhanpur (somewhere in India), with the heroine Roja singing and romping through the landscape.[1] In this rapidly-presented sequence—its slickness that of a TV commercial—we see Roja, sometimes accompanied by her youngest sister, driving a tractor (for fun, since they don't "work"), playing pranks on the older villagers, dressing up in men's clothes, wearing a graduate's convocation robes, and dancing through a field where women are transplanting seedlings. As in other Maniratnam films, actual labour serves as a backdrop that enhances the light-heartedness of the heroine. Then we see her and the other girl driving a flock of goats down a hill and across the road (not work but play

---

[1] I have chosen to focus on the Hindi version of *Roja*, although I am familiar with the Telugu version as well. The Hindi version was a national success, and marked a confident occupation of a "national" rather than just a "regional" space (in terms of political agendas as well as markets) by the new South Indian cinema. Unlike the Tamil version, which might have interpellated its audience along very different axes, the Telugu and Hindi versions were quite similar in their structures of address. However, the Hindi version of the film does flatten out and clarify some of the ambiguity of the Tamil and Telugu versions, especially around the question of language. Also, the question of "patriotism" would be attached to very different debates in the context of Tamilnadu politics. When the film was released in 1992 in Tamilnadu, many people are supposed to have seen it as an exorcism of the collective guilt felt by Tamilians over Rajiv Gandhi's assassination in Sriperumbudur the previous year.

again) to block the hero's car so that he can be scrutinized before he enters the village. Roja is a good deal like Geeta, in spite of the "rural" origins of the one and the "urban" background of the other. Both are portrayed as uninhibited, high-spirited, self-assertive, never at a loss for words. These are women whose articulateness has been made possible by the women's movement, which has created certain kinds of spaces for women and helped bring them a new visibility, although they are recuperated into the very spectacularization that some feminists might challenge. Interestingly, Roja's high spirits, like Geetanjali's, seem to be made possible by the exemption of the heroines from "real work", [1] so their assertiveness is not part of their interaction in a workplace situation. [2]

Rishi Kumar, the urbane hero, has come to 'see Roja's sister, since he wants to marry "a girl from a village". Not only that, he would like his bride to be from the beautiful village with which he has fallen in love ("I love the very soil of this place", as he says later). But clearly he will not marry just anyone—when the match

---

[1] Earlier commercial cinema also portrayed frolicking heroines exempt from the compulsions of the everyday world. What I'm trying to mark here is the difference in Maniratnam's young women, given the *realism* of the film's narrative style which distances it from dominant Indian commercial cinema, and which makes the women both "real" and "natural".

[2] This exemption from "work" helps contain the heroines' assertiveness, making it cute and attractive rather than threatening.

with Roja's sister falls through because she wants to marry someone else, he turns immediately to Roja, whom he has glimpsed exactly twice until then.

Roja, who is fair, sharp-featured, obviously upper-caste, is quite different from the village women of the neo-realist "art" films of Shyam Benegal, Adoor Gopalkrishna and others. She addresses her father as Daddy, has a television set at home, is accustomed to talking on the telephone; and, except that she does not know English, she is quite at ease in urban surroundings, adapting without difficulty to Rishi's upper-middle-class home and milieu. Roja does not therefore belong even to the genre of the "village belle" of older commercial Hindi and regional-language cinema. Her old world and her new one are not represented as opposed to each other; rather, they exist in an almost seamless continuum. Given the rapid urbanization of the rural upper class/castes, English is no longer a sufficient marker of cultural difference or even a marker of non-Indianness. Instead, "English" can be acquired through training in consumerism; what is more curious, English is closely associated not with the non-Indian but with that which is not only assertively Indian but clearly nationalist: as indicated by the words which signify Rishi's profession and his daily activity, a point to which I will return.

What the village stands for in Rishi's eyes is a newly formulated traditionalism: the "ethnic" wedding, so much unlike the hotel or function-hall reception now seen as so tasteless by the upper-middle-class, the colourful saris of the old women who dance for the couple, or the sexual frankness of the "rustic" wedding song, which is sung in playback partly by the rap musician Baba Sehgal. All this displayed ethnicity is not at variance with Rishi's cosmopolitan modernness; on the contrary, it helps strengthen its self-confidence. Except for the dhoti-kurta of his wedding day, Rishi usually appears only in jeans and shirt or sweater. On the other hand, the Kashmiri militants always appear in clothes which mark them as ethnically Muslim, it is an ethnicity which reveals them as anti-modern (therefore anti-national or anti-Indian), intolerant and fundamentalist, while Hindu ethnicity as displayed by Roja or Rishi is merely part of the complexity of being Indian. The Hindu wedding rites are so normalized that we do not pay them any special attention, or even mark them as "religious", just as we do not really see Roja's frequent attempts to pray to her idols as significant to the story. The militants, however, especially Rishi's main captor Liaqat, are always shown praying— an action shored up by intercutting and by the soundtrack in such a way as to make it seem not only an assertion of religious difference but a menacing or sinister portent. Whereas their religiosity is always portrayed as grim and humourless, Roja's prayers are funny and endearing, inviting the spectator to share her hopes and anxieties.

Rishi's occupation is "cryptologist", a word uttered in English and left unexplained, until he tells Roja in passing that she should get "security clearance" since he deals with "confidential matters" involving "coding and decoding" (all these phrases uttered in English). Rishi is shown a few times in front of a computer monitor and keyboard, working on decoding a message. His work, directly related to the security interests of the country, is presented to us as truly nationalist; and, interestingly, his nationalism, I would argue, is not anti-Western, but although never stated as such, anti-Muslim. It has been asserted by some writers that since Nehruvian nationalism was pro-Western but not anti-Muslim, the argument about contemporary nationalism being pro-Western and therefore inclined to be anti-Muslim cannot be sustained.[1] There is, it seems to me, a major difference between 1950s Nehruvianism and 1990s middle-class neo-nationalism.[2] The conjuncture of

---

1 See Arun Kumar Patnaik, "Idealist Equations", *Economic and Political Weekly*, vol.xxix: 32 (6 August 1994), p.2108.

2 To elaborate this, we would have to look into the composition of the citizensubject in India. As Susie Tharu and I have argued in "Problems for a Contemporary Theory of Gender", in *Subaltern Studies IX*, the "Indian" in the nineteenth century emerges marked, or *coded (since* the marks are not visible) as upper-caste/middle-class, Hindu and male. The Indian comes into being, as several scholars have demonstrated, simultaneously unequal to the colonizer and claiming superiority to him in certain realms. The post-Independence Indian, therefore, professes to be more egalitarian and more welfarist than the liberal citizens at the heart of empire, and claims to strive for the eradication of all forms of "backwardness". The secular Indian citizen, then, presents "him" self as transcending caste and community identities, the assertion of which work against the dominant narrative of emancipation.

nationhood and modernity in which the new citizen emerges also produces a secularism that proclaims its transcendence of caste and religion. The point to be made about Nehruvian nationalism is not simply that it was not anti-Muslim. (It was not simply pro-Western either, but that needs to be debated elsewhere and at length.)

The formation of the "Indian" in the 1950s was not explicitly dependent on an anti-Muslim discourse, because the citizen-subject was coded, among other things, as Hindu. Today, in the context of globalization, the hidden markings of the Indian citizen-subject are being revealed, and claimed without embarrassment by the upper-caste Hindu middle class.This lack of embarrassment can go unremarked in a post-Cold War "new world order" in which Islam is being relentlessly demonized. One kind of display of the markers of "difference"—here, difference as privilege and not inferiority—emerges as part of the positive agenda of liberalization and globalization. Difference as mark of privilege is linked, I would like to suggest, to the comprehensive claiming of the space of the nation by the new middle class. This kind of claim is clearly manifested in the middle-class representation of the Kashmir "problem".

When Rishi's boss, who is supposed to go to Kashmir to help the army, falls seriously ill, he asks Rishrto take his place. His "You don't mind going, do you?" is answered by Rishi's "Of course not. I'll go anywhere in India. Isn't Kashmir in India?" (loud audience applause.) Roja insists on accompanying her new husband, although she has initially rejected all his advances due to a misunderstanding. So, like many earlier Hindi-film honeymooners, they arrive in "Kashmir". But to an official welcome, to be put up in a five-star hotel where there are obviously no other guests. As they are driven through deserted streets, Roja asks why the town looks so empty and Rishi merely answers "curfew". When asked why there should be curfew, he uses a favourite word: "security". No other explanation is seen as necessary for the spectator-position the film creates. Hardly any ordinary Kashmiris are shown in the film, except for a newspaper boy and some people selling souvenirs. In two fantasy/song sequences, we do see Kashmiris—either women, or children dressed in elaborate costumes. All the other Kashmiris (with one exception) are militants, and male. This depiction helps mark off Roja as the bearer of both femininity and Indianness, both implicitly marked as Hindu.[1]

Coming in search of Roja, who has gone to the temple

---

[1] Ravi Vasudevan's assertion, that "regional identity in the figure of the woman ultimately seems to elude its translation into the rationality of the nationalist self (Vasudevan, "Other Voices: Reading 'Roja' Against the Grain" , *Seminar* 423, November 1994), pp.43—4 is an interesting one that could be explored further. However, it seems to miss the crucial fact that Maniratnam's films increasingly construct an "ethnic" identity rather than a specifically "regional" one. This might account fot the phenomenal success of his films in "South Indian" languages as well as Hindi.

to pray, the hero is kidnapped by the militants who have been following him, and who demand in exchange for his release their captured leader Wasim Khan. Roja goes to the police, to report that "raakshas jaise aadmi" ("men like demons") took away her husband, who is a deshpremi (patriot, lover of the nation). The aid of the state is invoked for the "good citizen" against the militant "demons". Roja, although all she demands is her husband's return ("I don't care about the country"), is patriotic by implication, through her representation of both Rishi and the militants, as a patriot and as monsters respectively.

Rishi's love for the nation is driven home through two dramatic acts performed by him in captivity. First, when his captors want him to speak into a tape recorder and ask for the release of Wasim Khan, all he says into the machine is a firm "Jai Hind". Even after repeated blows which leave his face bleeding, he continues to say the phrase over and over again, making the audience cheer aloud. When the news arrives that the government has refused to release their leader, one of the militants picks up an Indian flag and rushes outside holding a flaming torch with which he sets fire to the flag. Rishi leaps through a window, shattering a glass pane, knocks over the militant, and throws his body on to the burning flag, driving the audience delirious. Having put out the fire, Rishi rises to his feet, partially aflame. In his jeans and sweater, with the flames licking his clothes, he looks uncannily like the fullcolour pictures with which the media glorified uppercaste anti-Mandal agitators in 1990, agitators who claimed that they were truly secular because they did not believe in caste but only in merit. Whereas in the anti-Mandal agitation, caste difference was coded as lack of merit, in Roja religious or ethnic difference (specifically Islamic) is portrayed not only as antinational but as signifying lack of humanity. In this encrypted image, as Rishi "burns", the soundtrack rises to a crescendo, the words of a nationalist poem blending into a triumphant chant. Throughout this sequence, intercut shots show the militant leader Liaqat deep in prayer inside the building, unconcerned about the struggle over the burning flag outside.

At the end, however, Rishi does escape, with the help of Liaqat's sister, who is mute throughout the film, though always depicted as shocked/weeping/distressed at the militants' rough treatment of their captive, and at the death of her youngest brother. The girl's femininity and her humanness ultimately oblige her to help the patriot, make her overcome her loyalty to her community, thus attaining the secular and, presumably, becoming Indian. In spite of Roja's determined appeals to the army and to the minister who arranges to have Wasim Khan released, the exchange of prisoners does not take place, and Rishi, although he is an employee of the state, does not depend on the state to regain his liberty. Roja pleads with the minister who is inspecting the army in Kashmir: my husband is not a big man, but "Bharat kipraja to hai" ("he is after all a citizen of India"), and we need security. The new middle class, in claiming its complete identification with the nation, has to demonstrate that demands made on the state are not met. The new class has to show its self-reliance instead, for the state apparatus is outworn, out of date, however large and impressive it may seem.[1] This middle-class imperative to detach itself from the state to mark its coming to maturity can be seen, as I have suggested earlier, as a rejection of the Nehruvian state which had been compelled to write into its policies a vision of democracy and egalitarian socialism. (I see the absence of the mother in Geetanjali as another symptom of this rejection.) Among the consequences of these failed policies, the middle class would argue, is the situation in Kashmir, which can no longer be dealt with by the state but only by individuals like Rishi, who has shaken Liaqat to such an extent that the militant lets him go even when he has a rifle trained on him. Liaqat is shown to have been made human, through suffering and through Rishi's goodness (i.e. patriotism). Go, he says, "ugravaadiaansupochegd" ("the militant

---

[1] While acknowledging the point made by S.V. Srinivas, "Roja in Law and Order State", EPW, vol. xxix: 20 (14 May 1994), pp.1225—6 and Arun Patnaik, "Idealist Equations" about the increasingcoercive activity of the state in the time of liberalization, I would argue that this is one of the signs of the changing state which indicates reallocation of functions, that is, different things are now being demanded of the state as it evacuates its older functions.

will wipe histears"). Rishi's patriotism or nationalism, I would contend, is not centred around the nation-state; in fact, the state in this film is one that has failed in all respects—it cannot defeat the militants, cannot rescue its employee, cannot help Roja; its failure, then, can be made to justify a middle-ciass rejection of it in favour of a new economic order which in endorsing privatization will ensure greater efficiency.[1]

If Rishi is in many ways the central character of the film, Roja is integral to his vision of love for the nation. What makes this film's portrayal of the heroine different from older representations of womanas-nation (such as Mother India) is that the woman is no longer mother but lover. In the song "Rojajaanemari" for instance, in Rishi's reverie the rose (red/green) he sees outside his cell merges into the figure of his bride (who is especially towards the end of the film dressed in green sari/red or saffron blouse or red sari/green blouse). In turn, the beauty of the Kashmiri landscape blends into the physical beauty of the heroine, who appears in this particular song-sequence dressed in Kashmiri clothes and jewellery, followed by little children also wearing Kashmiri dress. The early autonomy and assertiveness shown by Roja before marriage all but disappears

---

[1] This is where I disagree with Venkatesh Chakravarthy and M.S.S. Pandian who have argued that "the apparent inability of the state in the film actually masks its silent and powerful ability". See their "More on Roja" EPW, vol. xxix: 11(12 March 1994), pp.642—4.

in the sober woman who attempts to win back her husband's life, and whose agency actually comes to naught.

In the concluding sequence, Rishi sprints to safety across a bridge while Roja runs towards him and falls at his feet, woman-as-nation grateful for his return, before he lifts her up for his embrace. It is evident from Roja that the conjuncture between romantic love and nationalism does not provide the same kind of space for the woman as it does for the man. For Roja, the conjugal space is configured very differently from the national space, and her love for her husband finds utterance in statements such as "I don't care about the country, all I want is my husband back". For Rishi, on the other hand, love for wife and love for nation converge, as in the 'Roja jaanemari song sequence, so that romantic love comes to be figured nationalism. The authentic subject of modernity in the post-national-modern, then, is the one who can be both lover and citizen, in fact is lover-as-citizen. The narrative logic does not permit Roja the heroine to be this desiring subject, for she has to be assigned the role of that which is desired. The representation of her agency in the film, therefore, relates to her function as the crucial mediator who enables the manifestation of love as nationalism.

The Secularism of Love

The good citizen accomplishing what an inefficient state

machinery is incapable of is as central to the narrative of Bombay as it is to Roja. In Bombay, the capacity for romantic love is not only a significant marker of modernity, it is also seen as the highest form of secularism. The film was the focus of intense controversies in several parts of India. Let me take the example of one city, Hyderabad.

Bombayi (the Telugu version of Bombay) was released all over Andhra Pradesh on 10 March 1995, playing to full houses in every theatre. On 14 March, screening of the film was banned in the twin cities of Hyderabad and Secunderabad as well as the adjoining district of Rangareddy.[1] Newspaper reports indicated that stray incidents of audience violence and representations to the Home Minister from the Majlis-Ittehadul-Muslimeen and the Majlis Bachao Tehreek had resulted in the ban order. It was also reported that leftist organizations such as the Students' Federation of India (SFI) and the Democratic Youth Federation of India (DYFI) as well as the right-wing Bharatiya Janata Yuva Morcha had opposed the ban. A statement by the SFI and DYFI declared that "the film depicted nationalist feelings and had nothing communal about it".[2]

The reaction to Maniratnam's films in Hyderabad may not

---

1 The film was re-released with three cuts a few weeks later.

2 Report in *Newstime* (15 March 1995).

be representative of a general South Indian response to them, nor of the response in Andhra Pradesh either. Due to its atypical demographic profile (a Muslim population that is over 50 per cent in the old city and over 20 per cent even in the new city), Hyderabad's political scenario and the space occupied in it by the agendas of specifically "Hindu" and "Muslim" parties may very well be unique in southern India. Maniratnam's earlier film Roja, first in its Telugu version and then in Hindi, had elicited considerable applause in new Hyderabad for its unabashed patriotism and its categorical denunciation of Kashmiri militancy. A national (ist) commonsense about what constitutes the truly secular was articulated here in its convergence with Hindutva; in fact, "secularism" in Roja was indistinguishable, as it is in other contemporary cultural formations, from the attitudes produced by the making invisible of a "Hindu" ethnicity. Bombay is in many ways not very different from Roja in its portrayal of the secular and the Indian. It is worth investigating, therefore, why the film seems to have evoked from the minority community, which made no public protest about Roja, a very different kind of response. In my view, the response allows us to reflect anew on major questions of cultural politics today, in particular the question of what constitutes the secular.

While the film follows Roja in the framing of its central problem—the question of the nation and the question of communalism (community identity in Roja) —it is, to my mind, marked by a certain stuttering, not so evident in Roja, when it comes to the issue of gender. This might partly account for the hostile reception in certain quarters of a film that, compared to a Roja which depicted the Muslim almost entirely as terrorist and anti-Indian, represents in its syrupy secularism "nothing... that hurts Muslim sentiments", [1] and indeed is framed as an attempt to "[balance] the viewpoints of the opposing communities".[2] "How sad", exclaims a journalist writing in The Hindu, "every time sincere efforts have been made towards national integration we end up in protests and riots".[3] There appears to be a general consensus that Maniratnam is indeed a "nationalist" filmmaker, as evidenced by Roja winning the 1993 award for national integration. It is perhaps then the very composition of the national-modern—a composition which legitimises some identities and marginalises others—that was being contested by those who were demanding a ban on Bombay. And it is precisely around the question of gender, I would suggest, that the fracturing of this composition became visible.

But first, an outline of the narrative. Shekhar, a young upper-

---

[1] Nasreen Sultana, "Lift Ban on 'Bombay' ", Letter to the Editor, *Newstime* (20 March 1995).

[2] Interviewer (Lens Eye), in "Truth or Dare", interview with Maniratnam, *Times of India* (2 April 1995).

[3] Bhawna Bomaya, "The 'Bombay' Problem", *The Hindu* (31 March 1995).

caste Hindu from Bheemunipatnam, Visakha District, has just finished his studies in Bombay and started working as a proof-reader in a newspaper, with a view to becoming a journalist. On a visit to his village he sees Shaila Banu, the daughter of the Muslim brickmaker Basheer, and instantly falls in love with her. After a brief courtship, and after encountering the hostility of his family and Basheer's to the possibility of his marriage with Shaila Banu, Shekhar returns to Bombay, to be joined there by the girl. They commence wedded life as paying guests in a rickety old apartment building; Shekhar gets promoted to reporter, Shaila Banu gives birth to twins; Shekhar's father Narayanamurthy (who has tried to send bricks marked "Sri Ram" to Ayodhya as penance for his son's act) comes to visit, fearing for the safety of Shekhar's family after the fall of the Babri Masjid, and is overwhelmed to learn that the twins are named Kabeer Narayan and Kamal Basheer. Shaila Banu's parents also come on a visit at the same time. The January 1993 Bombay riots take place; the parents of both hero and heroine die in a fire; the children are lost; amidst scenes of rioting the chief protagonists search for the twins. In the concluding scenes, Shekhar makes impassioned speeches to the rioters to stop killing each other, and the children are found, even as Hindus and Muslims drop their weapons and hold hands. This bare narrative cannot possibly account for the many ingenious ways in which Maniratnam achieves his cinematic effects, some of which I shall refer to.

What I earlier called the "stuttering" of Bombay has to do, it seems to me, with the portrayal of the Muslim woman. When the film was first shown, some of the audience kept asking why the protagonists could not have been a Muslim man and a Hindu woman. Given the logic of gender and nation in Maniratnam, this equation would have been clearly impossible. The (Hindu) female in Roja, for instance, is shown as imperfectly secular, imperfectly nationalist, because her concern is not for the security of the nation but for her husband. It is the Hindu male, therefore, who must take on the task of making the Muslim "human", which implicitly means becoming secular and nationalist as well. Whereas in Roja it is the male militant Liaqat who is portrayed as being made human, his silent sister who helps the hero escape is shown as already human by virtue of her femininity. By aiding the hero, she transcends her community identity and in the process stands revealed as both human and "Indian", rather than Kashmiri and militant-separatist.

Bombay is even more subtle: Shaila Banu marries the Brahmin Hindu hero (who is never shown as marked by caste or community) but does not give up her religion; neither does she dress like a South Indian Hindu woman, especiallys' ince she does not wear abindi except in two song sequences. The secular hero is obviously tolerant about all this, is in a sense attracted by the very "difference" of the heroine. While male Muslim ethnic markers in the film (prayer caps, or scenes of mass praying for example) are ominous portents of the rioting to follow, female Muslim markers of ethnicity—the burqa, primarily—are glamourised and eroticised.[1] Shekhar's first glimpse of Shaila Banu is when the wind accidentally lifts up her veil, and many of his subsequent encounters with her, including on the night when they consummate their marriage, the matise this visibility/invisibility as tantalising.

While in Roja the hero tries to change the militant Muslim's beliefs without necessarily comprehending why the latter might hold them, in Bombay the secular citizen attempts to understand the ethnic other, but it is an understanding that can only be accomplished through the erotic gaze. It is the feminine other who is the embodiment of the erotically mysterious and unapproachable, and who therefore compels an unveiling in the act of making intimate, while the relationship of the secular nationalist with the ethnicised male can only be contentious and combative. This ethnicised male in the logic of these films, and indeed in the dominant cultural logic of our times, cannot possibly be the hero of a narrative about the need for national integration. The only acceptable hero is the urbanised, westernised Shekhar who, like

---

[1] I should point out that BJP/Shiv Sena men are also shown in the film as engaging in aggressive public worship of Hindu gods. I would see this, however, as part of the problematic equalizing of Muslim and Hindu "fundamentalism" in *Bombay*.

Rishi Kumar in Roja, does not need to draw attention to his caste or religion because in espousing nationalism he has transcended such identities.[1] If one examines the composition of the Indian citizen subject of the 1990s, the Hindu female appears as the necessary bearer of ethnicity. Thus, the initiator of the integration process, or the initiator of the romantic relationship in the film, cannot but be a man from the majority community. Bombay, then, could not have had a Muslim hero and a Hindu heroine.

This inevitability is also related to the sharp demarcation of gendered "secular" spaces in Bombay. While the hero's secularism (read tolerance) does have a domestic aspect to it, it is made manifest in this sphere only as playfulness, as in the scene where a relay of little children conveys to his bride his question—"Shall I change my religion?" or the song sequence ("Halla gulla") in which he briefly dons Muslim headgear. His publicly secular acts, on the other hand, are shown as acts of consequence, when during the riots he berates his two colleagues for claiming to be Hindu and Muslim instead of saying they are Indian, or in the climactic scenes when he splashes petrol on his body and urges the rioters to burn him in order to shame them into throwing down their arms. In contrast, when Shaila Banu makes a rare appearance outside the home, it is most visibly when she and Shekhar are looking for

---

[1] It is not entitely fortuitous that the actor Arvind Swamy plays both Rishi Kumar in *Roja* and Shekhar in *Bombayi*.

the children during the riots, and she is called upon only to show distress and horror. Early on in the film, the heroine expresses her secularism in a mode reminiscent of popular Western feminist analyses of Islamic women: running to meet Shekhar of her own volition, her burqa snags on a piece of rusting metal (actually an old anchor!) ; she tugs but cannot loosen it, and finally (in slow motion) leaves it behind and dashes towards the hero.

The domestic space is constantly defined in the film as a counterpoint to communalism; the increasing familial harmony (the birth of the twins, the reconciliation of the grandparents, Shekhar's desire for more children) is matched against increasing communal tension in the city. Integration, the film seems to suggest, can be accomplished within the family.[1] In the domestic space, Shekhar does not have to undergo any sort of transformation to prove his secularism. In any case, his "religion" is not central to his identity. Also, by virtue of being the breadwinner, there are other conventional asymmetries in relation to male and female roles that he need never challenge. It is crucial to the narrative that the couple have children, for the film's logic suggests that it is the urbanized nuclear family which can solve the problem of communalism. This problem, indicates the film, is one of senseless

---

[1] In an interview, Maniratnam says: "The family is the most invincible institution of our country. We lead our entire lives in the family's folds." *Times of India* (2 April 1995).

hatred. Communalism is imaged here, as in some analytical accounts of recent events in India, as the resurgence of ancient hates, primordial hostilities. Thus it becomes a residue, a mark of the non-modern, or backwardness, [1] and, as I have suggested earlier, the anti-national comes to be staged as community (or caste, for that matter). Secularism or nationalism, therefore, appears as the "other" of communalism; [2] however, in the 1990s, in a historical space where the privatization of secularism seems to be taking place, this nationalism need not be part of apolitical agenda.[3] As Roja demonstrated, the middle-class attempt to delink itself from the state results in a transfer of functions to that class. The efforts of the new citizen will accomplish what state policy can not, what indeed it has worked against; it is not only state economic enterprise that needs to be privatized, but also the solution to "cultural" questions such as that of communalism. For if the problem is diagnosed as one of hatred, the solution has

---

1 This depiction makes invisible the large-scale participation of the "modern" middle class in the Bombay riots.

2 For a useful discussion of this process in the colonial period, see Gyanendra Pandey, *The Construction of Communalism in Colonial North India* (Delhi: OUP, 1990), especially chapter 7, "Nationalism versus Communalism".

3 The new nationalism is of necessity detached from anti-imperialism, the differences between the BJP and the RSS over the *swadeshi* campaign notwithstanding. Nationalism, then, becomes a purely internal question, to be asserted against non-Hindu. I use the word privatization here to invoke also the current changes in the Indian economy regarding the transformation of the public sector.

to be located in the possibility of love. Humanism, too, becomes a question of good individuals, happy families. And love in its modern form, as Bombay shows, achieves its most exalted and exemplary expression in romantic love, the love between individuals. It might, then, be worth asking whether the demand for banning Bombay, on the basis that it offends Muslim sentiments, was simply an expression of "fundamentalism" or of Muslim patriarchal attitudes. Was it perhaps an indication that the liberal analysis and solution (communalism is caused by "hatred" and can be cured by "love") is unacceptable—as inaccurate, simplistic and patronising—to those who comprise the majority amongst the victims of communal violence?[1] Could it point to the need to rethink whose tolerance the dominant notion of secularism embodies, and whether "love" and "tolerance" can be recommended in equal measure to both the majority and minority communities?

It is the burden of both Roja and Bombay to create the contemporary convergences between the human, the secular and the nationalist and to dramatize the condensation of these characteristics in the Hindu male who has discarded marks of caste and community. The question of the nation is posed in these

---

[1] I use the word "patronising" to indicate the tone of those, like Shekhar in *Bombay*, who exempt themselves from communalism by their modernity. Reduced to hatred, communalism becomes an emotion reserved for the non-modern and the irrational.

films through the depiction of the Kashmir situation on the one hand and the Bombay riots on the other. In both, the modalities of the question's "framing" collapse any challenge to the national-modern, or the post-national-modern, into a simple assertion of religious identity. Simultaneously with the gradual erosion of the nation's economic sovereignty and the ongoing process of market consolidation, an earlier anti-colonial nationalism turns into one for whom the "enemy" is within and needs to be either transformed or expelled. The figure of woman, indeed the agency of women, I have been suggesting, is central to the formation of the new nationalism. If the changes taking place today are being crucially mediated by popular cinema, figures like Geeta, Roja and Shaila Banu are active mediators of such changes. Characterizing women in this fashion will allow us to form a perspective somewhat different from those analysts of Maniratnam's films who see these women simply as the hapless victims of Hindu patriarchy, Muslim patriarchy, sexism and male chauvinism.[1]

---

1 Chakravarthy and Pandian (More on *Roja*, pp.642—4) see Roja's desire as repressed by the Hindu patriarchy whose numerous representatives include Rishi Kumar as well as state institutions. Swaminathan S. Anklesaria Aiyar, who hails *Bombay* as "a passionate plea for humanity to rise above sectarian mayhem", denounces the Muslim groups seeking a ban on *Bombay* for their "sexism" and "male chauvinism". He adds: "The concept of women as independent human beings with a right to choose their husbands, jobs or religion is alien to traditionalists of both communities". "Objecting to 'Bombay' : Sexism More Than Communalism", *The Times of India* (15 April 1995).

To my mind, the ground prepared for a feminist politics by the latter approach allows women to engage only in certain kinds of protest: in a peculiar coming together of filmic portrayal and filmic critical analysis, Shaila Banu must cast off her burqa to escape from Muslim patriarchy, reaffirming in the process the stereotype of what constitutes the oppression of the Muslim woman, and reaffirming that the Muslim community is both "backward" and patriarchal. Roja too is not merely a victim of patriarchy but a key figure in its reconfiguration. I would argue, then, that a discussion of the narrative functions of characters like Geeta, Roja and Shaila Banu and of the centrality of romantic love in these films can reveal for feminism the gendering of the new "Indian" as well as the complicity of "women" in producing the exclusions of caste and community which enable the formation of the citizen-subject. A rethinking of feminist politics provoked by the questions raised by films like Maniratnam's might well have to proceed from a rethinking of those structuring terms of our daily experience as well as our politics: nationalism, humanism and secularism.

"印度当代新思潮读本"系列是"西天中土"项目出版计划的第一组丛书,是专为以下系列论坛编辑的参考读本:

"从西天到中土:印中社会思想对话"

项目总监: 张颂仁

学术主持: 陈光兴　高士明

主　　办: 第八届上海双年展
　　　　　　中国美术学院展示文化研究中心

支　　持: 汉雅轩　梦周文教基金会

Readers of Current Indian Thought is the first series of publication of the West Heavens Project, which coincides with the following academic forums:

"West Heavens: India-China Summit on Social Thought"

Commissioner:

Chang Tsong-Zung

Academic Curators:

Kuan-Hsing Chen, Gao Shiming

Presented by:

The 8th Shanghai Biennale, Institute of Visual Culture at China Academy of Art

Supported by:

Hanart TZ Gallery, Moonchu Foundation

在想像世界版图的"西方"时,
尚有一个离感官更远而脚程更近的"西天"。

再访天竺,自明中土

从社会思想和当代艺术两个角度去亲近印度,
进行视觉文化和亚洲现代性的文化比较。

从西天到中土:印度当代新思潮读本
West Heavens: Readers of Current Indian Thought

阿希斯·南迪	民族主义,真诚与欺骗
ASHIS NANDY	*Nationalism, Genuine and Spurious*
帕沙·查特吉	我们的现代性
PARTHA CHATTERJEE	*Our Modernity*
迪佩什·查卡拉巴提	后殖民与历史的诡计
DIPESH CHAKRABARTY	*Postcoloniality and the Artifice of History*
杜赞奇	历史意识与国族认同
PRASENJIT DUARA	*Historical Consciousness and National Identity*
吉塔·卡普尔	印度艺术的现代主义时刻
GEETA KAPUR	*When Was Modernism in Indian Art?*
特贾斯维莉·尼南贾纳	重塑民族主义
TEJASWINI NIRANJANA	*Nationalism Refigured*
萨拉·马哈拉吉	元化扩散
SARAT MAHARAJ	*Elemental Scatterings*
霍米·巴巴	全球化与纠结
HOMI BHABHA	*Globalisation and Ambivalence*

出　　品:亚际书院
丛书策划:张颂仁　陈光兴　高士明
丛书编辑:陈　韵　梁　捷
英文编辑:张　菁

Presented by: Inter-Asia School
Series initiated by: Chang Tsong-Zung, Kuan-Hsing Chen, Gao Shiming
Editors: Chen Yun, Liang Jie
English Editor: Gigi Chang

图书在版编目(CIP)数据

重塑民族主义:特贾斯维莉·尼南贾纳读本/张颂仁,陈光兴,高士明主编.—上海:上海社会科学院出版社,2018

(从西天到中土:印度当代新思潮读本)
ISBN 978-7-5520-2425-8

Ⅰ.①重… Ⅱ.①张… ②陈… ③高… Ⅲ.①文化-研究-印度 Ⅳ.①G135.1

中国版本图书馆CIP数据核字(2018)第188502号

重塑民族主义:特贾斯维莉·尼南贾纳读本

主　　编:张颂仁　陈光兴　高士明
责任编辑:唐云松　刘欢欣
封面设计:周伟伟
出版发行:上海社会科学院出版社
　　　　　上海顺昌路622号　邮编200025
　　　　　电话总机021-63315947　销售热线021-53063735
　　　　　http://www.sassp.org.cn　E-mail:sassp@sassp.cn
照　　排:南京理工出版信息技术有限公司
印　　刷:上海文艺大一印刷有限公司
开　　本:787×1092毫米　1/32开
印　　张:11.75
插　　页:4
字　　数:230千字
版　　次:2019年9月第1版　2019年9月第1次印刷

ISBN 978-7-5520-2425-8/G·774　　　　定价:68.00元

版权所有　翻印必究